SPEECH COMMUNICATION

ERNEST G. BORMANN / NANCY C. BORMANN

University of Minnesota

SPEECH COMMUNICATION
A BASIC APPROACH/THIRD EDITION

1817

HARPER & ROW, PUBLISHERS, New York

Cambridge, Hagerstown, Philadelphia, San Francisco,
London, Mexico City, São Paulo, Sydney

Photo Credits
Page 1: United Nations; p. 3: Strickler, Monkmeyer; p. 19: Chester, DeWys; p. 31: ©
Marjorie Pickens 1980; p. 45: © Marjorie Pickens 1980; p. 62: Lejeune, Stock, Boston;
p. 77: Ursillo, DeWys; p. 93: Chwatsky, DeWys; p. 95: Reeberg, DPI: p. 111: Dietz, Stock,
Boston; p. 124: Mezey, DPI: p. 142: Siteman, Stock, Boston; p. 155: Patterson, Stock,
Boston; p. 157: Southwick, Stock, Boston; p. 175: Burnett, DeWys; p. 190: Wolinsky, Stock,
Boston; p. 204: Grimes, DeWys; p. 225: Eagan, Woodfin Camp; p. 238: Forsyth,
Monkmeyer; p. 258: Patterson, Stock, Boston.

Sponsoring editor: Alan M. Spiegel
Project editor: Karla Billups Philip
Text and cover designer: Gayle Jaeger
Production manager: Jeanie Berke
Photo researcher: Myra Schachne
Compositor: Lexigraphics Inc.
Printer and binder: The Murray Printing Company
Art studio: J & R Technical Services, Inc.
Cover photo: Michel Craig

SPEECH COMMUNICATION: A Basic Approach, Third Edition
Copyright © 1981 by Ernest G. Bormann and Nancy C. Bormann

Library of Congress Cataloging in Publication Data

Bormann, Ernest G
      Speech communication.

      Includes bibliographies and indexes.
      1.   Oral communication.   I.   Bormann, Nancy C., joint
author.   II.   Title.
P95.B67   1981   001.54'2   80-23854
ISBN 0-06-040865-0

CONTENTS

PREFACE

We have revised *Speech Communication* to meet the need for a brief, clear, readable book for the basic performance course in public speaking and interpersonal and small-group communication. We have kept in mind that for many students the first course will be their only chance to make a systematic study of the vital area of oral communication, and we have revised earlier editions to make our level of presentation and approach more basic and practical.

Our guiding assumption is that speech communication has a core of basic information that applies to various communication forms and situations. If students first learn the fundamentals, they can then apply them to the demands of their daily communication. Instructors who ground their courses on basics can reduce repetition and concentrate on the unique aspects of specific situations and occasions.

We have based this revision on the most recent research and theory about communication. Included is material on communication anxiety, psycholinguistics, nonverbal communication, interpersonal and small-group communication, persuasion, and humanistic psychology. We have also used the time-tested basics from the study of rhetoric, rhetorical criticism, and public speaking with regard to such matters as evaluating communication, the use of evidence, analysis of audiences, and the preparation, organization, and delivery of speeches.

Speech Communication has three parts. Part One presents the core of basic principles that relate to the communication needs of the contemporary student. The remainder of the book applies these basics to typical communication forms and practices. Part Two deals with interpersonal and small-group communication; Part Three, with public-speaking theory and practice.

Part One begins with an overview of modern communication and rhetorical theory, including a model of the basic process of communication. It also includes a discussion of the anxiety associated with communication and how to deal with it, an examination of the oral uses of language, the essential findings relating to nonverbal communication applied to practical problems, the basic techniques of listening to public speeches and to others in two-person and small-group communications, and directions for evaluating communication for the student as a beginning speaker sharpening his or her skills and as a consumer of important messages in a mass-media society.

Part Two consists of four chapters that make specific application of the basics in Part One to the most important and common of the two-person and small-group situations. Part Two contains two chapters on interpersonal communication and two chapters on small-group communication.

Part Three consists of seven chapters that adapt the communication basics to public speaking and provide a complete treatment of speech preparation, audience analysis, and speech organization and delivery. In addition, Part Three examines in detail special forms of public speaking, including the persuasive speech, the informative speech, and speeches for special occasions. Also included is a practical discussion of the business presentation as an important form of modern communication.

Although we include more chapters on public speaking, we do not slight interpersonal and small-group communication. Instructors who wish to emphasize interpersonal and small-group communication but also include a unit on public speaking can easily do so because of our treatment of fundamentals that are common to all communication situations. Those who wish to emphasize public speaking while also dealing with interpersonal and small-group communication will find our proportioning of materials well adapted to their needs.

We have organized *Speech Communication* as a teaching aid to help structure a student's learning experiences. Each chapter is a self-contained essay, and instructors can rearrange the chapters in the best order for their classes. Our order of materials is a widely used and pedagogically sound one in that the book moves from considerations common to communication contexts in general to specific applications. The applications form a logical progression from two-person conferences to small-group meetings to speeches involving communication with larger audiences on special occasions.

Over the years, as teachers have worked with the first two editions of this book, we have sought their advice and help to make it an even more useful teaching resource. We have tried to tailor this edition to their needs. Many of these instructors were teaching basic speech-communication courses in community colleges, liberal-arts schools, and state universities. We have put our emphasis in this revision on those topics where we found the needs of the beginning students in these classes overlapping. We have kept the growing need for meaningful, marketable communication skills strongly in mind as we prepared this revision. Our presentation has been adapted to the growing student interest in education that is useful for career preparation.

The teachers we have consulted advised us that, above all, we should stress solid information the student can use throughout life; keep it businesslike, practical, as free of jargon as possible; and write a book that the student will be able to read, absorb, and use. We have tried to follow this advice.

Ernest G. Bormann
Nancy C. Bormann

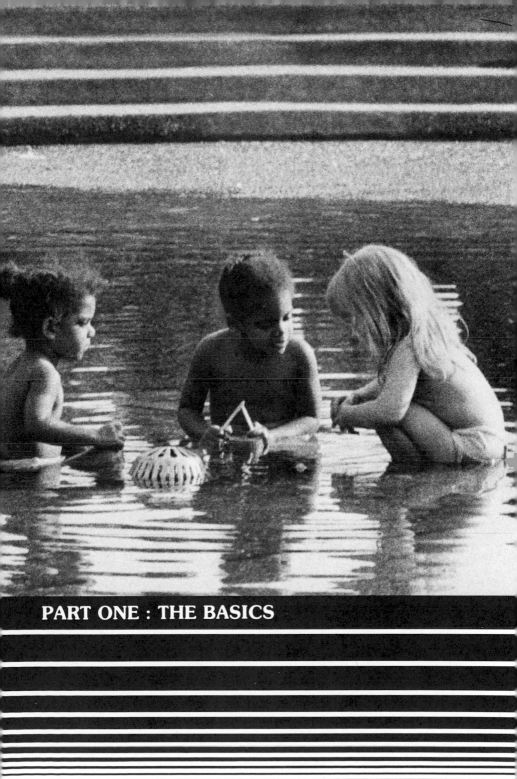

PART ONE : THE BASICS

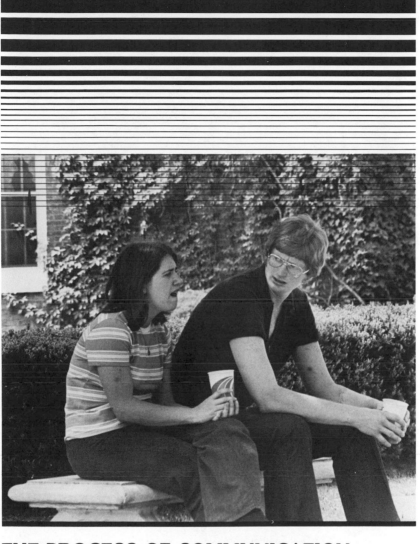

THE PROCESS OF COMMUNICATION
CHAPTER 1

FIGURE 1: ELEMENTS OF THE COMMUNICATION EVENT

When people talk together, we can think of what happens as a communication event. In this book we will examine the communication events that are most important in our daily lives, including such things as two-person talks to deepen relationships or work through interpersonal problems, small-group meetings and conferences to transmit information and do common tasks, and more formal occasions when one person delivers a carefully prepared message to an audience.

We have difficulty studying communication events because in all the settings we have mentioned, so much is going on when people talk with one another that we have trouble keeping track of everything. Communication events have the characteristics of a dynamic process. By *process*, we mean a series of give-and-take moves by which some end is reached. By dynamic, we mean the process unfolds and changes over time. Processes contain forces that push and pull the parts and set them in motion. Sometimes we are caught up by the way a speaker seems to be center stage; sometimes one member of a discussion is speaking in dramatic terms and we forget that the listener is also influencing the event and that the occasion makes a difference as well. The expectations of the people who are communicating with one another also play a part.

In this chapter we present a description of the basics in the process of communication. To understand a process, we need to know the major parts that make it up, how these parts fit together and move, and the nature and roots of the forces that power the action and reaction.

THE PARTS OF A COMMUNICATION EVENT

We will use the letters S M C R as a key to remember the parts of a communication event. Figure 1 presents the basic elements of the process. The S stands for *source*. The source is the person or group who decides to communicate with some other person or persons. If you meet someone in the hall and say "Good morning," you are the source of the communication,

The M stands for *message*. In our example the message is the words *good* and *morning*, plus the way you gesture and emphasize the words to indicate, "I really mean it is a pleasant morning" or "I am glad to see you again" or "I am saying these words because I always say these words even if the day is lousy and I feel terrible."

The C stands for *channel* or channels through which the message moves. Television messages come through channels. People can receive messages by way of their senses—sight, smell, taste, hearing, and touch. Thus, a message may travel through several channels at the same time, as is the case with television, where a viewer both sees the picture and hears the sound. You are most likely to hear, see, or read a message, since the most popular communication channels are through the eye or the ear.

The final letter, R, means *receiver*. The listener or viewer is the receiver of the message. When you greet someone in the hall you are the *source;* the words and the way you say them are the *message;* the message goes through the *channels* of sound (hearing) and light (sight) to the *receiver*.

Now that you know the *S M C R* way of looking at communication events, you can examine different situations and decide whether they are complete examples of the process of communication. For example, if John telephones Mary for a date, is that communication? Is there a source? A message? Channels? A receiver? All the parts are there: John is the source, what John says is the message, the channels are the telephone and hearing, and Mary is the receiver. Take another example: The national committee of a political party buys time on a television network and runs a short political announcement on nationwide TV. Is this an example of communication? Again all the parts are there. The national committee is the source; the television waves, television set, sight, and hearing are the channels; and the people at home who see and hear the announcement are the receivers. One more example and then you can think up some other situations and see if they are communication events. A candidate for student-body president is talking from the auditorium stage to an assembly, urging the audience to vote for a platform to improve the school. The candidate is the source, the message is what he says and the way he says it, the channels are the light waves (sight) and sound waves (hearing), and students in the auditorium are the receivers.

The *S M C R* key to the study of communication covers every sort of communication. We have seen the four basic parts in a telephone call, a television message, and a public speech. If we learn how the spark plug works to cause the gas to explode in an engine cylinder, we know a lot about many different car engines. In the same way, if we learn about the source of messages, we know a good deal about many different kinds of communications. We can say the same for what we learn about messages, channels, and receivers.

A PROCESS MODEL OF COMMUNICATION

To illustrate the way people talk to one another, we will use the basic situation of a two-person conversation. Our approach is to describe an ideal communication event, which contains all the possible parts operating under good conditions. Our description of idealized conditions results in a *model* of the event. A good communication model contains all the main parts of a typical conversation in standard form, in their usual places, functioning at peak efficiency.

Assume a situation in which one person wishes to give another person some important information. The first person arranges for a conference with the second. The person who calls the conference has something he wishes to discuss, and he tells the listener about it. If the listener understands the message, the first person has succeeded in communicating with the second.

Can we locate the *S M C R* parts in the process of communication in our model of the two-person conference? The source is the individual who makes the appointment. The message consists of the words, gestures, and vocal melody the source uses in talking with the listener. The channels in this instance are sight and hearing. The receiver is the individual called in for the conference.

Our model of a communication event perhaps seems relatively cut and dried. Actually, what happens when two people talk with each other is very complicated. Probably the two people in our hypothetical conference spent some minutes passing the time of day before the source began to talk about his business.

Perhaps the person who requested the appointment was a worker who wanted to talk to the boss about a raise, or it may have been the boss who wanted to talk to the worker about improving performance on the job. In either case, the fact that one was boss and the other worker would affect the communication. We could develop a long list of things that affect the two people.

Probably the first message failed to achieve a meeting of minds, and the participants had to try, again and again, to come to an understanding satisfactory to both.

Because of the unpredictability of human beings, we must describe many possible choices and behaviors to explain adequately the process of human communication. We will begin our explanation with a simplified situation and then move to the more complex. We start with the simplified situation in which the receiver is completely predictable. We are referring to the process by which a person talks to a machine.

Assume that we want to talk to a computer. The first step is to decide what we want the machine to do. We then plan a message to reach our goal, put the message into symbols the computer can understand, and taking care that each sentence is in the correct form, and that no information is left out, we punch the message onto cards and feed it into the computer. The computer reads the cards until it comes to a sentence with a mistake in it. Perhaps we forgot to put in a comma where we should have. The computer stops and its typewriter prints out a sentence that tells us we have made a mistake. We then go back to the card that caused the trouble, check the sentence, discover the mistake, put in the comma, and replace the card in the computer. Now the computer understands; it keeps on in this way, either understanding completely or stopping and asking for a

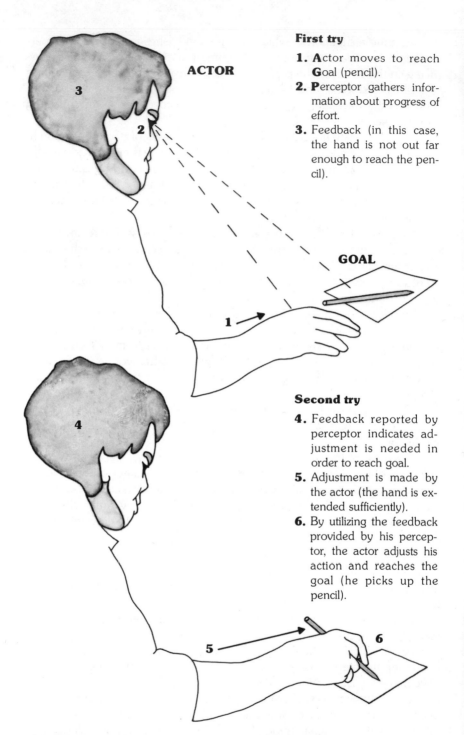

First try

1. **A**ctor moves to reach **G**oal (pencil).
2. **P**erceptor gathers information about progress of effort.
3. Feedback (in this case, the hand is not out far enough to reach the pencil).

Second try

4. Feedback reported by perceptor indicates adjustment is needed in order to reach goal.
5. Adjustment is made by the actor (the hand is extended sufficiently).
6. By utilizing the feedback provided by his perceptor, the actor adjusts his action and reaches the goal (he picks up the pencil).

FIGURE 2: THE CONCEPT OF FEEDBACK (*AGP*)

correction or for new information. Thus we work together with the machine to achieve understanding.

Remember that we defined process as a series of give-and-take moves by which some end is reached. The linking between the human being and machine is a communication process. Note that when we talk to the computer we start the communication and continue it until the computer fails to understand a part of the message. The back-and-forth part of the process is clear because the machine prints out an error statement indicating that it fails to understand. Although we start the process, and the machine is helping us reach the goal, we still have to talk the machine's language and follow the rules of the machine's thinking if we are to succeed.

When the computer indicates it does not understand a message, it feeds back information to the programmer to clear up the misunderstanding. *Feedback* consists of information about the errors in the message that enables the programmer to clear up the machine's lack of understanding.

Feedback plays an important part in the communication process. We can explain feedback in much the same way that we used $S\,M\,C\,R$ to refer to the parts of the communication event. We will use the letters $A\,G\,P$ as the key to the process of feedback. The A refers to an *actor* (a person or thing) that does something to reach a goal (G). The P indicates the *perceptor* built into the actor to provide information on how she is doing so she can correct mistaken attempts to reach her goal. We will examine some simple events in which feedback is important and then show how it works in communication.

Let us say you see a pencil on the desk and decide to pick it up. You stretch your hand out for the pencil, and as you watch your hand you see that you are going to overreach the pencil so you tighten certain muscles in your arm and shoulder and slow down the movement. You keep watching your hand and now see that you have slowed down too much and your hand will fall short. Again you adjust the push you give your hand until your fingers land on target and you pick up the pencil. One action loops back and causes another.

Does the situation of picking up the pencil contain the necessary parts for a feedback loop? You are the *actor* (person or thing) with the *goal* (picking up the pencil), and you sense (the *perceptor*) through your eyes information about how your arm is moving in comparison with where it ought to be if you are to reach your goal. Using the information you get from watching the path of your hand, you change your reach to hit directly on target. The situation illustrates all the parts, $A\,G\,P,$ of feedback as presented in Figure 2.

To return to the person talking with a computer, notice how the person (A) has a goal (G) to have the computer programmed to solve a problem or process data. The person sends the computer messages and

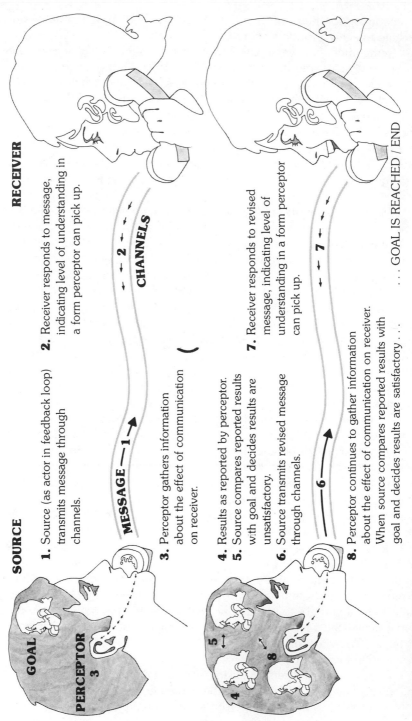

SOURCE

1. Source (as actor in feedback loop) transmits message through channels.

MESSAGE — 1 →

CHANNELS

2. Receiver responds to message, indicating level of understanding in a form perceptor can pick up.

← - 2 - ←

RECEIVER

3. Perceptor gathers information about the effect of communication on receiver.

4. Results as reported by perceptor.
5. Source compares reported results with goal and decides results are unsatisfactory.
6. Source transmits revised message through channels.

← 6 →

7. Receiver responds to revised message, indicating level of understanding in a form perceptor can pick up.

← - 7 - ←

8. Perceptor continues to gather information about the effect of communication on receiver. When source compares reported results with goal and decides results are satisfactory . . .

. . . GOAL IS REACHED / END

GOAL

PERCEPTOR
3

FIGURE 3: A MODEL OF THE PROCESS OF COMMUNICATION

the computer sends back information when it fails to understand. Thus the programmer can perceive (P) the actual level of understanding in the machine and check it against what is needed to reach the goal.

One important feature of the feedback loop is that only one person or thing has the goal. The pencil does not have a goal; the computer does not set up a different goal and fight the programmer over what they ought to do as a team. (You know, of course, about some dramas based on the idea that our machines begin to have goals of their own and start to take over the world, but up to now such stories remain science fiction.) In this simplified situation, feedback is information that enables the source to modify the message so the receiver understands it and the goal can be reached.

When people communicate with one another, the process is similar, but it is highly complicated by the fact that when another person is the potential receiver we cannot predict behavior as completely as we can the response of a machine. The message source begins a communication event with another person much as a programmer begins talking with a computer. The message source has some end she wishes to reach, and keeping in mind the receiver's ability to use language and her way of thinking, the source plans a message to reach her goal and speaks to the receiver.

The largest difference between person-to-machine and person-to-person communication is the machine's willingness to be bossed around to achieve the programmer's objective and a person's tendency to resist being the receiver of messages.

In our model of the process of communication (Figure 3), an important element is the fact that the message source has an end in view and sends out messages to achieve that goal. The communication process is a step-by-step, give-and-take interaction between source and receiver by which the source reaches the desired goal. The idea of feedback includes the notion that the source receives information so she can correct her attempts to reach her goal. The programmer gets error statements from the computer so he can rephrase his program until the computer understands it. The computer is willing to take the programmer's directives and accepts the programmer's goal without question. When the target for the message is another human being, the receiver often is not willing to be controlled and does not accept the objectives of the source.

What often happens in the conversation between people is that after a first attempt by one person to be the source of messages in a communication event, the other person tries to be the source also. When both try to be the source, neither gives the other feedback. The result is a battle over who will control the situation and whose ends will be achieved by the talk.

Even when a person willingly accepts the listener's role and tries to achieve understanding, the response of a human being is much more

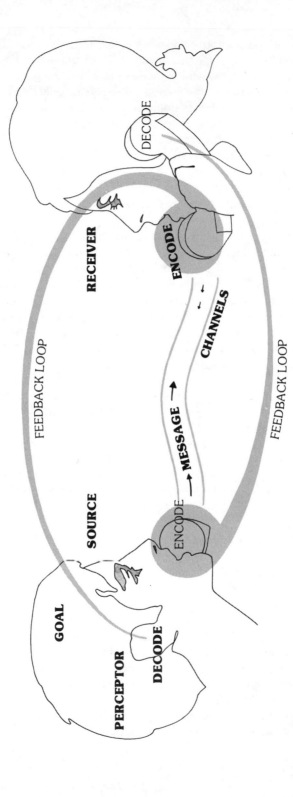

FIGURE 4: COMPLETE COMMUNICATION EVENT

complex than that of a machine. A person who listens to a message must, like the machine, receive the sentences in the right form, made up of words that can be understood. If you understand computer language, you can always tell when somebody has made a mistake in writing a sentence because the machine accepts only messages put in precisely the right form. A message for a computer is like an arithmetic or geometry problem in that you can tell whether the message can be understood simply by checking its form. But people can understand messages whether or not they are expressed in proper grammar. Of course we cannot put together just any bunch of English words and expect people to understand them. Within limits, our grammar must be correct to be understood. We are not talking about the difference between "it don't make no difference," and "it doesn't make any difference." Our point here is that, in order to be understood, we have to put our ideas into the right form according to some basic rules of American English.

Even when communication does not at first appear to make sense, people will try to find out the meaning of grunts, one-word exclamations, unstructured poetry, and ideas expressed in improper grammar. In that respect, people are much different from computers, and while the difference is helpful because it enables people to talk about complicated ideas and complex feelings, it is a disadvantage because while the computer never proceeds until it understands completely, people often plunge deeper and deeper into misunderstandings.

Like the computer, human beings can feed back error statements and thus indicate when they do not understand the message. As a matter of fact, people ought to be much better than a machine at giving feedback, because they can explain in greater detail exactly what they do not understand. In practice, however, people are often much worse than a machine at providing a speaker with feedback. People often hear only a few words of a message and then get the idea that they know what it is all about without listening to the rest. ("I know, I know, I've heard it a hundred times," says the teenager as he starts out with the family car.) People often hear what they expect to hear instead of what a speaker is saying. If a teacher assigns a difficult term paper, the student may not hear the assignment. Finally, and most important, people tend not to ask questions even when they do not understand because they are afraid a question may make them appear stupid, or they feel that if they keep quiet, at least nobody will know how little they understand. We are all guilty of bad communication habits at one time or another.

A model of the complete communication event is useful to the student of communicative interaction (see Figure 4). Remember that we are trying to picture a dynamic process, and a moving picture would do a better job. Without this moving picture, you must add your imagination. The parts of the process are put into the model, but they are actually parts in motion; as you look at the picture, imagine them in a give-and-take, step-by-step way.

Notice that the model in Figure 4 has two new terms to indicate the last important ideas about communication that we need to complete the picture. Between the source and the message we have placed the word *encode* and between the message and the receiver we have placed the word *decode*. We know that special codes or code words are used by soldiers or spies in wartime to keep secrets. Breakfast food companies often use decoder rings or other secret code devices as prizes to get children to buy their products. When spies decode a secret message, they discover what it means. The other term, *encode,* is not as widely used, but it means putting the ideas into a code and is the opposite of *decode.*

Look again at Figure 4. Before sources communicate with receivers, they must make a message out of something that can be sensed by the receivers. People who wish to communicate must make some link to establish contact. (Some people believe that contact can be made without going through the senses and they try to communicate with the spirit world or with others by means of extrasensory perception, or ESP.) When a person makes a message she encodes her ideas into a form the receiver can take in. Breaking the code, understanding the message, is the decoding process.

THE NATURE OF A CODE

To encode and decode messages we must have a *code* that can bridge the gap between source and receiver. You may think first of such things as the Morse code or a secret code such as the one you can make by giving each letter in the alphabet a number and then writing notes in numbers to others who know the code. The important thing about any code is that the people who use it must know all its parts and how they fit together into sentences. If a person has a private code, it is useful only to himself. Sometimes people write personal diaries in a secret code known only to themselves. If a code is to carry meaning between a source and a receiver, though, both parties must know the code.

Usually we know the code being used in a communication event, and we can concentrate on trying to use it. Sometimes, however, we think we know the code but find, in the middle of the conversation, that "we don't seem to be talking about the same thing." At that point we have to check to be sure everybody involved is using the same code. Have you ever talked with people from another country who speak English as a second language? From time to time they wish to say something in English but do not know the right English word. Often people who speak in a second language have to ask for the right word by pointing or gesturing, by using words that help their listeners come up with the word they are seeking. The difficulties people encounter talking in codes are easy to see when we talk about a second language and its problems, but there are problems in the use of codes even when all parties involved speak the same native language. They, too, may have to stop from time to time to check and make sure that they are using words that mean the same things to both. Words are highly personal, in that for each word, each of us carries his or her own mental image, or meaning, or several meanings.

All natural languages are codes. For most Americans, the common code or language is English. But there are many other kinds of codes besides languages such as English, Spanish, French, German, and so forth. Some, like the Morse code, use dots and dashes to represent letters and are simply added onto a language such as English. Other codes are not composed of words at all. For example, the American Indian tribes developed a sign language in which certain hand movements meant certain ideas. Although each tribe had its own language and often a member of one tribe could not talk with someone from a different tribe using language, all the tribes knew the sign language, and though it was somewhat limited, they could communicate with one another using the sign code.

The English language has certain words that stand for certain things. Thus the word *dog* stands for an animal of a certain kind. There is nothing about the animal that makes the word *dog* the one and only word that can stand for it. Other languages use other words: German, *Hundt;* French, *chien.* When we talk in a language, we must learn how the language is used, what the words mean, and how they can be put together in a sentence. For several people to talk to one another, they must all understand the words they use to mean pretty much the same things. When a person has in mind a furry, four-legged, domesticated animal that barks and eats meat, and she encodes a message that has the word *dog* in it, the listener who hears the word *dog,* should not decode it to mean, a two-legged bird that cackles and is good to eat southern-fried.

Among the important codes used in interpersonal communication are several that use not words but gestures, such as the Indian sign language. For example, when a person looks at another, smiles, and nods his head up and down, this behavior may be part of a code and mean agreement. Shaking the head from side to side, looking the other person in the eye, frowning, moving away, looking at the ground, and other such gestures may also be part of a nonverbal code. Everybody who knows the code understands what these actions mean.

Another important code, which is added onto speech, is like the melody that enhances a poem set to music. The code includes the way the voice changes pitch, the rate of speech, the changes in loudness, and the pauses that separate words and clumps of words. Thus if two people speak the same body and vocal codes, one can say a great deal to another by the way he draws out the sound "ooo" and at the same time smiles, and holds up his right hand in front of his shoulder and forms a circle with his thumb and forefinger.

When we speak to other people we punctuate our comments with pauses and changes in the rate of speech, loudness, and pitch. By proper use of vocal punctuation we can make the same sentence mean several different things. Take the sentence, "Youth today is revolting." Can you read the sentence aloud so it means two different things?

We will call the body codes and the vocal melodies *nonverbal* communication. While we can think of many other languages, and some of these are fun to play with, our concern in the book will be with speech communication that uses some dialect of American English as the verbal code and uses the nonverbal codes common in North America.

One final point about nonverbal communication and our model of the communication process will be complete. Many gestures and voice changes are not part of a code. A person may shift her eyes, jerk her head, and move her shoulders as she speaks, and other people in the same culture may still not know what all the body movements mean. For example, when Joe talks he makes a lot of movements that nobody else makes and these do not mean anything to anyone who does not know Joe well enough to have learned that when Joe gets red in the face, moves his head from side to side, and starts to stammer, he will soon begin to hit somebody or kick or throw something.

For the most part we must study the people we often talk with to try to find the nonverbal cues that indicate their feelings and attitudes. When Father meets you at the door with anger written all over his face, he does not even have to ask, "Why are you so late?" But when we talk with strangers, the best we can hope to do is learn the nonverbal codes—that is, the gestures everybody knows mean something in the same way all people who speak English understand the word *dog* to mean a certain kind of animal. A tight face puts us down, an open face helps us to relax and invites communication.

KEY IDEAS CHAPTER 1

• A good communication model contains all the main parts of a typical conversation in standard form and working in the usual way.

• The first attempt at communication usually fails.

• A process is a series of give-and-take moves by which some end is reached.

• The *S M C R* model of the communication process consists of a *source* encoding a *message* and transmitting it through *channels* to be decoded by a *receiver*.

• During the communication process the receiver feeds back information to the source about what the receiver got out of decoding the message.

• Feedback consists of information about the errors in a message that helps the source clear up misunderstandings.

• One important feature of the feedback loop is that only one person or thing has the goal.

• People tend to resist being the receivers of messages unless they trust the source or think they stand to gain from working to achieve understanding.

• People have greater potential to provide feedback than machines but often fail to do so.

• People often hear what they expect to hear instead of what is being said.

• People who wish to communicate must make some link to establish contact.

• When people make messages, they encode them into a form their listeners can take in.

• American English is a code.

• Codes such as the English language have no natural connection with the objects of the world.

• Among important codes for communication are several that use gestures.

• Another important code that adds meaning to speech is like the melody that enhances a poem set to music.

• By proper use of vocal punctuation we can make the same sentence mean several different things.

• Body codes and vocal melodies are nonverbal communication.

• Many gestures and voice changes are not part of a code but are simply personal characteristics of the speaker.

SUGGESTED PROJECTS

1 • The class is divided into pairs. Talk with each other for the time specified by the instructor. Learn as much about each other as you

can. Then, separately, write a short paper in which you discuss how well the communication model in Chapter 1 explains what happened during your conversation. Did the two of you alternate playing the roles of source and receiver? What was the nature of feedback during your talk? Were there important things happening that the model could not explain?

2 • The class is divided into groups of five or six. Each group creates a *code* suitable for communicating among themselves. This code may be a verbal one, a nonverbal one, or it may combine both verbal and nonverbal symbols. Each group has a few minutes for members to communicate with one another, using their code, in front of the class. The class then has 10 minutes to try to "break" the code. After all the groups have finished, there is a general class discussion of the nature of codes and how they work in the communication process.

3 • This is an exercise in feedback. Each student prepares a five-minute oral message. After one minute of the presentation, the instructor announces, "Feedback begins." Class members may then call out "What do you mean?" whenever they do not understand what the speaker is saying. Class discussion deals with how silence may not indicate understanding and how much more time is often required to explain ideas when the audience has an opportunity for feedback.

SUGGESTED READINGS

Berlo, David K. *The Process of Communication.* New York: Holt, Rinehart and Winston, 1960.

Mortensen, C. David. *Basic Readings in Communication Theory.* 2d ed. New York: Harper & Row, 1979.

Watzlawick, Paul, Janet H. Beavin, and Don D. Jackson. *Programatics of Human Communication: A Study of Interactional Patterns, Pathologies, and Paradoxes.* New York: Norton, 1967.

Wiener, Norbert. *The Human Use of Human Beings: Cybernetics and Society.* Garden City, N.Y.: Doubleday (Anchor Books), 1954.

COMMUNICATION ANXIETY
CHAPTER 2

Talking and listening are among the most important things we do; yet we begin talking and listening at such a young age that we often take oral communication for granted. Our communication skills and our feelings about communication are so ingrained that we seldom think about them and analyze what they are and how they might be improved.

Sometimes the hardest thing we have to do is to talk to someone or to a group of people. Usually those moments when we cannot talk easily are the very times we want most to talk smoothly, clearly, interestingly, and convincingly. Why do we feel tense and excited when we think about talking in certain situations in general or to certain individuals and groups in particular? Tension comes when much is at stake, when we feel failure will be unpleasant, perhaps even punishing to us, and when success will be pleasant and rewarding. The body alerts itself for verbal battle or for flight.

The fight or flight response is an old one that we have inherited from our prehistoric ancestors, who often faced personal danger. Whether they stood and fought or turned and ran, their bodies needed to be keyed up for maximum physical effort.

Our bodily symptoms when we become alerted to a communication situation where much is at stake tend to vary from person to person; they usually include such things as sweaty palms, increased heartbeat, dryness in the mouth, and shortness of breath. We often report these feelings in terms such as the clichés, "I had butterflies in my stomach," or "My heart was in my mouth."

A number of investigators have studied the relationship between the emotional feeling people report they have and physical measures of bodily changes such as increased heartbeats. These investigations reveal that some subjects will interpret such arousal as a positive and pleasurable emotion, while others will interpret the same physical changes as anxiety, fear, or dread.

A good way to understand how vital speech communication is to you personally and how you tend to interpret the physical tension associated with it is to set down your own feelings over the last couple of days. Did you get churned up in an argument with a friend, with a date, with your wife or husband? Did you dread having to talk to an intimate friend or relative about something important? Did you feel nervous and excited in class because you wanted to say something but were afraid of what others would think of you? Were you ill at ease at a party where you did not know anybody? Did you turn your face away and avoid having to talk to somebody because you felt that particular conversation might be uncomfortable? More to the point, how did you feel about the prospect of taking a course in speech communication, where you might be asked to participate in interviews, discussions, and exercises in which you would have to talk up? Or were you looking forward to, or dreading, a situation where you might have to get on your feet and speak to an audience?

One of the biggest mental barriers to the study and practice of speech communication is the often unreasonable fear of speaking in public, which is called *stage fright*.

In this chapter we examine the fear of speaking and what can be done to deal with it.

THE NATURE OF COMMUNICATION ANXIETY

We will define *communication anxiety* as mental distress, worry, uneasiness brought about by the fear of punishment or misfortune as a result of communication.

The emotional arousal that goes along with fear of speaking prepares people for either going ahead and meeting the situation or taking flight from it. The too common response, however, is to avoid communicating if possible.

The first point about the fear of speaking is that almost everybody has stage fright or fears a communication situation from time to time. The second point about communication anxiety is that people vary a great deal in terms of how often and how strongly they experience it. At one extreme, some people seldom feel anxious about communicating, and at the other extreme, some people are usually fearful and anxious about many different types of communication. The bulk of the population falls somewhere between these two extremes.

Toward the extremely anxious end of the population are those people who have a severe problem, one that requires special attention. To sort out those who have the normal experiences of communication anxiety from those with special problems, it is useful to note the differences between *state* and *trait* anxiety.

State anxiety

The normal experience of most people is to have off-and-on feelings of anxiety. When they feel anxious, it is because of a specific situation such as a job interview, or because they are scheduled to give a speech to a difficult audience. People normally get into an anxious state for brief periods of time, and when the specific incident is over they go about their normal communication activities without trouble.

The most common off-and-on feelings of anxiety have to do with thinking about acting in a play, singing a solo, playing an instrument in front of an audience, giving a public speech, and so forth. In similar fashion, most athletes feel anxiety before playing a big game before a large audience. Some years ago a nationwide survey of American adults discovered that the most frequently reported fear was of speaking in public. Of course the results of such surveys often change over time, but the fact that stage fright was so high on the list is interesting and in line with our own experiences in teaching students, in working with management training programs, and in teaching seminars for organizational leaders.

Off-and-on fear of speaking is a normal and understandable response to exciting and important situations in which successful communication means a great deal to you. Such off-and-on feelings of tension are to be expected, and people who do not feel them are probably the abnormal ones.

Trait anxiety

People who have trait anxiety tend to suffer from a vague and general fear about their communication. They dread communication situations that the majority of people take for granted.

Considerable research into the nature of trait anxiety indicates that it can be an important personal problem well worth special attention from counselors and instructors trained to work with such anxiety. Our concern in this chapter is with the majority of students who experience off-and-on normal bouts of communication anxiety and who, according to the research, can benefit from the experience and professional help they typically get in a course in speech communication.

Our report on the major findings of the effects of trait anxiety on those who really have a problem with fear of speaking will be brief and we present it primarily to indicate how much of a problem dread of speaking can be.

People with high general speech anxiety are often introverted and lacking in self-esteem. They avoid communicating if possible. For example, highly anxious people who take part in group discussions avoid the seating positions that are typically seen as the center of communication and interaction, such as the head of the table. Students with high levels of anxiety prefer large lecture classes and do not often ask for help from teachers and teaching assistants. They avoid seats in the front and center of classrooms and prefer seats around the edges. They avoid speaking with strangers, and if they date, they tend to go steady. They avoid jobs that require much communication, particularly positions that involve meeting the public.

One of the unfortunate by-products of avoiding communication is that others perceive anxious people as unattractive socially, sexually, and as work partners. One of the discoveries of studies of leadership emergence in leaderless group discussions is that members eliminate quiet participants from consideration for leadership.

If you suffer from such unusually high and general fear, you should discuss your problem with your instructor. For the great majority of readers who do not have trait anxiety, we only want to indicate that some time and attention to those times in which they experience state anxiety will help them improve their communication practices.

One of the authors was coaching an executive in a major financial institution on communication skills related to formal presentations. The executive's position required that he give frequent presentations of complicated financial material to influential clients. To an observer he seemed to be fluent, articulate, and poised. His nonverbal communication suggested confidence and competence. During a private meeting with the author in which we were playing back a videotape of a presentation for evaluation and coaching, he confessed that he suffered from stage fright whenever he had to give a presentation. He testified that the continual bouts of anxiety made his life miserable. He was not going to give up an excellent position, but he did want to do something about the problem. Discussing the problem revealed that the executive did not suffer from trait apprehension but had fallen into the habit of working himself into a state of anxiety about this one particular recurring kind of presentation. When we talked about the problem and he changed his attitude toward the situation, he did not change his way of giving a presentation or his calm manner but he did feel better about it both before and during the presentation.

THE INTERPRETATION OF SPEECH TENSION

Investigators studying speech anxiety have used instruments to study physical changes such as increased heartbeats, have trained observers to rate speakers on their apparent nervousness, and have asked subjects how nervous they felt while speaking.

Some scholars have surveyed a number of studies to see whether the three ways of studying communication anxiety are comparable. They tried to find out if people who said they felt nervous seemed nervous to trained observers. They also compared measures of bodily changes taken by instruments to the speakers' reports of feeling nervous and the observers' ratings of how nervous the speakers looked. The results of such surveys indicate, as we noted earlier, that the three things do not go together as much as one might think. You may feel physical excitement and interpret it as anticipation and enthusiasm rather than fear. Observers may evaluate a confident inexperienced speaker as nervous and an anxious experienced speaker as confident. Sometimes people who say they felt nervous while speaking looked as though they were bored or tired.

The point is that studies matching body symptoms to emotional feelings have found that while instruments indicate that the same things are happening physically, people *report* they are feeling a wide range of emotions. What causes you to decide that your pounding heart, sweaty palms, and dry mouth are evidence of love or hate or fear or anger is the context in which you have these feelings and how you interpret them.

In our culture there is a widespread idea that if you are to give a speech you should feel nervous and dread the experience. Your friends may kid you about it or take pity on you as though you were going to some torture chamber. Some people suggest you should be afraid, so you are encouraged to interpret the excitement that is a normal reaction to thinking about an important event in your life as fear or anxiety.

We do not have to follow the suggestion that the usual response to speaking is fear. We can interpret our aroused state as excitement, as pleasurable anticipation. A good skier standing at the top of a long, challenging slope may have the same feelings of butterflies in the stomach, pounding heart, and dry mouth as the speaker standing before an audience, but the skier may find the excitement pleasurable while the speaker may interpret the feeling as fear.

A good way to manage the physical tension surrounding important communication events is to develop a positive interpretation of what they mean. In our personal fantasies we often daydream about doing things we are interested in. If we are interested in playing baseball, we may daydream about going to bat with the bases loaded in the last half of the ninth with a chance to win the game. If we are interested in sports cars, we may have a daydream in which we drive our favorite model.

In our wishful daydreams we often hit the home run, win the game. We could, however, play out the story so it becomes a dreadful experience in our imagination. Instead of dreaming of the feel of the bat on a solid hit and the sounds of the crowd cheering, we could see the fast ball heading for our head, and feel the sharp pain as it hits our cheek, or we could feel the shame of striking out. We could anticipate the skid on the ice as we drive our dream car, the terrible crash and pain following the crash. People who fantasize all the scary things that can happen when participating in athletic events will tend to avoid them. Those who emphasize the dangers of owning a car are unlikely to buy one. The physical arousal that comes with the daydream will be similar but the way the person interprets that feeling, as pleasant or unpleasant, depends on the interpretative fantasy.

You often have the chance to seek out an important communication event, such as striking up a conversation with someone you would like to date or arranging for an interview for a job that you would like to have. Sometimes circumstances make it hard for you to avoid giving a speech, such as when you take a course in speech communication or when you are elected to a position of leadership in a student organization.

When important speaking occasions arise you can daydream about them in scary negative ways. You may see yourself making a stupid comment or "putting your foot in your mouth." You may feel your knees knock together, your voice quiver, and your hands shake. You can see yourself before an audience giving a speech when suddenly your mind goes blank and the audience grows more and more embarrassed and you panic and freeze. If you daydream along these lines, you will certainly interpret your normal and desirable physical tension before giving the speech as fear. Unfortunately, movie and television comedy routines have used all these negative situations frequently.

You may choose your own daydreams, however. You can see yourself before the audience hitting the equivalent of a home run—poised, trying out an interesting line of thought, holding the audience, receiving a standing ovation at the conclusion. If you begin to view your speaking in positive fashion, you may interpret your tension prior to speaking as a heady excitement similar to that felt by the skier at the top of the slope. Indeed, giving a successful speech can be as exciting and pleasant as making a good run down a ski slope.

USING COMMUNICATION TENSION PRODUCTIVELY

In this section we discuss the productive use of speech tension while giving a public speech. Anxiety about taking center stage to perform or give a speech is normal and to be expected. Our suggestions about using tension productively while giving a public speech can be easily adapted to less tense situations, such as participating in a conversation, an interview, or a group meeting.

The first rule is to pick topics that excite you. If you talk on subjects you feel strongly about, you will soon discover that your interest in what you are saying is genuine and taking your mind off yourself.

The second rule is to prepare thoroughly. A good way to get the tension under control is to feel satisfied and confident that you are well prepared. A thorough preparation serves to put your mind at ease about that common bugaboo of speakers—forgetting what you want to say.

Some people try to assure that they will not forget by writing the speech out and reading it. Speakers sometimes need a written manuscript for other reasons in addition to making sure they do not forget what they want to say. If you are speaking on radio or television or making an important announcement where you are likely to be quoted in news media, you may need to write all your comments carefully and be sure to read the exact language you have worked out. The speech manuscript does put your words right in front of you so you need not worry about what you will say, but it also causes some problems.

Reading a speech tends to put a barrier between the speaker and the audience. You must be a skillful reader to overcome that barrier and communicate with the audience when you are tied to your manuscript. Few speakers manage to deliver a speech effectively under such conditions. American presidents since the advent of radio have tended to read their broadcast speeches to the nation. Aside from Franklin Roosevelt in the 1930s, almost all the rest have been poor oral readers, and their speeches have often been dull and ineffective as a result. The manuscript itself becomes a distraction often for the audience. Of course you can use note cards, but a speech of any length written out on cards will grow to quite a deck, too large to handle easily. The way you shuffle this deck and the possibility of getting the cards out of order all contribute to possible difficulties, all easy distractions for an audience.

If you write the speech and memorize it, you can sometimes overcome the barrier put up by the manuscript. If you have the speech memorized, you can practice its delivery and polish up your use of voice, your timing, and your gestures. Memorizing a speech takes a good deal of additional time, however, and you always run the danger of forgetting. When you forget a memorized speech, you often have to be prompted to get back on the right track. For the beginner who tries to memorize a speech, the result may be a patterned use of voice and gesture that seems unnatural to the audience.

The extemporaneous speech is one in which you prepare a careful outline and the supporting ideas you plan to use, but you do not write it out and memorize it word for word. You may rehearse the speech aloud by talking from the outline until you have it well in mind. You might commit the main points of the outline to memory or write them on note cards or a sheet of paper and use these main points to jog your memory while you talk with the audience. If you prepare an extemporaneous speech carefully, you still have the freedom to change your comments as you watch the audience response. Should you forget a point or a story or an example, you can continue on with the next section of your speech without prompting. A well-prepared extemporaneous speech is one of the best ways to deal productively with speech tension.

Thus if you have followed rule one and picked a topic that excites you, and prepared thoroughly, the second rule, you can add the third rule for using communication tension productively, which is to develop an audience-centered approach to speaking. Keep your mind on the listeners and their responses. Watch individuals. Did the audience like some example you used? Did an analogy work well in getting one of your points across?(Was there nodding of heads in agreement, for example?) Can you think of other analogies or examples that you might insert to increase audience interest and involvement? Is the audience getting bored? Do any members of the audience look confused? As in the trite but true advice to young people who want to learn how to get over self-consciousness in social situations, get your mind off yourself! By concentrating on the audience, you can take your mind off yourself and your performance. Self-centered attitudes are primary causes of stage fright.

The fourth rule you have probably guessed by now: act as though you were confident both before and during your speech. If the beginning speaker is anxious and the audience finds out about it, it is largely through nonverbal cues. The speaker's hands may shake, his voice may quiver, he may have difficulty looking at the audience, and he may remain poker-faced, wooden-looking. An audience is quick to pick up cues about the way a speaker feels about himself. If the speaker regards his own nonverbal cues as showing that he is worried about his performance, the audience will get the correct impression that the speaker has stage fright. They will begin to worry about him and his feelings and be distracted from the ideas in his speech. Then the speaker not only has trouble getting his ideas across to the audience but also must combat their view of him as someone with not much to offer them, someone they need to help through the difficult task of giving a speech. Interestingly enough, the same body motions, if perceived by the speaker as symptoms of his intense involvement with, and high regard for, his subject and the occasion, can make a strong positive impression on an audience. We cannot stress too much the importance of how the speaker perceives himself. This perception of yourself is the first thing you communicate to any audience.

If the speaker can control her tension so that her gestures, posture, and facial expression are appropriate to what she is saying, the audience will seldom know she is anxious. Every good speaker gets keyed up before she goes on. But like the athlete who is nervous and keyed up in the dressing room but feels fine two minutes after the game starts, the good speaker uses these feelings of nervousness and tension to key her up to do a better job.

The point is that you do not want to stop feeling excited and keyed up about giving a speech or standing before a crowd. You want to learn to use this tension to make your mind sharper and less likely to forget, and to give your whole body more focus and concentration on communicating with your audience.

While waiting for your turn to speak, force yourself to sit erect and gaze about with confidence. Pick a spot in the front of the audience and when you are introduced, get up from your chair, pause, pull yourself erect, and firmly and calmly force yourself to walk to the spot. When you reach the spot you picked, pause again, stand erect, and with the weight balanced comfortably on both feet, look out at the audience and, for just a moment, let your eyes run over the listeners. Be sure and look at the people in the audience *until you can see them.* Some beginners, when they feel particularly nervous at the start of the speech, are unwilling actually to look at the audience. Since they do not know what the people look like or what they are doing, they find themselves growing more and more nervous as they proceed. We are all afraid of the unknown, and if the speaker is not watching the audience, he has no way of knowing what it is doing. In all speaking situations, it is far better for you, the speaker, to look at your audience, to see the friendly faces, the smiles, the frowns, the questioning looks—to realize that an audience is made up of human beings much like yourself, that they usually wish you well (particularly in a speech-communication class), and that they want you to be a good speaker.

And so, having looked directly during this pause at the people to whom you will be talking, take a good deep breath as quietly as you can and begin your speech in a strong voice. By standing erect, by acting confident, by pausing, and by beginning in a good strong voice, you complete the illusion of confidence for your audience.

Furthermore, you will discover that if you can give the audience the impression that you are a poised and confident speaker, their impression will affect you, and you may soon feel more confidence and find that you can keep your tension under control.

KEY IDEAS CHAPTER 2

• Communication tension is the old fight-or-flight response to situations that seem to offer strong rewards or punishments.

• Communication anxiety is the mental distress, worry, uneasiness brought about by the fear of punishment or misfortune as a result of communication.

• The common response to communication anxiety is to avoid communicating.

• Almost all people have feelings they interpret as stage fright from time to time.

• State anxiety refers to the normal feelings of uneasiness related to a specific situation which are brief and leave when the communication is over.

• Off-and-on feelings of tension are to be expected, and people who do not feel them are probably the abnormal ones.

• Trait anxiety refers to the general and continual fear about communication that seems to be a permanent part of a person's makeup.

• People with trait anxiety tend to avoid communicating as much as possible.

• Others often stereotype people with trait anxiety in negative ways.

• People with trait anxiety can benefit from special counseling and training programs.

• Our approach in this chapter is geared to students with normal state anxiety about communicating.

• The results of surveys of research indicate that bodily changes, looking nervous to others, and feeling nervous are three different things, not closely related.

• Body symptoms tend to be about the same for many different emotions.

• Our interpretation of our bodily states is important in our emotional feelings.

• A good way to manage physical tensions about communication is to develop a positive interpretation of your emotional feeling.

• Communication tension can serve to lessen your effectiveness or to key you up for more effective speaking.

• The first rule in giving public speeches is to pick topics that excite you.

• The second rule is to prepare thoroughly.

• The third rule is to develop an audience-centered approach.

• The fourth rule is to act as though you were confident.

SUGGESTED PROJECTS

1 • Prepare an analysis of your feelings about communication. Show this initial response to your instructor, then keep it throughout the course. It is to be your personal record, so be completely honest. Begin with a brief discussion of types of communication experiences in which you interpret your feelings as anxiety. Write a brief description of physical symptoms that you notice at such times. Keep a record of your communication experiences throughout the term and describe in some detail your feelings during each class exercise. For those exercises that trouble you, write down all the negative thoughts you have beforehand and examine them to see how likely they are to happen. For each negative thought, write down a positive one. Compare your responses to communication tension toward the end of the class with your initial analysis and particularly with your program in managing communication tension.

2 • This is an exercise in getting acquainted in a realistic way with the audience situation. The first part is an exercise in the speaker's pause. Your instructor will have you walk to the front of the class in pairs. You are to stand erect and look at the audience in a poised, expectant way

as though you are about to speak. You will not actually say anything but, for about thirty seconds, look at the audience directly so you can really see what they look like. Next, your instructor will combine your pairs into groups of four. You will come forward and, while sitting or standing in a relaxed fashion, will each briefly introduce yourself to the class.

3 • This is an assignment that you should prepare with the express purpose of managing your tensions productively. You will be given three or four minutes to come forward and tell the class about an emotional personal experience. The assignment is to make the audience feel what you felt by describing what you saw, what you heard, what you smelled, what you tasted, what you touched. Describe what you sensed in such graphic terms that your listeners will be able to see it in their mind's eye and smell and taste the experience. Select a topic about which you have strong feelings; prepare your comments carefully; concentrate on the audience. Be prepared for a response, because they will get caught up in your description. Write a report of your feelings prior to and during your talk.

SUGGESTED READINGS

Freimuth, Vicki S. "The Effects of Communication Apprehension on Communication Effectiveness." *Human Communication Research* 2 (1976) 289–98.

Fremouw, William J., and Michael D. Scott, "Cognitive Restructuring: An Alternative Method for the Treatment of Communication Apprehension." *Communication Education* 28 (1979): 129–33.

McCroskey, James C. "Oral Communication Apprehension: A Summary of Recent Theory and Research." *Human Communication Research* 4 (1977): 78–96.

Phillips, Gerald M. "Rhetoritherapy Versus the Medical Model: Dealing with Reticence. *Communication Education.* 26 (1977) 34–43

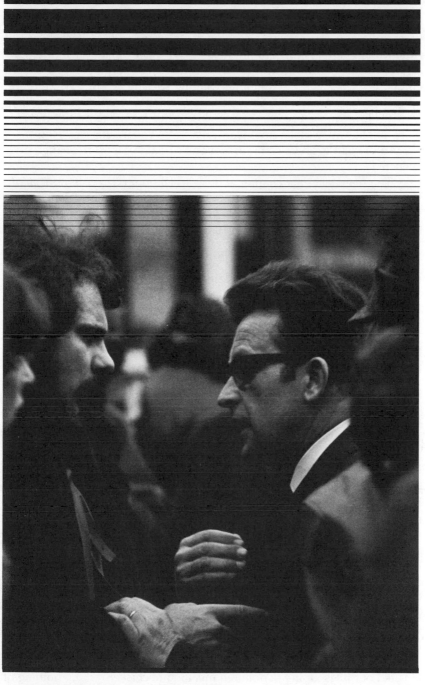

THE USE OF LANGUAGE
CHAPTER 3

In Chapter 1 we discussed the encoding and decoding links in the communication process. In this chapter we examine the effective use of American English in oral communication. We will examine such questions as the following: How do words work to transmit information? To arouse emotions? To suggest something without spelling it out? What is the difference between denotation and connotation? How can we define words? How can we use names and descriptive language persuasively? Is there a right way to speak American English? What are dialects? How does the use of dialects affect communication? Should you try to change your dialect?

The material in the chapter is basic to all your daily communication. How you encode and decode messages affects your informal conversations as well as your public speeches. Your use of words affects the impression you make in a job interview as well as your participation in a group meeting.

We begin the chapter with a discussion of the denotative and connotative use of language in general and then deal with specific cultural differences in language usage.

DENOTATIVE AND CONNOTATIVE MEANING

When we say a word *denotes* something we mean that the word points to, notes, stands for, or indicates the thing. Thus we can say that the word *chicken* denotes a certain kind of fowl that is a certain general size, is feathered, cackles, and lays our breakfast eggs.

The denotative meanings of a language are the ways the words are plugged into the perceptions of the participants in a communication event. Our decision to use a given word to stand for some object, person, or event is up to us. If the language is to work as a code for communication, however, we must decide which words stand for which objects, and we must agree about it and come to share the *common* code or understanding.

We cannot change the denotative meaning of words willy-nilly, because if we did, we would confuse people. Naturally language is continually changing, and we do change the denotative meanings of some words over time. We have inherited a tradition of using certain words for certain objects, however, and we learn its rules when we learn the vocabulary of our language. We all come to have a number of common denotative meanings for words in a language we use to talk with one another. If a waiter gives us fried dog when we order fried chicken, he has violated our rules for the denotative meaning of *chicken,* to say nothing of our sensibilities.

A common dictionary is a list of rules connecting words with denotative meanings, and we can read, write, and understand dictionaries because we share the same understanding of how words relate to things. We must point out the difference between the denotative meanings which are common to a number of people, and the individual responses we all have to words. Although we may all know what animal is meant by the term *dog*, we may respond to that word in different ways because of our past experience. One of you reading about the notion of *fried dog* may respond differently from another one of you, but both of you will have a clear idea of what the words stand for or denote.

Response to language is both individual and cultural. When we say a word *connotes* something, we mean it has additional meanings for a person or a group of persons that go beyond the denotative meaning. Often these additional meanings arouse emotional interpretations. Sometimes we respond to a word or an expression because of our personal experience. The word *chicken* refers to a certain kind of fowl. Both speaker and listener usually understand the denotative meaning, for the word to be the same kind of fowl. If the receiver has a violent dislike of fried chicken because of past experience, however, the response to the word will be emotional as well as reasonable. He may not only picture a chicken in his mind but he may feel a shudder of revulsion go through his entire body when he hears the word. Another person using the same dialect and in the same situation might feel a warm, pleasant glow when he pictures the same fowl, because of the favorite pet chicken he had when he was a little boy.

Sometimes a number of people share a common response to language because they share a common situation. Consider the example of two grade school boys arguing during recess. A circle of other children is soon ringed around them. The two boys become angry and one yells at the other, "You're chicken!" Probably none of the children watching the argument, however, think that the first boy is saying to the second that he is really a fowl capable of laying eggs and cackling. Denotative meaning is pushed into the background by the situation. The sentence expresses the source's emotional feeling and attitude, he breaks out with a cry of anger and frustration, and he might have expressed his feelings almost as well with a grunt or a shout as with the sentence. The other boy interprets the sentence in a similarly emotional fashion. The context and the culture which suggests that in a conflict the word *chicken* is a taunt and an insult come into play to form the response to the word. Every student of public speaking learns the importance of analyzing the effect of the situation and the occasion on the response of the audience. The speaker finds that an expression that is appropriate and gains him the desired response on one occasion may well be all wrong on another. Often when we are a message source, we have as our basic purpose telling the receiver something about the world. We are emphasizing the denotative aspect of language. For example, when we tell someone how to get from one place to another, we are informing her about the geographic location of various places. The basic content of a message discussing facts is *information*. A common dictionary definition of *information* is "a message about facts."

What are facts? *Facts* are those things which two or more people can see and agree on. We encode factual messages about such things as chairs, tables, cars, people, buildings, and their relationships to one another. Someone may come to a meeting, look about the room, and ask, "Where is John?" If you have the information, you may encode a message in reply as follows: "John just called. His car is stuck in the snow in his driveway and he will be late." The information in the message relates to things such as the human being called John, his automobile, his driveway, and the relationships among these things, for example, the relationship contained in the words "he is stuck in his driveway." Further, the message provides information about John's relationship to the building in which the meeting is being held: that he is in his driveway, that the driveway is some distance from the place of the meeting, and that he is there now and will be here somewhat later than expected.

We need to understand and have skills in the denotative use of language in order to make ideas about facts clear. Definition is the basic process we use to create denotative meanings as we communicate.

DEFINITIONS

Among the most important tools a speaker has to help make ideas clear is the ability to define a word. Before a person can tell someone about facts, she must decide whether her listener understands the word she hopes to use. If the listener does not know what is named by a word in the speaker's message, he is likely to misunderstand or be confused by the message.

When a speaker defines a word she tries to make clear to her listener the thing, property, or relationship she means to indicate when she uses the word in their conversation. If the source and receiver have the same meaning for the content words in messages—that is, they both use the same words for naming things and the same words to stand for properties and relationships—they can talk about the facts of their common experience. They can then talk about the things in a room. For example, one person might say, "Please sit in that red chair." Or, "Be careful of sitting on that red chair, because it is weak and may break." People can also speak about chairs that are not present at the time of their conversation. For instance, the source may describe the color, size, and shape of a chair which he is selling. Should the receiver decide to buy the chair, she will expect it to have certain properties because of the information she decoded from the message. If the chair is not what she expected, either the source misled her by claiming that the chair had certain properties it did not possess (her information was false), or the source and she did not have the same definition for the words in the message (the receiver misunderstood).

When you are trying to make an idea clear you must look carefully at the words you use in your messages. You must ask yourself, "Will all the people taking part in the communication decode a name as standing for the same thing?" If not, can you use another word that everybody will understand? If not, you must select the best word, in your opinion, for the thing to be discussed and carefully define it for your listeners.

One way to define a term is to find other words that say the same or nearly the same thing, and by using those other words, clarify how you plan to use the term in the communications to follow. Many of the terms that we have used earlier in the book have been defined in other words. The dictionary definition of a term usually supplies other words that mean the same thing. For example, one meaning of *communicate* in a good dictionary is "to give thoughts, feelings, or information by writing, speaking, and so forth."

Imaginary definitions

If one can describe the thing or events named by a term clearly in other words, the result is a definition. An interesting by-product of the process of definition is that we can describe an imaginary thing, person, or event, and give it a name. For example, we can describe a person who is "the present queen of the United States" and refer to such a person in our messages. Of course, the United States has no queen, so no real person is named by the definition. Yet we can go on talking about "Samantha Regina, the present queen of the United States," as though such a person existed. We can also pick a name such as *unicorn* and supply such a precise description of the beast that an artist can draw a picture of one, even though the animal does not exist.

Take the case of the *rockslide cornberet,* a strange gray bird the size of a crow with a crown of feathers resembling a beret. The rockslide cornberet gets its name from its love of corn, its beretlike headdress, and the female's peculiar practice of laying a single egg in some stones at the top of a mountain and then kicking egg and stones over the edge, thus starting a rockslide. When the rockslide comes to rest in the valley, the pile of stones serves to protect and incubate the egg so the female does not have to sit on it. Since neither source nor receiver can observe the nonexistent rockslide cornberet, if they argue about it they are talking about individual impressions and not about anything in the world that they can observe to correct their impressions.

We do not get into serious trouble talking about mythical animals or the present queen of the United States, but we do get into difficulties when we talk about *a conspiracy, a racist society, duty,* or *Women's Liberation* and cannot find any observations to correct our impressions. Much misunderstanding and many arguments come from discussions of terms that, like the rockslide cornberet, stand for nothing but the meanings we put into them. Equally important is the problem posed by defining terms such as *democracy, capitalism,* or *communism* without reference to actual events. The process of definition allows us to name a nonexistent economic system called *pure capitalism,* or a governmental arrangement called *pure communism.* Having named these fictitious things, we can go on to discuss them as though they were real events with real implications. If we define something called *world communism,* in terms of a powerful force of millions of people dedicated to the violent overthrow of capitalism, and the destruction of the United States, we may act as though the thing we have defined actually exists in the world. If the thing defined is as unreal as the rockslide cornberet, we might act foolishly because we are responding to definitions and not to things. What of the man who spends years in the Rockies with his camera, trying to get a photograph of the rockslide cornberet? The same thing can happen with definitions such as the *conspiracy* to raise gasoline prices or the *conspiracy* to overthrow the government by violent means.

If you wish to inform people, therefore, you should be sure that both you and your listeners understand whether the terms defined refer to the things of the world that can be observed and whose definitions can be checked or are names for mythical people or events or for abstract concepts.

In our efforts to transmit information we can strive to emphasize denotation and limit the secondary meanings, the connotative aspects of our words, as much as possible. Reporters for newspapers, for example, often try to write their stories in "objective" and evenhanded report language. However, people find connotative meanings even in such straightforward writing as the directions on how to use a product that you find on the label. Speakers may also load up their words with many secondary meanings either on purpose or without being aware they are doing so. Writers of television commercials and poets, for example, often try to pack as much emotion into their words as they can.

We can think of the range of denotation and connotation in messages as varying from report language with a heavy emphasis on denotation (take part A and fasten to part B with bolt of type Y) to the highly connotative words of a television commercial (my man wears Macho cologne or he wears nothing at all). We often refer to the highly connotative message as being *slanted* or containing *loaded* language. In order to sift out the information (denotative meanings), we need to get rid of as much of the slant, or load (connotative meanings), as we can.

Because emotional responses are so important in persuasion, we need to understand how connotative language works its word magic. Such understanding is useful in terms of our playing the role of message source. Often message sources fail in their attempts to communicate because they are unaware of the connotative aspects of the words they use. Understanding connotative usage can also help in a positive way in that message sources can use the secondary meanings in productive fashion.

Even more important, we need, as message receivers, an understanding of connotative language. Once you know how magicians do their tricks, you are no longer fooled by them. If you learn how it works, word magic will no longer arouse the automatic and unthinking response the "snake oil" salespeople hope that it will.

THE PERSUASIVE USE OF WORDS

Naming

One important persuasive skill is the ability to select exactly the right suggestive word to name a thing or event or to describe its properties and relationships. Mark Twain is supposed to have said that the difference between the right word and the almost-right word is the difference between lightning and a lightning bug.

Suppose people are talking about the same thing but are using different names for it. Even with these different names, they may all understand what is being discussed. Say that several people are talking about a college. They might name it *the college, the old alma mater, the institution, the nut house, the playpen with ash trays, the ivory tower,* or any one of the other names by which this college is known to its many students and alumni. No matter which name the person in the group chooses for labeling the college, all the others present know it is *the college* he is talking about. What, then, do we learn from the different labels? By the selection of a particular label for a thing, the source of a message indicates a lot about how he feels about the thing or event in question.

If several men are discussing female acquaintances, a given woman might be referred to a *darling, honey, my old lady, the little woman, that broad, that bitch,* or whatever happens to be the current slang words for attractive and unattractive females. And of course, women have a comparable vocabulary to describe the males they know. The name selected for a woman or man is a powerful indirect suggestion to all others present. The words we use are important parts of our persuasive messages.

Propagandists often use names that reflect attitudes. Two hostile bordering countries report an armed clash of their troops. Country number one calls the event "shameless naked aggression," while country number two calls the same event "a defensive retaliation." One country names the government of another "a totalitarian regime," the latter government refers to itself as "a democratic peoples' republic." Some revolutionaries set off a bomb in a public building. Sympathizers with the revolution call the bombing "a courageous act by heroic freedom fighters." Those who oppose the revolutionaries and dislike the destruction of public buildings call the same bombing "a cowardly, criminal act by mindless anarchists."

Describing

Selecting names heavily loaded with suggestion is but one way in which choice of words is important. The words a speaker uses to describe the properties or qualities of the things, events, or people designated by the names are equally important. One person says, "This cheese has a rich bouquet." Another remarks, "This cheese stinks to high heaven."

Compare the following ways of describing the qualities of a given individual, and see how words work to carry suggestion to the listener.

John is prudent.
versus
John is a tightwad.

Mary is courageous.
versus
Mary is reckless.

John is sensitive
versus
John is emotionally unstable.

We can also suggest attitudes by the words and phrases we use to describe relationships among things, people, and events. Consider these examples:

John was a love child.
versus
John is a bastard.

John and Mary have a deep and satisfying personal relationship.
versus
John and Mary are living together like a couple of alley cats.

In the last example we used a figure of speech to describe the relationship. Figures of speech are important techniques to suggest or state a comparison between two things. By associating a thing, person, or event with something pleasant, admirable, or good, we suggest that the thing itself is also desirable. By associating the thing with something unpleasant, or bad, we make the opposite impression. Compare "This cigarette has a springlike freshness" with "This cigarette reeks like a dumpyard incinerator."

One important persuasive technique is to describe a person in terms of an adjective or noun that connotes a positive or negative attitude toward that individual. Much of what people do when they persuade is to attack or defend other people and their actions. We often say that a friend has good qualities and an enemy has bad character traits. When a propagandist uses words with negative connotations to describe an enemy, we call the technique *name calling*. A politician using the name-calling technique might refer to an opponent as a *political hack,* a *crook,* a *left-winger,* or an *arch conservative.*

CONNOTATIVE MEANINGS LINKED TO CULTURAL DIFFERENCES

Some words and statements are closely tied to the structure of society and tend to arouse a common reaction from entire groups of people. Look at the following examples:

Drive slow.
She played it as she should.
Whom did you wish to see?
It is I.
It don't neither.
Dese cigarettes are better'n dose.
Andy, he be with us.
Y'all come back soon, heah?
I hain't seen 'im.

You probably found some of the examples odd and somehow not right, while others seemed quite right and comfortable. You might decide that some of the expressions were incorrect or bad grammar or showoff ways of talking that only affected people would use, or people speaking with a southern dialect or an urban-ghetto dialect. Your response to the expression reflects your reponse to the culture, the way of life, of those who speak the various dialects. Do you like the southern geographic region? Do you feel it is an area of pleasant, cultured, and gracious life? Do you feel the South is a closed society, racist and bigoted? All these feelings come into play when you hear a person speak in a southern dialect. Some critics of political speaking argued that former President Lyndon Johnson's Texas drawl damaged the effect of his television talks to the nation. Jimmy Carter's Georgia dialect and the Kennedy family's Boston speech also influenced the response of various segments of the American public to their speeches. Your response to an expression in black English likewise reflects your attitude toward race relations and your feelings about black culture. Whoever you are, wherever you live, you have to accept the fact that you speak a dialect. To someone from a different heritage and environment, the way you speak is strange.

Speech often reflects geographic regions, social classes, and economic, ethnic, religious, and racial differences. People in different geographic regions have developed different styles of speaking; working-class members use different forms of expression, different vocal inflections, different rules to form sentences, than do upper-middle-class people. People who live in the black urban ghettos of the North develop some unique patterns of speech as do bilingual members, such as our Mexican-American and Puerto Rican populations.

All the different ways of talking within the United States make up a single complicated system in which people move around from place to place, from one social and economic class to another. We must add to the system the effect of the mass media—film, television, and radio—which transmit a steady flow of messages in a standard dialect. Even within the same geographic regions, such as the southeastern United States, the lower class speaks differently from the upper middle class; the black worker speaks differently from the white worker. In practice, however, since all classes within a region talk with one another and all are exposed to radio, television, and film, the various expressions and ways of speaking rub off on one another. Thus you probably shift back and forth in your style of speaking, depending on how formal the situation is and on the people with whom you happen to be speaking at the time.

DIALECTS

We will call the different ways of speaking American English within the United States *dialects*. What is a dialect? The differences that make one group's way of speaking a dialect in comparison with another's are part and parcel of the entire language. Dialect differences include the way people say the individual sounds, such as the /r/ sound or the /aw/ sound. Differences include the way people say larger units, such as the word *pin* (denoting a small, slender, sharp thing useful for sticking pieces of cloth together) and the word *pen* (an enclosure useful for keeping babies confined in a small area). Differences also include the way people say clusters of words, such as "Charlie Aunt she be with us" and "Y'all come back soon, heah?"

A dialect differs from other dialects in vocabulary. Some words are commonly used in one dialect and not in another. The same word can denote different things in one dialect than in other dialects. For example, some dialects use the word *man* frequently as a word of emphasis, not merely to refer to a human male. A dialect may use a word to mean something quite different from the usual meaning associated with the same word in another dialect. The words *bread, grass,* and *trip* come to mind in this regard. A given dialect differs from others in the way the various sounds are made and in the way they fit together to form words, as well as in the way the words fit together into sentences.

Those people who first learned to speak in a given dialect tend to have a common set of emotional responses to it. People who do not know the dialect or who learn it later in life often have a different set of responses to the dialect than do native speakers. Language reflects, supports, and influences changes of class structure, race relations, and economic privilege, and people respond with deep and profound emotions to dialects and the changing of speech habits. Often a comment intended to correct a dialect is taken as a personal insult or a slur on a class, race, or region. Sometimes it actually is.

Hawaii has a rich, diverse culture composed of many races. For years, speech teachers in Hawaii tried to change the pidgin and other native dialects of students to conform to a standard white-middle-class dialect. Some years ago the entire program was reevaluated and changed so that the students are now allowed to use their native dialects and learn skills using them. In Brooklyn for many years, people who were studying to become teachers and who spoke native "Brooklynese" were retrained to speak with a standard American dialect. Washington, D.C. at one time had a program to teach black children from the city's ghettos a standard white-middle-class dialect. The program came under heavy fire and was finally discontinued because enough people felt it was racist and demeaning to black culture and to the students' pride in being black. Nevertheless, even within native dialects, most students need to learn to improve their communication skills. Some people are simply better able to communicate within their native dialect than are others, and most of us could improve our ability to communicate effectively with people whose native dialect is different from ours.

CONSIDERATIONS ABOUT IMPROVING VERBAL COMMUNICATION

Should you change your way of speaking if you use a dialect that is not the same as the standard general American speech of radio, television, and film? Should you change your grammar to that which is commonly used by educated and cultured people of all dialects? You now have an understanding of some basic facts about language and dialects to help you make that decision for yourself.

You should keep the following points in mind as you decide whether you need to change or improve your own language.

1 More middle-class speakers have skills primarily related to school language, but working-class speakers also have a wide range of verbal skills, including

many not mastered by middle-class speakers; and in the urban ghetto, speakers communicate in ways that demand ingenuity, originality, and complex language behaviors.

2   Black English and other nonstandard dialects are not deficient uses of standard English. They are logical outgrowths of the linguistic history of the people who speak them.

3   Because of the social, economic, and geographic anchoring of speech, people tend to make stereotyped judgments on the basis of the way you talk. Television announcers, schoolteachers, office managers, and so forth are stereotyped as having excellent speech with regard to their use of grammar, their articulation, and their pronunciation. A man who uses such nonstandard terms as *dem, dese, dose,* and *dat* and double-negative expressions such as "Don't never do dat to me agin" is stereotyped as a tough guy, one who probably fights a lot. Upper-middle-class and upper-class speakers are stereotyped as using correct grammar, pronunciations and articulation.

4   The more style changes you have at your command, the better you can communicate in a wide range of situations for a larger number of different receivers.

5   Your instructor can help make you aware of any differences between your dialect and the standard grammar and pronunciation. Simply becoming aware of differences will not teach you to use the standard dialect. Certainly what you learn in the classroom will not become an unconscious verbal habit. Probably the best you can hope for is a control such as when a person learns to use standard grammar at least in more formal speaking situations. Your casual speech will tend to remain much what it has always been.

6   The most important consideration is for you to decide what you plan to do with your life. Do you plan to adopt a lifestyle that requires talking with many different kinds of people? Do you plan to move from one part of the country to another? Do you expect to work with people from different social classes? From different ethnic backgrounds? Do you plan to work at a job in which your native dialect is basic and sufficient? Do you plan a career that would require you to use standard general American dialect and standard school grammar and do you speak this way now? In general, you should consider that life in the complex, shifting, urban, multiracial culture of the United States will put increasing demands on college-educated people to be able to shift styles of speech and dialect over a wide range.

KEY IDEAS CHAPTER 3

• **When a word denotes something it points to, notes, stands for, or indicates the thing.**

• **The denotative meanings of language relate to the descriptions of the world.**

• **We make a decision to use a word to stand for some object, person, or event.**

• A dictionary is a list of rules connecting words with their denotative meanings.

• When a word connotes something it has additional meanings for a person or a group that go beyond its denotative meaning.

• The basic content of a message discussing facts is information.

• Definition is an important process we can use to create denotative meanings as we communicate with one another.

• A description of a thing or event named by a term results in a definition of the term.

• Definition can also be the process that creates imaginary things or abstract concepts and assigns names to them.

• Abstract names such as *democracy, capitalism, communism, youth,* and *nationalism* can cause communication problems when used without reference to actual events and things.

• The highly connotative message is slanted, or loaded, to suggest a positive or negative interpretation of the information.

• An important persuasive skill is the ability to pick the right word to suggest the connotative meaning the speaker has in mind.

• Speakers can arouse connotative meanings by skillful use of descriptive words to characterize people, things, or events.

• Whoever you are, wherever you live, you speak a dialect.

• Belittling a dialect can cause emotional responses, conflict, and misunderstanding.

• Most people can learn to speak their native dialect more effectively than they do.

• No dialect should be singled out as better than all others.

• A person is often stereotyped on the basis of his or her dialect.

• People who want to be effective communicators in a mobile society are well advised to develop the ability to shift from native dialect and use other dialects when appropriate.

SUGGESTED PROJECTS

1 • Select a newspaper article that reports some dramatic news event involving interesting people. Rewrite the news story in two ways. First, emphasize the denotative factual reporting of the event. Try to keep the names, the relational terms, and the descriptions as neutral as possible. Second, slant the message to create an emotional response

to the event. If time permits, tape record the two versions for playback to the class.

2 • Select a highly persuasive television commercial, printed advertisement, or political speech and analyze the word choice and descriptive language to discover how the copywriter or speechwriter manipulated connotative meanings to suggest that the message receiver do or think or believe something.

3 • Your instructor will provide you with a chance to record your voice either in conversation or in reading a short selection. Either in small groups or in the entire class the recordings will be played without letting the listeners know who did the recording. Listen to the voices and try to make a description of the dialect and various ethnic, religious, geographic, and national influences heard in them. After you have heard the voices, there will be a further discussion of the stereotypes that are associated with the use of language.

SUGGESTED READINGS

Clark, Margaret L., Ella A. Erway, and Lee Beltzer. *The Learning Encounter: The Classroom as a Communications Workshop.* New York: Random House, 1971.

Farb, Peter. *Word Play: What Happens When People Talk.* New York: Knopf, 1974.

Labov, William. *The Study of Nonstandard English.* Champaign, Ill.: National Council of Teachers of English, 1970.

Shuy, Roger W. *Discovering American Dialects.* Champaign, Ill.: National Council of Teachers of English, 1967.

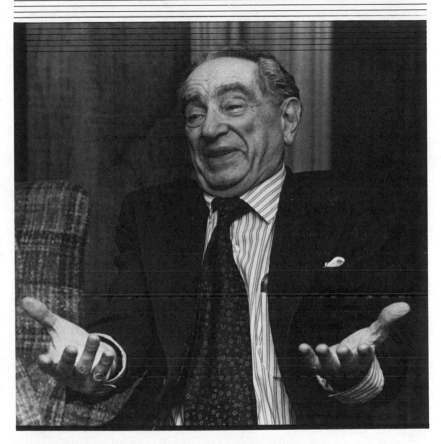

NONVERBAL COMMUNICATION
CHAPTER 4

NONVERBAL COMMUNICATION DEFINED

We will define nonverbal communication as (1) what people do on purpose, intentionally, in order to get something across to others, and (2) what people do out of habit or because of spur-of-the-moment feelings—even if it is without their being aware of it—if other people can generally get the same impression about relationships among the participants from the action.

While we have limited our definition a good deal so we can emphasize some basics, you should remember that an emphasis on *context* is a good one for the student of contemporary communication. We must remember that others may read more (or less) meaning into our dress, smell, physical appearance, hair style, fidgeting, facial expressions, home surroundings, and office arrangements than we do. The influence of context or scene is important and cuts across all communication situations.

CATEGORIES OF NONVERBAL BEHAVIOR

The technical name for the contemporary study of the nonverbal features of spoken communication related to voice productions and the articulation of sounds is **paralinguistics.** *Para,* a prefix borrowed from the Greek language, in this instance means "beyond." *Linguistics* refers to language. The term *paralinguistics* thus means "beyond language" and refers to that part of talking that goes beyond words.

The technical term for the study of nonverbal behavior that involves the motion of the body is **kinesics.** We define *body motion* to include gestures and facial expressions that support, mimic, or pantomime in parallel with verbal communication and either reinforce or reverse the content of what the person is saying—the overall posture, facial expression, eye movements, and so forth that support, modify, or reverse the content of verbal messages.

The technical term for the category of nonverbal behavior that includes the position of the participants in a communication event in relation to one another and to any other objects around them is **proxemics.** We define *proxemics* to include what is known in theatrical terms as the stage blocking of a play and what theater people call *stage business.* A play director will often tell the actors exactly how to stand, move, and gesture in order to communicate the meaning of a scene. The spontaneous and unrehearsed situations are, of course, much more prevalent and are of more interest to us as we look at nonverbal communication.

LEARNING NONVERBAL COMMUNICATION

One question that keeps coming up in the study of nonverbal communication is: To what extent is nonverbal behavior something you are born with because you are a human being, and to what extent is it something you have learned to do? Some studies have tried to see if certain physical actions are always interpreted as "meaning" the same emotion, even when the subjects for the study come from different cultures.

Four factors are involved in the nonverbal communication of each of us:

1　We learn a general way to communicate nonverbally from our particular culture. We learn this general nonverbal language as children, just as we learn to speak in the verbal code of our family. The cultural body language includes such things as how closely people stand when they talk to one another, whether people touch one another when talking, whether people look one another in the eye when they are angry or embarrassed, whether a vigorous nodding of the head accompanies agreement or disagreement.

2　Every individual, within his or her culture, develops a nonverbal language and vocal inflections to help communicate. We may use nonverbal gestures while talking to emphasize our verbal messages, or we may use nonverbal gestures alone to convey our meaning. To some extent nonverbal communication is cultural, but to some extent it is individual and varies from person to person. Some people are skilled and can use nonverbal communication to emphasize, even to contradict, what they are saying.

3　Every person develops characteristic ways of talking and moving, of standing or sitting while listening, of using the hands while excited. This is highly individual, and often nonverbal communication of this sort is more an interference than a help in conveying meanings to another person. If an individual's gestures call attention to themselves, not to the message intent, these gestures should be modified to allow more meaningful gestures to enhance communication.

Examples of the contextual cultural basis of much nonverbal communication are numerous and striking. In the last decade, middle-class white teachers in urban ghetto schools had difficulty communicating with young black children because they did not understand some of the black nonverbal communication unique to that place and time. The teachers were from a culture in which eye contact while conversing indicated interest, sincerity, careful listening, and genuine concern. The teachers thought of a person who looked down, even away much of the time, as being uninterested or insincere, perhaps even untruthful. The children were from a culture in which eye contact indicated anger. No wonder the children were disturbed by teachers who always seemed to be angry with them!

The Japanese tend to smile in a certain way when apologetic, embarrassed, and disturbed. When a manager in a Japanese factory calls a mistake to an employee's attention, the employee smiles. Before American managers working in firms in Japan learned of this cultural way of communicating, they often were upset by the smile. One manager broke off, reprimanding the employee with a curse, and forbade the employee to smile like that when discussing an important problem.

When you talk with someone from a different culture, whether that culture is within the United States or outside it, you need to be aware that the culture-based silent language of body position, relationships, and motion can hinder successful communication. We have many different cultures within the United States that affect the nonverbal part of communication. Some authorities maintain that poverty produces its own culture. We are becoming increasingly aware of, and are emphasizing, cultural differences in the minority groups in our national culture. Regional differences affect communication. The dialects of the Deep South are not just matters of forming sounds, they also relate to the vocal inflections and the body motions that accompany them. The same is true of the Yankee dialects of the New Englander or the speech of the Far Western Mountain Region.

PARALINGUISTIC FACTORS

Proper articulation is a matter of being intelligible—of being able to make all the sounds of a dialect so that someone else can understand them. *Pronunciation* is a matter of being able to use well-made sounds in words, with the emphasis in the generally accepted order for a particular dialect. One might articulate the sounds properly and still mispronounce a word.

The phonemes (sounds) can be divided into two main categories. *vowels* and *consonants*. (Phoneticians point to other important distinctions, but for our purposes, this one *major* difference needs to be stressed.) All vowels require a sound wave of a regular frequency, produced with the oral breath channel open. The tone of the voice and its musical characteristics are therefore a function of the way we say the vowels. Because the vowels are phonated—that is, because the vocal folds are always in vibration to produce them—they contain more sound energy than many of the consonants. The vowels also carry your voice quality. If a person has a pleasant musical voice, it is because of the way the vowel sounds are formed and the resonators utilized. If a person's voice is breathy, nasal-sounding, weak, harsh, or in any other way distinctive, the vowels are largely responsible. That means that if you want to improve your voice *quality,* you should work on improving the way you make the vowel sounds. You have doubtless all heard the old line "How now brown cow." It is a senseless sentence, the repeated saying of which makes much sense. Now to the other speech sounds, consonants.

The importance of articulating consonants

Consonants are produced by stopping, blocking, or diverting a sound wave. Most consonants are short and cannot be drawn out the way vowels can. Because of the shortness and noisiness of most of them, consonants do not carry the musical or voice quality features that the vowels do. Their main function is to distinguish among the various parts of an oral code such as the English language. The differences among words such as *bit, hit, sit,* and *bit, bill, big* are in the consonants that surround a common vowel.

The consonants often contain less sound energy than the vowels. One of the weakest sounds in English, for example, is the consonant /t/. Because the consonants generally have less energy in them, the listener cannot easily hear them. As a result, the receiver cannot always decode the words; if the consonants are not heard the message is lost. Often we can overhear a conversation without understanding it because all we can distinguish are the vowels, and we hear something like "oh, ee, awww, ooo." On the other hand, we can use the same vowel in every word of a sentence, and if the consonants are clear, we can understand the words even though the conversation sounds strange and stilted. For example, say the following sentence using the same vowel every time. "Mu futhur dummunds thut u gu to culludg."

The lesson to be learned from the nature of consonants is clear. If you want to be understood, in the most basic sense of the receiver's getting the words you are saying, you must articulate consonants clearly. The reason the mumbler is often not understood is that the receiver simply cannot hear the consonants well enough to decipher what words the source is saying.

For example, if you are talking over the telephone and find that because of a bad connection the person on the other end of the line cannot make out the words you are saying, the best procedure is not to yell the vowels more loudly but to articulate the consonants with great care and clarity. The vowels are probably being heard, but the consonants are what counts. Talking more loudly to slightly deaf people often makes them angry, but articulating your consonants more slowly and more clearly helps them to understand.

To communicate effectively, a person must both articulate clearly and pronounce the words correctly. Of the two skills, clear articulation is the more basic. If a person articulates clearly, others will probably be able to decipher the words even though they may wince at the way a dialect's conventions for saying those words are being broken by mispronunciations, but if a person does not articulate well, the receiver may not be able to decode the word the source intends.

Major articulation errors

As a child learns a language, he tends to begin speaking by omitting certain sounds and may first say something like "I wa I tee tone" for "I want an ice-cream cone." As the child becomes more proficient, he tends to add the sounds, but because some consonants are more difficult to form than others, he may substitute easier sounds for the more difficult ones. Finally, at the later stages, a child may realize the substitution is an error and try to say the right sound, but fail in the effort and, as a result, distort the sound.

Sometimes, because of bad habits, we continue to omit, substitute, or distort sounds on into our adolescent or adult years. No one bothers to point out our error, and we do not listen to ourselves critically as a rule. A common word illustrating two articulation problems is *just,* which ought to have a final /t/ sound but is often articulated as "jɪs." When one says "jɪs" for "just," not only is he omitting the sound at the end, he is also substituting the easier sound /ɪ/ for the /u/ sound. Learn to listen for this in your own speech and that of others. You will hear "jɪs" frequently. Other common substitutions include "git" for "get," "goin" for "going," "run-nin" for "running" and "beaudy" for "beauty." An occasional misarticula-tion is of little importance, of course, but many people have evolved bad habits of articulation, and their speech is filled with such mistakes.

When a person consistently omits and substitutes sounds in running speech, the result is a mumble that is difficult to understand. Read the following sentence aloud to see how difficult misarticulation is to understand. "Hey, Joe, jeet yet? Lesgo grabbasanwish." Now read the following sentence, carefully forming each phoneme. "Hey, Joe, did you eat yet? Let's go grab a sandwich."

No matter what dialect or dialects you speak, you ought to check your articulation, and where it is inaccurate, you should work to improve it, simply for the sake of being understood—to make your speech intelligible.

Pitch

Pitch is the perception of changes in a sound wave as tones on a musical scale. The pitch of a speaking voice should be neither too high nor too low for general, comfortable use, and every speaker should learn to use variations in pitch to best advantage.

The way a speaker varies the pitch of her voice is an important nonverbal technique to emphasize the meaning in a message or to indicate that the meaning one would normally associate with certain words is to be discounted or interpreted as irony or sarcasm. One can communicate a great deal by the skillful use of changes in pitch in such vowels as "oh" or "eee." You can experiment with the usefulness of pitch variations as a nonverbal technique of communication by saying "oh" so that it expresses different emotions and meanings. "How delightful," "I don't believe you," "That's nothing new," or "How disgusting."

Pitch changes are among the most important voice techniques for nonverbal communication. Generally, pitch changes are a result of stepping up or down in pitch, either from syllable to syllable or from word to word, or of gliding from one tone to another while prolonging a vowel sound. (Recall that the vowels carry the musical quality of connected speech, and that pitch changes within syllables are usually associated with vowels.) The pitch variations in Oriental languages often convey different meanings: The same sound pitched at four different tonal levels may be decoded by an Oriental listener as four distinct words.

You should select some sentences, experiment with shifting pitch in a steplike way from word to word, and then read the same sentences and shift pitch on the vowels in order to get the feel of the two major techniques to suggest mood and meaning with pitch variations.

Loudness

The ear perceives changes in air pressure in the sound wave as changes in loudness. Loudness levels of voice have one basic and vital function in speech communication. The message must contain enough sound energy to travel through the channel to the intended receiver, so it can be picked up and decoded.

Above the minimum required for decoding, loudness changes provide another technique of nonverbal communication. Loudness variations add emphasis by making certain ideas within a message stand out. A speaker can make important elements in a message stand out by saying them either more loudly or more softly than the surrounding verbal padding. We sometimes forget that speaking for a time at one level of loudness and then suddenly dropping the voice and saying the important words softly can emphasize them as much as suddenly raising the voice to a shout.

Try reading the following line in the two ways suggested by the stage directions in parentheses, to get the feel of loudness variations as a nonverbal communication tool:

(Normal level of loudness) When you say that, mister, (drop loudness some) you better (pause, then very softly) smile.
(Normal level of loudness) When you say that, mister, (louder) you better (very loud) smile.

Rate

The speed with which one utters syllables and words is the rate of speech. Rate is the third major dimension of voice related to nonverbal communication. A rapid rate is usually associated with excitement, danger, the need for sudden action. A slow rate often communicates calm, tiredness, sickness, resignation. Speaking rates tend to vary depending on what section of the country a speaker was brought up in, and much of what we call speech accents are actually variances in rate.

In many respects, variations of rate, like variations in pitch and loudness, function to add emphasis.

Pauses

Pauses can be thought of as part of the rate of utterance, but they play such an important role in the nonverbal encoding of messages that they deserve separate treatment.

Perhaps the most important feature of the pause is its function as oral punctuation. Comedian-pianist Victor Borge had a comedy routine in which he substituted strange and bizarre sounds, such as whistles, squawks, and clicks, for the various punctuation marks. The result was a hilarious example of the fact that the spoken as well as the written message needs to be properly punctuated to carry meaning successfully.

Generally, short pauses are useful as dividing points, to separate short thought units or modifying ideas, much as commas are used in writing. Long pauses serve to separate complete thought units, much as periods, question marks, and exclamation points do in writing. Notice how pausing punctuates the following sentences so their meanings are changed.

> The captain *(pause)* said the mate *(pause)* was drunk again last night.
> The captain said *(pause)* the mate was drunk again last night.
> Woman *(pause)* without her *(pause)* man is a beast.
> Woman without her man *(pause)* is a beast.

Pauses of longer duration may communicate nonverbally in the context of an interview or small group meeting or before an audience. The famous "speaker's pause"—when a public speaker takes the podium and before starting to speak looks out over the audience and waits for several moments—communicates confidence, a collecting together of important thoughts; it often catches the attention of the listeners, who expect something to happen at once, and when it does not, grow curious about why the speech has not begun.

Within the context of an interview, also, a pause may be interpreted as meaningful. An interviewee who pauses for an appreciable length of time before answering a question may be communicating something such as, "That is a difficult question and I am not sure I know how to answer it," or, "I know how to answer that question, but I am not sure I want to do so right at this point." When a respondent stops talking and the interviewer does not say something in turn, the pause may be interpreted as, "Please go on; I would like to hear you continue talking about this matter."

THE FUNCTIONS OF VOICE AND GESTURE

To enhance the words

A speaker may enhance or flesh out the words of a message with the nonverbal. The nonverbal can increase the expressiveness of the speaker and can add in making information clear. The message source can repeat meanings (add redundancy) by saying the same things nonverbally as verbally, so that gestures, vocal melody, and words reinforce one another. When the receiver sees gestures that support the ideas he is hearing, another communication channel is being used, which adds more information, thus increasing the chance of getting the idea across from source to receiver.

Body motion may also serve to add to the vocal sounds, to frame or package an utterance for a speaker. The speaker may use head nods, arm gestures, or hand and finger motions to show where a comment begins and ends, to underline or emphasize certain parts of the comment, to indicate complete thought units, to separate modifying words, clauses, or phrases, and to point out which of the expressed ideas are more, and which less, important in relation to one another.

Some gestures serve as a tipoff that a person wishes to speak. Maybe that person will lean forward, make mouthing movements, and tense the body as though to move even farther forward, and others will notice that this individual wants the floor. Once a person starts to speak, she may use nonverbal cues such as facial expressions to display emotions and attitudes similar to those encoded in words. The speaker may say, "I don't understand," and accompany the words with a puzzled facial expression. Other gestures may resemble or demonstrate what the speaker is saying. The person returning from a fishing trip says, "You should have seen the one that got away. I swear it was over a foot long," and indicates a size by holding her hands apart. A speaker may say, "I bought that picture in Paris," and point to the picture. A speaker may emphasize the intensity of his verbally expressed emotion or resolve. The coach shouts, "We're going to get going next half or I'll know the reason why!" and kicks a locker or pounds his fist on a table.

To detract from or reverse the words

A speaker may detract from or reverse the verbal message with the nonverbal. The speaker who says one thing verbally and another nonverbally introduces *ambiguity* and makes the message less clear. The speaker implies, "I mean this, but on the other hand, maybe not." On the other hand a persuasive speaker can use the nonverbal to reverse the verbal for purposes of irony and sarcasm. A skillful speaker can say a great deal with a few words by using irony and satire.

As feedback

Nonverbal communication can serve a powerful function as *feedback*. Indeed, nonverbal gestures, facial expressions, eye movements, postures are all among the most useful ways in which someone playing the role of receiver can indicate confusion, understanding, agreement, apathy or lack of interest, involvement, acceptance, or rejection as related to the *content* of the verbal message. Nonverbal communication can function to indicate the subtleties of relationships and can display emotions. Since so much of our social conversation is directed to how people relate to one another, nonverbal expression during the beginning and evolution of interpersonal relationships is extremely important.

Double-edged messages

Double-edged messages are communications that say one thing verbally and another thing nonverbally. The double-edged message may have either a positive or negative function, depending upon the context. The positive functions include the fact that the double-edged message may at one and the same time make one sort of comment on the content of the words, and another on the relationship between the speaker and listener. If a woman believes that a man who has just traded in his old car for a newer model has wasted $1,000 she may say to him, "You dumb nut;" but if she smiles and touches him sympathetically as she says it, she expresses her dissatisfaction with this action but indicates that she still cherishes their relationship. By sending the positive relationship message through the more potent means of body motion, she indicates that the relationship is more important to her than her dislike for the thing that he has done. Should she reverse the selection of channels and say, "Aren't you the smart one?" but punctuate the sentence with nonverbal cues which suggest, "You dumb nut! Where are you going to get another thousand bucks?," she achieves sarcasm and indicates that the negative comment (nonverbal) is more important than the positive (verbal). She may well get an unequivocal message from him, in which the nonverbal supports the verbal to the effect, "What do you mean by that? It's my money, isn't it? If I want a new car that's my business, isn't it?"

Sarcasm and irony often make points with a sharper cut than long explanations can manage. "How was your date last night?" asks a friend. The woman answers, "He was a nice boy," punctuated with body motion which says that he was nice in the way that a pampered and protected twelve-year-old male can be nice, which makes a point with considerable force for the listener who interprets it correctly. The danger, of course, is that the nonverbal part of the message may fail, if not delivered skillfully, to reverse the verbal, and the listener may end up confused. "She says he was a nice boy, but I don't know for sure what she means." One reason why the study of public speaking includes specific training in voice and gesture is to enable its practitioners to deliver double-edged messages effectively.

By using the double-edged message, a speaker can make a statement with irony or sarcasm and leave an escape route in case the results begin to be punishing. The speaker finds it more difficult to "weasel out" of a clear, unequivocal statement. The woman discussing the purchase of the car in the example above can, if she chooses, answer the challenge. "It's my business, isn't it?" with, "I said you are a smart one, didn't I?" If she changes the nonverbal way she says the latter sentence so that it is now supportive of the words, she has hinted at her displeasure but escaped from the storm.

The double-edged message can, however, have a negative effect. If people who are in a close personal relationship use many double-edged messages, they may well carry on their power struggles largely on the nonverbal level. They may hint at problems and conflicts but not resolve them. The fact that much of our theory about nonverbal communication has come from psychiatry is an indication of the toll that inconsistent messages can take on the cohesiveness of groups and the emotional and mental health of individuals.

The double bind

If a person keeps getting double-edged messages from a friend or relative, the relationship between them is likely to deteriorate; or if the relationship is difficult to break off, the first person is likely to be in a double bind, if the messages are in the form of contradictory instructions: If the person follows the one instruction, the other cannot be followed. One instruction is usually in words and the order is countermanded by the nonverbal. The woman who asks a man, "Aren't you going to kiss me?" verbally, but who nonverbally indicates that she'd just as soon he didn't, puts the man in a double bind.

Think how a child often learns from his family to do things that are directly counter to the parents' pious pronouncements. "Don't," a father says, "make the mistake I did and drop out of high school. Get a good education. You can't get anywhere these days without it." At the same time the father says this, however, much of what he does suggests to the son that he thinks reading books is a waste of time, that he views colleges with suspicion, and that he sees college professors as strange, impractical people. The father communicates in a thousand nonverbal ways that he does not believe his own advice, and then this same father is unable to understand why his son quits school just as he himself did. There is much truth in the old saying that "teachers teach as they were taught, not as they were taught to teach." You must be sophisticated indeed in all aspects of communication to be totally aware of what you are communicating, nonverbally as well as verbally, when you send out messages.

PROXEMIC FACTORS

One important factor in the way people communicate with one another relates to the distances that separate them. We can divide up distances into four important regions.

The first is *intimate distance,* which varies from touching to a space of one or two feet. Intimate distance is appropriate for only the most intimate conversations, usually between adults who are well acquainted and friendly, or between parents and children, particularly young children. When we are forced into such close contact on a crowded bus or elevator we usually protect ourselves by not conversing. For important and personal communications, however, the intimate distance is often the most rewarding.

The second distance is *personal* and is roughly 2 to 2.5 feet. When two people meet in an office building or on the street and strike up a casual conversation, they usually remain approximately this far apart. Watch the people around you for the next day or so, and see if your own observation bears out this theory and if you behave this way too.

The third distance, *social* distance, varies from about 4 to 7 feet. The social distance is good for impersonal business. The job interview, for example, is often conducted at this distance.

The final distance is the *public* distance, which starts at about 12 feet and extends as far as is feasible in a large room or auditorium. (You may wonder what happens in the areas between the zones covered, such as the distance from 7 to 12 feet. Other things must be taken into account, and the student of nonverbal communication might be able to determine whether the design of a given room for a speech, a presentation, or a discussion will place the participants in a public or personal zone if they are going to be talking to one another at a distance somewhere between 7 and 12 feet. These distances are simply rough rules of thumb to indicate that distance is an important feature of communication.)

As important as distance is the geographic location of the participants—where people are in relation to one another. If an employer calls an employee into her office to discuss something in a two-person situation, the arrangement of the furniture and the seating of the two people influence the communicative setting. If the boss sits behind her desk and the worker sits in front of the desk, the fact that one is the boss and the other the employee is always part of the situation. With the proxemic nonverbal dimension so strongly a part of the interview, a discussion of personal matters would be difficult. Clearly, the boss who sets up a conference on this basis wishes to keep some distance from the employer as a person and to stress the status difference between them. If the boss comes from behind her desk, pulls up another chair, and sits beside the employee so they can talk at a distance of one or two feet or even touch (a tap on the shoulder to indicate personal concern or emphasis), the situation has been drastically altered by the changed geography of the communicative setting.

The geography of the small group meeting is a fascinating study. In some settings, a place at one end of a rectangular table is viewed as a position of power. Watching the way people sit at a meeting tells a wise observer a good deal about who likes whom and who is competing with whom for position or influence. During the course of the discussion such gross bodily movements as leaning back in a chair, leaning forward and placing the elbows on the table, turning slightly and pulling away from the speaker, or turning toward the speaker respectively indicate interest, boredom, acceptance, or rejection.

In a large group, the position of the listeners in relation to one another and to the speaker is a matter of considerable importance. If the speaker is located on a stage, standing behind a podium some distance from the audience, the speaker's relationship to the audience not only indicates formality but also stresses the separateness between speaker and audience. Should the speaker jump down from the stage and walk up and down the aisles as he speaks, such bodily movement would communicate a desire to break the public distance and move in the direction of more personal space to convey his message.

The distances among the members of the listening audience also affect the suggestibility of the audience. If a few individuals are scattered throughout a relatively large room, with many chairs empty, the effect is much different than if the audience is packed tightly together and some people are sitting on the floor around the edges of the room or standing along the walls. When the audience reacts sharply to a speaker by a sudden tightening of bodily tension on the part of a majority of the listeners, or by a sudden intake of breath, a sigh, a laugh, or a groan, the speaker and the listeners get the message and respond with emotion as well as with interest.

The functions of proxemics

To indicate boundaries and to defend territory. Nonverbal communication can function in terms of *territoriality* and personal space. Recently, evidence has been assembled to indicate that human beings stake out various territories in which they live, work, and play, just as animals do. A student may sit in the same chair every time he attends a given class and be disturbed if someone else takes his territory. They exhibit some of the same behaviors in defense of their territory as other species do. In addition, people act as though they had a bubble of personal space surrounding them that they like to keep free of others. The size of the bubble seems to grow larger or smaller depending on the context and nature of their meetings.

People talking with one another often define territorial limits in a given situation nonverbally. Members of a small discussion group in a classroom will frame or outline the boundaries of their group's territory by the way they arrange the chairs in a circle, by the way they look at one another and away from other people in the room, by the way they hold their arms and legs to protect their turf. When the group finishes its "meeting," the participants often move in ways that say, in effect, "OK, we have finished now, and we give up our hold on this territory." They pull back their chairs, lean back, look around; some may get up, while others stay seated.

To frame a communication event. Body position and motion can serve to indicate that an informal and spontaneous transaction is to begin, can define the details of the order of speaking and listening and the tempo of the give-and-take, and can mark the end of communication. For example, John sees Mary walking down the hall toward him. He slows up, changes direcion so he will walk closer to her apparent path, lifts his eyebrows, widens his eyes, raises his head, holds up his right hand, and says, "Hello, how are you?" The way John emphasizes the words and his body motion invite the forming of a transaction. Mary can answer, "Hi." The way Mary acts as she says the word may reject the invitation, and John may swing back on his former path and go on his way. On the other hand, Mary may respond with a big smile, walking directly toward him until she is within three or four feet and then stopping. John may then continue with, "Classes keeping you awake today?" As Mary answers, he notices an acquaintance, Harry, coming down the hall. Harry smiles and says "Hello," but Johns nods to him briefly over his shoulder, while turning a bit to close off the turf of the twosome he has formed with Mary. Even though Mary has turned with her head up, looking expectantly at Harry, whom she has not met, Harry gets the nonverbal message from John and walks past them. In the same way, after they have chatted and John has indicated nonverbally a desire to extend and make the transaction more intimate and Mary has replied nonverbally that she is not interested in doing so at this time, she may indicate nonverbally that the transaction is coming to a close. John may accept her cues and nonverbally agree, and they will go their separate ways.

To indicate interpersonal relationships. Nonverbal communication may also function in relationships that are beginning or evolving among the participants in a communication event. One of the most important ways in which nonverbal messages comment on relationships is in terms of saying "I like you" or "I dislike you." Most people are always on the alert for cues relating to how they are being accepted or rejected by others. Often a verbal response to another person is restricted by custom, norms, or style. The participants in a business meeting are restricted by the norms of our society from saying such things as "You arouse me sexually."

Innocuous verbal comments can, however be accompanied by nonverbal messages that suggest the evolving relationship. Frequently, too, expressing dislike or loathing in verbal messages is "not the thing to do" in many social situations, but nonverbal cues may get the message across nonetheless.

Another important relationship that nonverbal messages often communicate is that of power. If there is a "pecking order" in the relationships of two or more people and they are meeting together, the nonverbal messages often communicate their pattern of dominance and submissiveness. Nonverbal cues often reveal if one participant is of higher status, has fate control over others, or is in a "one-up" relationship.

When status is clear and accepted, the participants who communicate with one another tend to have routine nonverbal patterns that indicate that the power relationships are known and accepted by all involved and that the communication can continue based on those relationships. The members do not have to consciously expend effort in building or rebuilding status relationships. Clear and accepted power relationships tend to free the time of the participants to concentrate on information processing and would thus represent a good situation. In other words, with comfortable and acceptable personal relationships established, participants can keep their minds on the content of the messages and use both the verbal and nonverbal channels to support the same information, with a better chance of achieving understanding. When the relationships are disturbed and begin to get in the way of the work, then our recommendation would be to tend to those relationships and get them back into harmony, so the participants can once again concentrate on the task at hand.

In intimate communication, on the other hand, we tend to emphasize evolving relationships as people grow—for example, from acquaintance, to liking, to love. For the participants, the relationship itself often becomes a focus of concern, and both verbal and nonverbal messages deal with relationship matters.

When relationships are evolving, people emit nonverbal messages that are not routine or habitual: they exhibit courtship cues and cues of rejection or acceptance; they exhibit dominance behavior, conflict confrontation, submission, and so forth as they go about evolving relationships.

KEY IDEAS CHAPTER 4

• **Nonverbal communication consists of the body language and vocal melodies that accompany a speaker's words.**

• **The technical name for the contemporary study of the nonverbal features of voice production is *paralinguistics*.**

• The technical term for the study of body motion related to speech is *kinesics*.

• The technical term for the physical relationships among communicators is *proxemics*.

• We learn a general body language from our particular culture and also develop a highly individualistic way of communicating nonverbally.

• Proper *articulation* is a matter of being understood.

• Proper *pronunciation* is a matter of using the generally accepted sounds in the proper order with the proper emphasis.

• The vowels carry the quality of the voice.

• The main function of the consonants is to carry the code that furnishes the meaning of an utterance. Therefore, if you want to be understood, you must articulate the consonants clearly.

• If you want to have a pleasant and expressive voice, you must articulate the vowels clearly and vary their pitch, loudness, and duration.

• When a person consistently omits and substitutes sounds while speaking, the result is a difficult-to-understand mumble.

• The most important feature of the pause is its function as oral punctuation.

• Kinesics and proxemics may function to enhance words, to indicate boundaries, and to frame a communication event.

• Nonverbal communication often indicates relationships such as liking or disliking, and power and status differences.

• Nonverbal communication is an important means of providing feedback.

SUGGESTED PROJECTS

1 • Each student records his or her voice both talking informally and reading. The reading should be from simple prose exposition, *not* dramatic reading. With the help of the instructor and the other students, each class member analyzes his or her nonverbal communication in terms of vocal monotony, flexibility, quality, pitch, rate, loudness, and clarity of articulation. Each student writes a brief paper describing his or her own vocal strengths and inadequacies, and in consultation with the instructor and if necessary plans a program of exercises that can be used to improve his or her nonverbal vocal communication.

2 • Divide the class into coeducational pairs, if possible. Each pair has two minutes to communicate a mutually agreed-upon emotional relationship between two people, using only a variation in the intonations of the words *John* and *Mary*. No other words may be used. The male member of the pair will say, "Mary," and then the female member will say "John," and they alternate these words for two minutes. Gestures and facial expressions should be kept at a minimum. The situation portrayed could be as impersonal as two strangers meeting on a bus and striking up a conversation, as personal as an intimate family incident, a lover's quarrel, or merely two friends gossiping. The class tries to figure out the relationship between the two people from the verbal intonations alone.

3 • Five members of the class are given a current, preferably controversial topic to discuss. They go to the front of the classroom and conduct a brief unrehearsed discussion. Half of the remaining members watch and make notes about the proxemics of the discussion group, their nonverbal gestures, postures, and facial expressions. The other half of the class watches the nonverbal proxemics and gestures of the entire classroom, including the instructor. After the discussion, a general class meeting analyzes the nonverbal dimension of the discussion group and the entire classroom setting.

SUGGESTED READINGS

Birdwhistell, Ray L. *Kinesics and Context: Essays on Body Motion Communication*. Philadelphia: University of Pennsylvania Press, 1970.

Knapp, Mark L. *Nonverbal Communication in Human Interaction*. 2d ed. New York: Holt, Rinehart and Winston, 1978.

Leathers, Dale. *Nonverbal Communication Systems*. Boston: Allyn & Bacon, 1976.

Sheflen, Albert E., and Alice Sheflen. *Body Language and Social Order: Communication as Behavioral Control*. Englewood Cliffs, N.J.: Prentice-Hall, 1972.

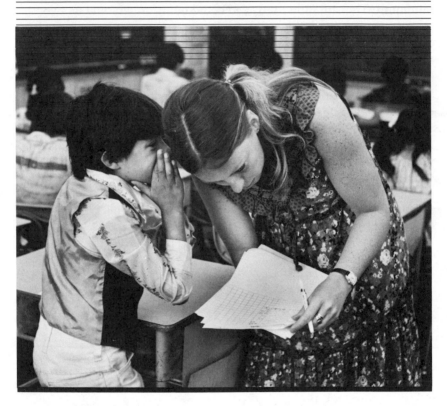

LISTENING
CHAPTER 5

When we explain the importance of listening, most people say, "You know, you're right! I never thought about it much, but listening is important. From now on I'm going to pay better attention, I'm going to listen better." Like most communication skills, unfortunately, listening is not much improved merely by trying to "listen better."

Speaking and listening are learned skills, learned in much the same manner as reading and writing. The major difference is that we all learn to speak and listen at such an early age, long before starting formal schooling that we tend to feel that everything we need to know about speaking and listening is already learned before we start school; many come to the mistaken conclusion that we do not need to study speaking and listening. We learn to walk and to run long before we enter school, too, but any person with a talent for running dashes can profit from expert coaching and diligent practice, and it is the same with speaking and listening skills. Anyone can learn to listen more efficiently and effectively given increased awareness of the factors involved plus practice guided by an expert in listening.

LISTENING TO PUBLIC SPEECHES

Often members of an audience listening to a public speech do not listen carefully, and as a result they do not comprehend all the ideas in the speech, nor do they critically evaluate those ideas they do comprehend. Some members of the audience may be poor listeners because they are taking flight from the situation, doing anything but listen. There are a dozen places they would rather be and a dozen things they would rather be doing. Playing the role of listener is a time-consuming, tension-producing job. A person must often exert effort to keep his attention from wandering.

If we are at all creative, our attention can find materials more interesting than the speaker's comments. We have a colleague who claims that for years he has organized his next week's lectures every Sunday morning during the church sermon. Mental energy that could be used for listening is often spent in less constructive ways than organizing our week's work, however; perhaps the speaker has interesting mannerisms of speech or gesture, and we can count the number of times he says "y'know" or the number of times he twitches his eyelids, looks at the floor, or tries to put one hand in a nonexistent pocket in the back of his coat jacket. Perhaps a young man is attracted to a woman sitting three rows in front of him in the audience and spends his time thinking how he will get acquainted with her after the lecture is over.

Deciding to listen

All too often, our minds drift away from, then back to, a speaker; we thus unthinkingly listen for a while, then fail to do so, then find ourselves back in the role. It often happens that if we work at listening carefully to the people we least want to hear, we are amply rewarded by what we learn. In any case, we would be wise to make a conscious choice about whether to listen; we should think about whether we will concentrate in a listening situation and not leave the matter to chance.

Think through your own experiences and list some situations in which you were unwilling to listen. From time to time the decision not to listen is probably justified (as our colleague insists is the case for him when he sits in church), but the question of when you should be willing to listen and when not deserves more study than it usually receives.

For the remainder of this chapter we will concentrate our analysis on those situations in which you have decided that you *will* try to listen. Even when you willingly take the part of a listener, you will discover that the role requires some specific skills that need to be understood and practiced in order to increase listening competence.

Controlling your attention

A runner may tire at the midway point in a race but force him- or herself to continue, despite pain and fatigue. A person listening to a public speech can do much the same thing by forcing his or her attention to stay on what is being said. Concentrated effort to focus on the message and understand it can overcome listening fatigue and the natural tendency of our attention to wander.

A little practice can help you become aware of those moments when your attention begins to waver. As you listen, you need to keep part of your mind on how well you are listening; you can learn to pull yourself back to the message when you catch yourself losing interest. If the speaker is developing an idea that seems dull, trite, or uninteresting, or if he or she is going so slowly that we find ourselves thinking ahead, we may be tempted to relax and indulge in daydreaming.

One way to keep from drifting away from a dull speaker's slow-moving train of ideas is to anticipate what point he will make next. By guessing where he will go, we can arouse our interest in checking to see if, indeed, we were correct. And if we have guessed correctly, we have then thought about the idea twice and are more likely to remember it than if we had not made the prediction. If we guess incorrectly, we still may wonder why the speaker took the turn he did instead of the one we thought he would take, and in either case, we have tricked ourselves into attending to what he is saying.

Another tactic that can help combat the boredom of listening to a slow speaker is to take 10 to 20 seconds from time to time to review quickly what the speaker has just said. You will find that summarizing from time to time helps you recall the important ideas later.

We have to focus our attention on any message before we can begin to interpret it. You will no doubt recall the old story about the farmer who told his neighbor he was going to teach his mule how to drag a log by a chain. After announcing his intention, the first thing the farmer did was pick up a big board and hit the mule over the head with it. "What'd you do that for?" the startled neighbor asked. "I thought you were going to teach him how to drag logs!" "Yup," the farmer said, "but first I have to get his attention."

Focusing on message structure

If we now know how to force our attention to the speech, we can learn further techniques of effective listening. We should focus on the structure of the message. People who listen for factual details tend to have trouble recalling the main ideas, and seldom remember many of the facts, either. They thus end up with a vague idea about a mass of undigested material. All of us tend to remember patterns more easily than isolated details. Whole systems of memory improvement depend on connecting the things to be remembered with something we know well. For example, when we meet a number of people at a party and wish to remember their names, if we can connect each person and each name with a house on a street that we know well, we can often recall the names of the persons later. Simply trying to remember a series of names without associations is difficult.

If you practice listening for the main outline or structure of a message, you will find your understanding increasing. You will know that you are a professional listener when you can hear a badly organized message and refit its parts into your own organizational pattern. You may, indeed, be able to recall more of what a rambling speaker said during an impromptu speech than the speaker himself can if you organize the material more effectively than he did.

Controlling emotional reactions to language

Finally, an important key to misunderstanding, even when a person is seeking actively to listen, is related to the connotative aspect of language, discussed in Chapter 3. Certain words arouse our emotions. Moreover, a speaker's dialect may cause us to respond with anger, suspicion, or fear. The power of words to cause emotional responses is a factor in poor listening. A person in an emotional state is generally upset and acts to some extent as though he were in shock. He loses his ability to think clearly, just as he loses his ability to make small, isolated, subtle physical movements. Even when we want to listen, we may respond emotionally to a word or phrase and lose some of our listening abilities. Just as we lose our ability to make fine adjustments with our fingers when we are nervous and upset, we begin to mishear.

Of course, a certain amount of excitement can improve our ability to listen, just as stage fright can be used to help us give a better public performance. Excitement, under control, makes us function better. People can experience a considerable level of excitement and high feeling and be keyed up to more efficient use of skills and talents.

In listening as in speaking before an audience, the trick is to be genuinely involved, interested, and efficient. Remember that when you find yourself getting boiling mad, you are also losing your ability to listen well.

After we have learned the techniques of keeping our attention on a message, or structuring the message as we hear it, and controlling our emotional responses to language, we can listen with *understanding*. When we listen to a speech with the aim of understanding, we *comprehend* the message.

Much of the difficulty we experience in working with one another we attribute to communication problems. Marriages are often said to fail because of a breakdown in communication. A colleague of ours argues, in an ironic way, that if it were not for misunderstandings, we would have a world with much more conflict and violence than we do have. He argues that most people filter their incoming communications in such a way that they protect their self-image. Thus they often rearrange what others say so that it fits in with their own comfortable preconceptions, biases, and prejudices. If we always had a clear understanding of what other people were trying to say, he argues, we would come in conflict with them much more often! His point is worth making, if only as an antidote to the popular assumption that communication problems are the basic causes of all conflicts.

Nonetheless, interpreting a speech to mean something other than what the speaker intends can cause difficulty, and most occasions require that we at least comprehend what the other person is saying before the conversation can proceed to either agreement or disagreement.

Listening critically

Many times we need to do more than just understand what denotative meanings a speaker wishes to convey to us. We must also critically evaluate the speech. We need to examine the speaker's assertions to see if they accurately describe the purported facts. If we can check what is said by observation, we can discover whether the message is true or false. Once we discover a message is false, although we understand what the speaker is saying, we do not accept the statement as an accurate depiction of events.

We should listen carefully and criticize speeches reflecting rumor, propaganda, and persuasion. People encounter rumors frequently and usually listen to them with interest. Rumors are messages in general circulation which cannot be factually confirmed, such as gossip, unofficial messages based upon guesses, or incomplete hints. Many times the rumor relates to official organizational secrets that are of considerable importance to the people in the organization. Rumors in the form of gossip often relate to matters that are socially unacceptable, and thus the concerned parties will keep them secret if possible. Gossip may relate to such things as the boss's wife becoming an alcoholic, the know-it-all neighbor's daughter's illegitimate baby, the professor who passed out drunk at the president's party—the list is endless. Most people enjoy listening to gossip.

If a rumor is the best source of information about something of importance to us, we should try to figure out what the facts are as best we can, remembering how things get distorted as they are passed on by word of mouth.

LISTENING IN INTERPERSONAL COMMUNICATION

How to listen for information

One of the important distinctions between the role of message source and that of message receiver in the *S M C R* model is that the evaluation of good or bad communication is dependent on the ability of the participants to achieve the source's intent jointly. The receiver may legitimately later become the source in another, consecutive exchange of information, but for purposes of judging how good or bad a portion of the communication is, we must judge the feedback of the listener in terms of how well it helps the source know that its message has been understood. The critic using the model will judge the fidelity of the transmission in terms of the information the source intended to transmit. Or if the source intended control, the critic will evaluate success in terms of whether or not the message achieved the source's intended control. When one person talks with another with the purpose of transmitting information, therefore, the problem of whose goal will control the communication must be faced early in the interchange.

When the apparent listener in a communication episode that is getting under way comments in a manner designed to assume the role of a message source, then what the person says and does is not feedback according to the model of communication. Recall that feedback refers to those verbal and nonverbal cues that the receiver provides about how the message is being decoded. The respondent who tries to assume the role of source encodes a message to achieve a different goal; the comment of the respondent is thus not feedback at all.

Nonverbal communication can help establish that a conversation is to begin, can set the ground rules for the talk, and can help the participants keep on the track. When you begin to communicate, assuming that you will be allowed to be the message source, you must be very alert to the verbal and nonverbal response of the others involved. In this regard you must "listen" with your eyes as well. You must make sure that your listener or listeners are playing the role of receiver and providing feedback rather than trying to assert a different role.

The case of the unwilling receiver

Often people refer to a situation where nobody wants to be a receiver and everybody wants to be a message source as an instance of poor listening. "We were all talking at once. Nobody was listening. We all had something we wanted to say, and we didn't even hear what anybody else said. We've got to start all over again and *listen* to one another." The problem in such cases probably is not lack of listening skills so much as the unwillingness of the participants to take on the role of receiver at that time. When two people both try to play the role of message source and encode messages aimed at achieving different personal goals, the results do not fit the communication model; instead we have two incomplete communication events that happen to take place at the same time. We have the not unfamiliar spectacle of two people talking past each other, or of two people talking in each other's presence without talking with each other. In terms of the ideal model, two message sources speaking in each other's presence are certainly not communicating. The critic of communication calls such events a failure or a breakdown in communication.

Unwillingness to be the receiver of messages often stems from poor interpersonal relationships, particularly when people are forced by organizational structures to talk over a common task. Above we referred to those informal communication transactions that are signaled and marked by nonverbal communication and tend to be maintained or broken off by mutual agreement. The meetings required by formal structures often cannot be terminated in the same way. The doctor and patient may be required to talk about the case history of the patient's illness; the applicant and the personnel director may be required to conduct a job interview; the supervisor and the subordinate may have to discuss the details of a job. Sometimes, two people trying to work on a common task and needing to talk effectively should switch from talking business to discussing their relationships and their communication process. After having created a suitable relationship, they can then switch into the task-oriented interview or conference more comfortably. The person who does not know the one who is the source of a message may be ill at ease, tense, and unsure and may not be willing to play the role of receiver until the source is better known. The person who is suspicious, hostile, or antagonistic to the message source often refuses to assume the role of receiver, because to do so would be to help the source achieve an objective, and the last thing the respondent wants is to be helpful. For all these reasons it is vital to remember that listening is not a passive state that just happens; listening is an activity, and a person has to agree to listen, be able to listen, and work at doing it well.

Playing the role of receiver effectively

When participating in a conversation for the purpose of exchanging information, you should willingly accept the role and duties of message receiver at appropriate points in your talk. If you anticipate conflict, you should allow the source to develop a complete message first, and then you should provide feedback and work to understand the message until both of you are satisfied that you understand each other. Then if you decide that you are not going to cooperate to achieve the source's intent, you ought to assert yourself clearly in the role of source for another round of communication. Conversely, the other person should willingly assume the role of receiver until your message is understood. Understanding does not assure harmony and cooperation. People may still disagree or grow to dislike one another, but they will do so on a more realistic basis and not because of misunderstandings stemming from lack of communication skills— particularly from either's lack of willingness to play the role of receiver—if they first come to understand one another.

Once you have agreed to play the role of message receiver, the communication skills of good listening come into play. Some of the same psychological powers of focusing intention, searching for structure in the message, predicting and summarizing ideas that were important in listening to a public speech or lecture are equally necessary to the listener in the informal communication event. The receiver tries to attend carefully to what is said, to decipher denotative meanings, and to provide continuous feedback. The speaker, in turn, willingly plays the role of message source, searches constantly for feedback, and keeps encoding new messages to achieve a satisfactory level of understanding. If both source and receiver play their roles willingly and with skill, the whole process becomes a classic expression of the basic model of communication.

Nonverbal feedback. The communication skills required of an effective receiver of messages include skill in providing nonverbal feedback. Facial expressions are extremely important.

The poker game, which is a situation which puts a premium on bluffing, lying, and systematically misleading other players, also encourages the "poker face," the careful suppression of any facial expression that might give away what cards a player is holding.

The poker face is a liability rather than an asset for the receiver. A skilled receiver makes clear facial expressions and gestures to indicate understanding, acceptance, misunderstanding, or rejection. When participating actively and willingly as receiver, you should smile, frown, look puzzled, allow a look of illumination to spread over your face when you see what the source is trying to say, and so forth. Head nods and shakes are another good technique to provide feedback. One of the authors of this book once took a driving examination for a license and was graded down because he drove across a set of railroad tracks without clearly turning his head first in one direction and then the other, although he stoutly maintained that he had looked carefully in both directions. The tester wanted to see an unmistakable swing of the head, first to the left and then to the right. (Said author then clued in your other author, and when she took the examination later the same afternoon, she looked so long and hard in both directions the tester chuckled and asked, checking the names on his list, "Say, was that your husband earlier. . . .?")

When playing the role of receiver, a person is as active as the individual playing the role of message source. Although the receiver may not say as many words as the source, the receiver will be providing nonverbal feedback continuously; his cues are intentional and done consciously.

Verbal feedback. Verbal feedback, too, is a communication skill necessary for an effective receiver of messages. The receiver can feed back error statements to the source indicating the nature of the problem: "You seem to think I know all about what the group decided last night, but I haven't any idea, really." "I'm confused." "Well, I thought I understood, but now I think it just doesn't make sense. Maybe you'd better . . ." "I don't think I heard that right." Questioning is an important technique for feedback: "What was that last word? Did you say 'would' or 'wouldn't'?" What do you mean by *entropy*?" "I'm sorry but that whole business about negative entropy confuses me. Would you go over that again, please?" The receiver can also give feedback by repeating, echoing, or rephrasing the message: "OK, now let me repeat what I think you just said." "Just a minute; here's what I got out of that." "Let's see now if I've got that straight." "Do you mean . . .?"

Individuals involved in a conversation that emphasizes information content of messages must take the initiative when necessary and stop the communication flow (just as a computer does, automatically) and indicate to the source, either verbally or nonverbally, (1) that there is a problem (misunderstanding), (2) what kind of problem it is, and (3) where the receiver is in terms of what is understood and what is not.

Creative listening

Creative listening goes beyond the process of transmitting information from source to receiver. Someone speaks and the listeners not only comprehend and evaluate the comment, but they also sometimes discover meanings in the message that had not occurred to the speaker. They search for nonverbal context and cues and try to understand the feelings implied by the comment as well as the denotative meanings encoded in the words. Much as a creative reader can discover more in a book than the author intended, a creative listener can make a comment that adds new meaning to the original statement. When the listener feeds back ideas into the event, the speaker may be stimulated to see a still deeper meaning in the messages that begin flowing rapidly between or among the participants, generating much increased excitement.

In discussions and conferences, people sometimes find themselves caught up in a chain of fantasies similar to the creative moments individuals experience when they daydream about a creative project or an important problem. Someone makes a suggestion, and the idea is picked up by another participant, then by another, and soon a number of people are deeply involved in the discussion, excitedly adding their reactions and ideas to it. Under the suggestive power of the group fantasy the constraints that normally hold people back are released, and people feel free to experiment with ideas, to play with concepts and wild suggestions and imaginative notions. This sort of idea interplay can also happen between two people who have reached a high level of supportive interpersonal communication.

The total involvement of the listener in communication with significant others creates a situation where the flow or meaning is no longer from source to receiver, but where all participants are adding to a common meaning until the result is greater than any one person could have managed by him- or herself. The final growth and insight and learning in such a communication event take place in both the person who originally discussed the topic and the individual who began as a listener. The creative involvement of all participants requires all the communication skills, including the highest levels of listening ability. Interpersonal trust, a positive social climate, skill in expressing ideas, sensitivity to dialect and suggestion, ability at nonverbal communication—all these components are important to the deep and important communication event.

An athlete does not spend all his time running important races at top speed; so, too, we should not hold up the pattern of deep significant communication as the formula for all communication. But when the time is right, and the people are in tune with one another, the deep and significant communication transactions in which we participate are among our most exciting and rewarding experiences.

LISTENING AS A SUPPORTIVE TECHNIQUE

Putting it too simply of course, the clinical psychologist or psychiatrist listens. You pay a great deal of money to have such a professional *listen* to you. Why? Because the kind of listening they do is a very special kind; they are trained to try to hear what you are *really* saying. There are times when all of us are aware that we are not saying what we really want to say because we are having difficulty getting the words out right, but professional helper-listeners are not listening for the right words. They are listening for the feelings that are being expressed—because the people themselves are sometimes not aware of the feelings, or do not know why they have these feelings or what they mean and why they are bothersome. In any case, professional listening designed to help disturbed people and all the research that has resulted from the study of this special kind of therapeutic listening have provided much interesting material for the normal person interested in becoming a more effective listener.

Defensiveness and communication breakdowns

Much of the material regarding communication breakdowns relates to *defensiveness* and its destructive effect on a person's ability to listen. The first step any good analyst makes is to try to break down the client's defensiveness so that a climate of trust can be built. Because disturbed people are more obviously upset or paranoid than normal people, their defensiveness is usually very apparent; they express their defensiveness verbally or nonverbally, either in an outgoing, obvious manner or by retreating into silence.

When people become defensive, their listening ability is lessened. All of us have to maintain sufficient defensiveness to protect our inner images. When we are insecure in a situation, always waiting for evaluation and criticism, we often hear only the "what you did wasn't up to your usual standards," and not the "but then, even second-best from you is better than what most people turn out!" that follows. All of us know people who seem to take nearly everything that is said to them the wrong way—or as we say, "personally." On a bad day even the healthiest of us can feel unduly attacked, and begin to respond defensively when it is not necessary.

Because defensive communication plays a part in everyone's natural communication behavior, but is so often an obvious source of trouble, it has been studied carefully. Jack Gibb discovered certain types of behaviors in messages that appeared to convey attitudes which set up defensive responses in listeners; he also recorded those messages and attitudes that seemed to set up a climate of support and acceptance in listeners. As you might expect, the supportive climates, as he calls them, are mirror images, exact opposites, of the defensive climates.

The defensive climates are generally manipulative in intent and include messages that are (1) evaluative (I'll tell you whether you're good or bad); (2) controlling (Me over you); (3) strategic (I've figured out how to get you to do it my way); (4) neutral (I really don't give a damn); (5) superior (You're a nothing, I'm "it"!); and (6) certain (It's going to go this way, and that's that). Our normal response to anyone communicating these attitudes is to be defensive. The problem, of course, lies in the fact that so often we are unaware of how much of this sort of defense-producing material creeps into our messages. And as listeners, we are often not fully aware why we are not listening well, when, in fact we have become defensive, riled up, angry, and probably hurt.

We all find it much easier to listen to someone whose messages create a supportive climate. Gibb includes among these (1) description (Tell me more about it); (2) problem orientation (What's the problem as you see it?); (3) spontaneity (Hey, let's see what we can do about this!); (4) empathy (You sure feel bad about it, don't you); (5) equality (Two heads are better than one, let's see what we might work out together); and (6) provisionalism (Looks like you feel you could go about it this way, or that way.) These are very brief statements derived from the Gibb article (which we have listed in the Suggested Readings at the end of this chapter), and you may well want to look into his account of defensive communication more thoroughly. Defensive climates are characterized by putdowns of the listener by the source, whereas supportive climates stress equality and a constant reassurance, verbally and nonverbally, that the listener is as valuable a human being as the source and has capabilities and feelings that matter. There is no evaluation of anyone by anyone going on in supportive-climate communication.

In terms of the S M C R communication model, when defensiveness interferes in the channel between the source and the receiver, it is that kind of psychological "noise" that makes good listening and accurate feedback almost impossible. Defensive communication builds barriers between people that make trust and openness and authentic interaction difficult, if not impossible. In terms of public speaking, to the extent that any speaker creates defensiveness in his audience, his effectiveness is lessened.

Active listening

Another form of listening that interests those involved in the study and practice of communication is that advanced by psychologist Carl R. Rogers. Originally conceived as a therapeutic technique for counselors, *active listening* contains principles well worth our consideration as we explore the facets of listening in contemporary communication.

Working with upper-level college students studying small group theory and techniques, we have become increasingly aware of how well the American educational system prepares its students for competition, and how poorly it prepares anyone for the cooperative skills necessary in our increasingly urban society and complex business and industrial organizations. We preach equality and reward excellence; we evaluate one another from babyhood on. Parents criticize so children "can learn." Teachers pit students against one another, "to get a little healthy competition going." Competition exists in most modern societies, in and out of school; but it seems unfortunate to us that the students we encourage to work together, in order to learn firsthand how group dynamics develop and how cooperation must be worked on throughout the class, report that this class is the first in which they *had* to cooperate to make the class work out. Most students have had to live with being ranked since kindergarten. Despite *every* device educators have come up with (no grades, no "smart" or "slow" groupings, no "failures"), students are constantly told, verbally and nonverbally, where they stand. No wonder our antennae are always out for cues about our personal worth.

We are so used to being evaluated, so used to having our statements accepted or rejected, that when someone actually listens to what we say *without evaluating it in any way*, we want to talk forever. There is an old Spanish proverb, "He who keeps silent consents." When someone listens so nonjudgmentally, we dare to assume he agrees with us, accepts us as we are, is "on our wavelength." This is the core of active listening, and yet there is much more to it. If as a listener you never respond, the person talking cannot be sure how you are responding; your mind could be a thousand miles away, or you could just be bored. The person talking needs some indication that you are empathetic to what he says.

If you are listening actively, as Rogers describes the concept, your mind is right with the person who is talking. You are trying to walk that mile in his shoes for the time involved, and you atune yourself to the person to such an extent that you cannot sit in judgment of him because you share his feelings from his point of view. Does it sound a little impossible? Perhaps it would take years of practice to become a totally supportive, nonevaluative active listener, but the basic premises and some of the techniques themselves have proved very interesting and useful to some of our students. They point out the slightly "manipulative" character of the technique: After all, you *do* have a purpose when you practice active listening; you are witholding yourself and your opinions for the express purpose of helping someone else discuss and sort out his or her own feelings and work out his or her own solutions. Even when you are asked, "What do you think? What's your opinion?," Rogers says you must turn the question back to the speaker and give neither negative nor positive evaluation.

Certainly in terms of basic communication skills, to be able to actively listen is extremely valuable, but such listening must be totally honest, verbally and nonverbally. You cannot "con" people by pretending to listen actively; if you try to use active listening as a manipulative tool, as we define *manipulate*—doing things for your own ends, not anybody else's—you will be found out sooner or later.

• Deciding to listen is not enough; guided practice in listening techniques is also necessary.

• Listening is as difficult as reading.

• A listener often must exert effort to keep the attention from wandering.

• We should make a conscious choice about whether or not we will listen to a speaker; we should not leave the matter to chance.

• People who listen for factual details have more trouble remembering what a speaker has said than people who listen for the main ideas.

• If we respond emotionally to a speaker's language, we lose some of our ability to listen.

• We need to understand what the other person is saying before we can intelligently agree or disagree.

• When we listen critically, we need to ask if the denotative meanings are true to the facts.

• Even after you understand a message, you should critically evaluate the propaganda elements within it.

• Feedback only takes place when some participants in the communication willingly try to understand the source's message and systematically provide cues as to how they are decoding it.

• Often what we think of as poor listening is due not so much to a lack of skill as to the unwillingness of the participants to play the role of receiver.

• The unwillingness of the participants to be receivers of messages often stems from poor interpersonal relationships.

• Once you have agreed to play the role of receiver, then the communication skills of good listening come into play.

• Creative listening discovers meanings in a message that go beyond a speaker's intentions.

• When you become defensive, your listening ability is lessened.

• Defensive communication climates often result from manipulative messages that imply evaluation, control, strategy, neutrality, superiority, and certainty on the part of the speaker.

• Supportive communication climates often result from messages that imply description, problem orientation, spontaneity, empathy, equality, and provisionalism.

• Active listening involves an empathic involvement with the other person.

SUGGESTED PROJECTS

1 • Make a list of words that tend to make you respond in such a way that you can hardly listen to what comes next.

2 • Think back to the experiences in communication you have had in the past week. Write a short paper analyzing your experience as a listener in an important situation.

3 • Select a group that is important to you—your family, your fellow workers, or your close friends. Analyze the listening skill of several other people in the group, and then analyze your own listening in that group. Can you suggest ways to improve the others' listening ability, as well as your own?

SUGGESTED READINGS

Barker, Larry L. *Listening Behavior*. Englewood Cliffs, N.J.: Prentice-Hall, 1971.

Bormann, Ernest G., William S. Howell, Ralph G. Nichols, and George L. Shapiro. *Interpersonal Communication in the Modern Organization*. Englewood Cliffs, N.J.: Prentice-Hall, 1969. "Listening to the Spoken Word," pp. 167–177; "Getting the Message," pp. 183–99; "Evaluating the Message," pp. 203–12.

Gibb, Jack R. "Defensive Communication," *The Journal of Communication* II (1961): 141–48.

Huseman, Richard C., Cal M. Logue, and Dwight L. Freshley. *Readings in Interpersonal and Organizational Communication*. Boston: Holbrook Press, 1969. "Communication Through Listening," pp. 457–96.

Lewis, Thomas, and Ralph G. Nichols. *Speaking and Listening: A Guide to Effective Oral-Aural Communication*. Dubuque, Iowa: Brown, 1965.

Nichols, Ralph G., and Leonard Stevens. *Are You Listening?* New York: McGraw-Hill, 1957.

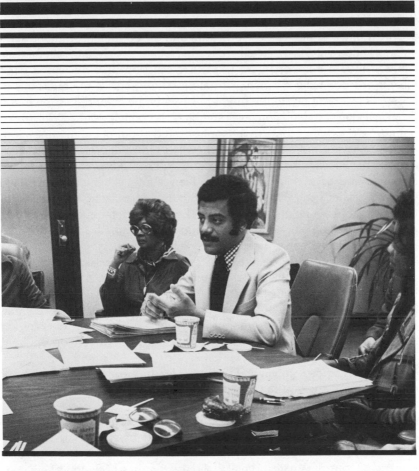

EVALUATING COMMUNICATION
CHAPTER 6

DAY-TO-DAY CRITICISM

We all evaluate communication events. Communication is such a vital activity that we all discuss our successful and unsuccessful communication attempts informally, just as we discuss films, plays, novels, and other artistic works if they are important to us. Our discussion may be of the basic I-like-it or I-don't-like-it variety. "I hate it when he asks me questions in class." "I just can't talk to my mother." "We had a great discussion in the dorm last night." "Can't you get something else on television? Politics is so boring." Or, as we become more sophisticated about our communication, we may provide more specific and detailed explanations of our evaluations: "I hate it when he asks me questions in class. Nonverbally he comes across to me as saying he is better than I am, like he is continually evaluating what I say. He also strikes me as manipulating me—trying to use me to make a point with the class. I get very defensive, but I'm in a one-down position, and if I told him what I really think he'd probably cut my grade." Or we may say about the politician on television, "Man, is he boring! His language is so abstract and filled with clichés. He never dramatizes. His organization is clear enough; fact is, it's so simple and he keeps repeating the points so often I begin to get the feeling he thinks I have the mind of a twelve-year-old. For a politician in national office, that man has got to have the most monotonous voice of anyone in Washington in the last twenty years. It's a real chore to keep your attention on what he's saying."

As this course continues you will learn more and more about communication and you can move from the haphazard day-to-day type of evaluation to more rigorous criticism.

In this chapter we provide you with the basics you need to begin evaluating communication. We provide a step-by-step analysis of the evaluative process you can apply to your communication assignments and to those of your classmates. We also discuss the uses of rhetorical criticism and provide directions on how to apply one approach to criticism so you can evaluate messages that are of special importance.

THE BASIC EVALUATIVE PROCESS

In order to evaluate communication, you must learn the basic principles relating to the processes involved. Once you learn the theory, you can examine a given communication event and apply the appropriate standards to it. The basic evaluative process consists of three steps: (1) selecting criteria for evaluation, (2) describing the communication event, and (3) applying the criteria to the description and making the evaluation.

Selecting criteria

Once you have picked the communication you wish to study, you can turn to the evaluation proper. The first step is to take from the applicable principles of communication a number of criteria to use in the evaluation. The process applies to casual conversations, interviews, business meetings, television programs, public speeches, and all other forms and contexts of communication. To illustrate our point, we will look at how you might criticize a public speech.

You could pick a number of criteria to use in evaluating a speech. You could evaluate how the speaker analyzes the audience and adapts the ideas in the speech to the audience. You could select the way the speaker argues the case, the quality of the evidence, the plausibility and consistency of the reasoning. You could pick the skill with which the speaker develops a persuasive platform personality. You could concentrate on the speaker's delivery, including gestures, facial expressions, voice projection, articulation, and so forth. You could focus on how the speaker dramatizes his or her avowed position and evokes emotions, creates positive and negative suggestions, gives directions, and arouses the listeners to action.

Usually we do not raise every possible critical issue that we can about every speech. For example, if your instructor gave you an assignment to give a public speech, he or she might emphasize the delivery or the organization or the persuasive content; when you delivered the speech, then, your classmates and instructor would look for the particular aspect assigned when evaluating the speech.

Describing a communication event

The second step in criticizing communication is to use the criteria as guidelines in examining a communication event (as it unfolds or as it is represented in a recording) and describing its features. Let us say that an assignment emphasized making ideas clear. You would then look at the speech and ask such questions as "Did the speaker use definitions? If so, what kind of definitions were used? Did the speaker use any of the techniques of explanation, such as listing parts and so forth? Did the speaker use any examples? If so, were they real or hypothetical examples? On the basis of the criteria, you would then describe the techniques that the speaker used in the speech in some detail. You might note: "The speaker tried to clarify the point about how high unemployment and economic recession could be accompanied by a high rate of inflation with a hypothetical example about a dairy farm that was losing money, was not milking all of its cows, and was still charging more for its milk."

Evaluating the event

The last step in the critical process is to make an evaluation of the speech according to the criteria. You might decide that the speaker did a poor job of clarifying the concept of recession and inflation because the example drawn from agriculture was poorly adapted to the audience, which was composed of students who were all from the core-city areas of a large metropolitan center and were unfamiliar with some of the technical details of dairy farming. The same sort of critical judgments could be made about delivery: "poor eye contact, mumbled, lots of fidgeting; I thought she was going to break her pencil in two at least five times during the speech"; about the audience: "The audience really sat there like a bunch of zombies; they did not respond at all"; and so forth.

The same essential critical process is used in all communication contexts. The critic evaluating organizational communication event might select as criterion the fidelity of information transmission and might make her evaluation by conducting a survey of how much information the employees of a company receive from messages that are sent downward through the organization's formal channels of communication. She might conclude, for instance, that employees comprehend or can recall only 25 percent of the information that upper management transmits down through channels to them. Another critic might examine the amount of information that a jury gets from the judge's charge by giving them a test of their comprehension of key ideas. The critic might also study videotapes of conversations or small group meetings for evidence of nonverbal feedback, which she could evaluate as to quantity and effectiveness.

A student might recall a deep discussion with close friends that dealt with important questions of human relationships and examine how well the participants expressed authentic feelings, developed trust, self-disclosed, and confronted and worked through their conflicts.

Evaluation is important in your role as a student in a communication class. Without evaluation of our communication so that we can discover what we are doing well and what we still need to work on, we cannot improve. Your evaluations can help your fellow students improve their communication. Learning to evaluate communication gives you an added understanding that you can then apply to your own speaking and listening.

We go beyond the basic principles of classroom criticism in this chapter, because as important as evaluation is to your own improvement as a message source it is even more important to your role as message consumer. You spend much more of your time listening, reading, and watching messages than you spend in writing and speaking. Unfortunately in our modern mass-communication world the slogan "Listener beware" is often the order of the day.

THE CRITIC AS CONSUMER OF COMMUNICATION

One of your purposes in this course should be to become a skillful and perceptive critic of the messages that bombard you so you can be a wise consumer of information, persuasion, and propaganda.

We live in an age in which we get messages from public speakers, but we also get messages while being hammered by disco music as we see images projected on a screen. Perhaps most effective of all modern persuasive messages is the television commercial—using music, slogans, dance, drama, still pictures, moving pictures, animated cartoons, poetry, and argument—all orchestrated into a tight, smooth sales pitch, crammed into 60 seconds or less. How many TV commercial ditties can you sing? Did you try to memorize the words? Or did the catchy tunes insinuate the persuasive message into your mind without your paying much attention?

Communication events are frequently aimed at mass audiences; messages are brief and polished, and they have to compete for our attention with hundreds of other messages. This fight for attention leads communicators to use every avenue of the senses to reach us, hold our attention, and persuade us to buy a particular model car, adopt a new hemline, or wash with a certain brand of soap.

Gullible consumers of film, radio, and television may come to live in a world of images, impressions, and stereotypes without being aware of how they got there. What kinds of people do what sorts of things in the messages we daily consume? Are the old people decrepit and useless, the butt of jokes about shuffling walks and squeaky voices? Are the drug users cool and admirable or sad and bewildered? Are women portrayed as superwomen easily juggling career, home, and family? Do you gradually get the impression that the mayor is a fool as you watch him answer reporters on news shows? Do you begin to wonder if the marines are vicious and the cops corrupt? Much of what we believe and much of how we act derives from the sometimes fringe impressions we get from the messages we see on the mass media—impressions that are reinforced when we talk informally with family and friends.

Huey Long, a colorful southern politician in the 1930s, gained a large following during the Depression with his slogan "Every Man a King." In a very real sense, every citizen is a ruler in a representative democracy such as the one in the United States. The basic assumption of our government is that with freedom of speech, of press, and of assembly, many points of view will be given an opportunity to be heard and the people, once they have heard the competing positions debated, will have the wisdom to choose the best policy and the best representatives. A citizen in a democracy has to be more responsible, more politically knowledgeable and active, than a citizen in any other form of society. An important part of training for citizenship is the ability to evaluate political communication critically, including not only the blatant sales pitches of the political advertisement but also the supposedly more objective political analyses of journalists and columnists.

We should be aware that candidates often hire ghostwriters to help them prepare messages for the public. At best the ghostwriter helps the candidate frame his ideas in more effective language; at worst the ghostwriter provides both ideas and language and may fool the public into thinking a poor candidate is a good one. Some candidates have teams of ghostwriters, and several people contribute to the preparation of a single speech. Most politicians running for important public offices now use the latest persuasive techniques developed by advertising agencies and public relations firms to produce their campaign messages. They often hire marketing specialists and professional survey firms to make elaborate polls of audience attitudes and opinions prior to developing the campaign persuasion. How can you know who you are voting for under the circumstances? If we have been conned by experts in merchandizing candidates, our elected officials may be inadequate for effective government.

Fortunately television not only encourages a candidate to use advertising agencies, short commercial-type announcements, and ghostwriters, but also forces politicians to appear on public-affairs programs where skilled journalists and political analysts ask probing questions and the candidate cannot rely on other people to answer for him or her. Indeed, on the better public affairs programs, the issues receive a fuller airing and more intensive probing than they do in the typical political address or rally speech delivered by a candidate to an audience.

To be a citizen in a democracy, therefore, a person needs to know how to analyze political persuasion—how to test the validity of an argument, the truthfulness of evidence, and the wisdom of policy.

We have pointed out in some detail the importance of developing skill at critically evaluating the political messages that we receive in order to function as citizens. We could make the same point in regard to religious messages; the rise of cults, the charges and countercharges of brainwashing and deprogramming indicate the importance of your becoming an aware consumer in that area. Similar concerns apply to our responses to advertisements about products, to messages relating to self-improvement, to leisure-time activities, and to a wide range of other topics.

We are all plugged in to so many message sources through the mass media that we are in danger of suffering from information overload. Most of us protect ourselves against such overload by ignoring the bulk of the messages that surround us. We simply do not have time to listen, let alone evaluate it all carefully. Some of these messages, however, are vital to our interests. We seek out these messages and pay careful attention to them. The vital and interesting messages are the ones we should learn how to examine with care.

USES OF RHETORICAL CRITICISM

The technical term for carefully criticizing important messages is *rhetorical criticism*. Rhetoric is the study of the arts of persuasion. Scholars have developed some techniques to guide the evaluation of important messages and have published studies that can help the general public in their role as consumers of information. Rhetorical criticism has three major uses: (1)

you may criticize messages as a way to present and defend your position in a discussion or debate, (2) you may criticize messages to upgrade the general quality of communication in society, and (3) you may criticize messages to discover how communication works to shape our dreams, impel us to act, and provide us with a vision of the world. All these uses of rhetorical criticism help us become wiser consumers of communication. Once we understand how the word magic works, it loses its spell over us. We begin to control our communication rather than to be controlled by it.

One good basic approach to rhetorical criticism is to take the steps of evaluating a communication event, described earlier in the chapter, and apply them to the messages you wish to study. The difference between applying these steps to classroom evaluations and rhetorical criticism is largely one of degree. The rhetorical critic will take more time and be more careful and rigorous in applying the steps. Rhetorical criticism begins with the selection of a set of messages to evaluate. Just as you might turn to information from consumer groups when you are about to make an expensive purchase such as a car or stereo set to see how they evaluate a product, so you might pick out what is for you a particularly important article, book, speech, television program, radio message, or other source of information to criticize in detail.

If the country is in the midst of a political campaign and you are interested in it, you might select a televised debate among the candidates or a speech or news conference for your rhetorical criticism. Following the steps of selecting criteria, describing the message, and applying the criteria, you might examine such things as the credibility of the message sources, the soundness of the ideas, and the propaganda elements in the communication.

Criticism as advocacy

In your discussions with others you may use the criticism of messages as a way to debate the pros and cons of a question. One way to make your point is to emphasize the high quality of the communication of those who are leading speakers for your position. Another way is to attack the shoddy communication of a person who symbolizes the opposition. Such criticism helps clarify public debate on important issues. When a number of people examine the communication surrounding a public issue, they often succeed in carefully and systematically evaluating the communication of pressure groups, one-issue movements, and established political and social institutions.

Another technique for taking an "advocate's" position by means of communication criticism is to examine how communication contributes to an undesirable condition in society. Critics might examine how the language of the mass media or the dramatizations of the media give an undesirable impression of a particular ethnic or minority group. In this regard, a critic might analyze the negative connotations of the terms associated with darkness or blackness (e.g., blackhearted) and argue that black people are victims of the language of a racist society. Or a critic might argue that Polish jokes reflect prejudice against Polish people. Or the critic might argue that the commercials on television present male parents as simpleminded dolts who are continually duped by their spouses and children. Or the critic might argue that girls are dramatized in the mass media magazines as nurturing, selfless, soft, and defenseless, while boys are portrayed as assertive, tough, and selfish. Or the critic might argue that sexist bias is built into the language in that all terms for positions of power are associated with the male gender—*chairman*, for example. (Under the impact of the latter sort of criticism, at our schools we now have *chairpersons* and *chair-ones*. One of our daughters received a letter from a college she was considering attending addressed to "Dear Freshperson.")

Criticism as social corrective

You will find rhetorical criticism useful in still another way. Some critics of communication are not involved as participants in an ongoing debate but are interested in criticizing the general quality of communication in a society. Their aim is to be objective and look at the communication on all sides and criticize it in an evenhanded manner. They strike out at shoddy communication no matter where they find it. They may examine the gobbledygook of bureaucratic communication or the murky, jargon-ridden style of some textbook writers. They may evaluate the decline in the quality of imagination and dramatization resulting from television commercials or the dull English created by ghostwriters for the television broadcasts of the president.

Criticism as an avenue to knowledge

The final kind of rhetorical criticism aims at discovering knowledge about human communication. Scholars criticizing public communication in this way are trying to understand human communications in all its varied forms. Rhetorical criticism thus takes its place as a liberal and humanizing art, a scholarly endeavor that aims to illuminate the human condition. It is particularly concerned with human symbolizing, which works to divide and integrate human beings, to interpret human problems, and to enable cooperative efforts to be made to solve them and to provide self and group concepts for human beings searching for meaning in their existence and endeavors.

We will explain in some detail one approach to rhetorical criticism that aims to discover knowledge about the human condition. You should understand that the approach we outline is but one of several; critics have used a number of other methods to make important contributions to our understanding of human communication. Since you are being introduced to the study of speech communication, you do not have time to go into all the intricate details of these major approaches to criticism, but you should understand the method of rhetorical criticism and how it illuminates the study of persuasion. The method we will use is simple enough that you can try your hand at criticizing discourse after you finish reading this chapter.

FANTASY THEME ANALYSIS

We call the approach a *fantasy theme analysis of rhetorical visions* and use the method to explore the social reality of a group of people who share a rhetorical vision. A fantasy theme is a dramatizing message, which contains characters (personae) in a dramatic situation acting out a scenario. Dramatizing messages occur in our talking to ourselves (our personal fantasies); they occur in two-person conversations, they occur in small groups, they occur in radio and television commercials, they occur in public speechs; they occur in radio and television talk shows, public-affairs broadcasts, and newcasts; and they occur in newspapers and magazines. In short, dramatic narratives are often part of messages. Dramatizing messages occur in all cultures and in all communication contexts.

The important feature of dramatizing messages for the rhetorical critic is the fact that some dramatizing catches people's attention. They come to identify with the "good people," to root for their welfare, and to hope they will win out in the struggle; and they come to dislike the "bad people," to feel suspense as the forces of evil threaten to overwhelm the forces of good. They begin to feel fear, hatred, or disgust for the evil ones and begin to experience the emotions of the good people, with whom they identify. When the heroine cries, they cry; when the heroine laughs with joy, they laugh; when the heroine jumps in fear, they jump and feel fear. You can document the chaining of a dramatization through groups of people by finding evidence that a given response to it is repeated in different contexts. Such evidence is available in written records as well as in audio- and videotapes.

The critic who discovers that a small group or community has shared fantasies has evidence that the people have established the first bonds of a rhetorical community. When a group of people come to share a common cast of heroes and villains, they have a common symbolism that serves to tie them together.

How to make a fantasy theme analysis

You begin a fantasy theme analysis by selecting a general topic area that you would like to investigate. Perhaps you are interested in political campaigning or you enjoy ridiculing television commercials; you may be intrigued by the process of religious conversion, by the communication associated with transcendental meditation, by the communication within a large corporation designed to increase employee morale, or by the communication of some pressure group or social reform movement. The communication you study need not be in the mass media; it can be messages produced by a discussion group or the conversations of two or three persons.

Once you have selected an area of study, you begin to collect evidence relating to the content of the communication. You can use video- or audiotapes or your own direct observation. Often you can find written transcripts or records of important public messages. You should try to restrict the scope of your topic of criticism, so that you can deal with it in considerable detail in the time you have for your study.

Discovering fantasy themes

You should next go through the communication and note each dramatic incident in the messages you have collected. When you have gathered a number of dramatic incidents, try to sort them into fantasy types. Is the same story repeated over and over again, with slightly different characters and minor variations? Put all instances of that story together. You have now discovered a fantasy type. The discovery of a fantasy type is evidence that similar fantasy themes are shared by an important community of people and that they are coming to share a common rhetorical vision. A rhetorical fantasy type is like the fantasy types used in television dramas. You may, for instance, find a dramatic series on one television network that features three police officers who deal competently with a series of incidents of a diverse nature, with some humor but with much seriousness. If you then find similar series on other networks you can lump them together as police-action fantasy types and examine all of the programs as a group.

Once you have a collection of basic fantasy types, you can begin to search the discourse again to see if the communicators themselves use fantasy types in their messages. If you find such use of fantasy types, it is further evidence that they share the same fantasies. A speaker can only use fantasy types in a message successfully if the listeners have previously shared a number of similar fantasy themes. For example, a political pamphlet for a senatorial candidate may contain a statement something like the following: "Senator James Early Courageous was the first to speak out against the corruption in the state capital. He was the first to take the unpopular stand of energy conservation. He was the first to demand greater participation on the part of the poor people, in local welfare programs. He was the first to . . ." etc., etc. The statement is essentially a fantasy type, and by alluding to but not developing the fantasies relating to each drama when Senator Courageous took an early and unpopular stand which later proved to be the right one, the overall type emerges. Namely, Senator James Early Courageous is an individual who characteristically sees the right thing to do before anyone else in government; he characteristically takes a stand for the right thing, and then, characteristically, those who are too selfish or too stupid to understand his farseeing statesmanship come forward to harass and attack him. Senator Courageous, however, stands firm for what is right and takes the blows and risks his career for these farsighted programs.

Reconstructing a rhetorical vision

Once you have discovered the basic fantasy types, you can reconstruct the vision of the people who have shared them. You can look for patterns of characteristics. Do the same people keep cropping up as villains? Are the same people generally praised and identified with as heroes? You can look also for similar scenarios. Do you find the same stories told over and over, or very similar ones? You can look to the setting of the dramas.

Once you can describe the general vision of the communicators, you can ask more specific questions about various elements of the rhetoric. How concrete and detailed are the characterizations of the heroes and villains? What motives are attributed to the bad guys and to the good guys? (Often those participating in the vision will try to act for the same motives that they identify in their heroes.) How are the members of the rhetorical community characterized? ("We Americans are always . . ."; "The farmer is . . ."; "Black people are basically . . .". Those of us interested in the anti-nuclear energy movement . . .") For what are the members of the community praised? For what are the enemies castigated? When you have made such an analysis of the heroes and villains you can decide what values are implied in the rhetorical vision. Are the heroes active and involved in the general welfare? If so, then the value of active involvement for others is implied, and so forth.

Where are the fantasy themes set? In the wilderness? In the urban ghetto? On the campus? In the classroom? In an automobile? Often the place of the drama becomes an important territory and serves to establish home turf. People searching for rhetorical community often find a symbolic ground useful as a unifying symbol.

What are the typical scenarios? What actions take place? What do the good people do? Do they demonstrate in the streets? Vote? Plant bombs? Go to jail and resist the oppressive system? Stay home and tend to their personal affairs? What do the bad people do? Conspire to exploit the innocent? Hypocritically mouth platitudes about freedom while acting in oppressive ways? Use violence to coerce the good people? What actions are celebrated and what actions are censored? What lifestyles are cele-brated as praiseworthy?

What meanings are inherent in the dramas? Where does the partici-pant in the vision fit into the nature of things? Where does the community fit into the rest of the culture? into the scheme of history? What emotions are aroused by the typical fantasy types that you discover? Does hate predominate? rage? pity? love? indignation? resignation? What motives are embedded in the vision? Would those committed to it work for or resist legal action if necessary? violence? One industrial psychologist has de-veloped a system of analyzing motives in fantasy themes that can be used to discover if a given drama reflects an affiliation motive (a love story), an achievement motivation (the Horatio Alger fantasy type), or mastery moti-vation (how the hero clawed his way to the top).

You can examine how the rhetorical vision deals with facts or the breaking news; you can discover the kinds of argumentation that are implied by the vision. For example, some visions dramatize a written text as the ultimate legitimizer of argument. Certain religions' rhetorical visions portray the Bible (or some other sacred text) as the repository of knowledge, and the participants' reasoning and argument consists of providing a conclusion and quotations from the Bible that support the conclusion. Some rhetorical visions celebrate observations of facts as the ultimate legitimizer of argument, and participants tend to argue from data gathered in scientific studies, census surveys, and other systematic obser-vations. Some rhetorical visions dramatize precedent, or previous human experience, as the ultimate legitimizer of argument, and the participants submit prior instances and the way these instances were handled as arguments in behalf of a certain conclusion.

You need not, and often a brief rhetorical criticism cannot, raise all of the above questions about a given speech or series of messages, but for an in-depth study of a single message a critic might ask more of the questions and search for more details.

Once you have analyzed some of the major features of a rhetorical vision in terms of the questions posed above, you can answer some more general rhetorical questions. You can learn of the hopes and fears, the emotional tone, and the inner life of a group by examining how it deals with basic, universal rhetorical problems. Such insight flows from answers to questions such as these. How well did the communication deal with the problem of creating and celebrating a sense of community? Did it help generate a group and individual self-image that was strong, confident, and resilient? How did the rhetoric aid or hinder the community in its adaptation to its physical environment? How did the communicators deal with the rhetorical problem of creating a social reality that provides norms for community behavior in terms of the level of violence, exploitation, dominance, and injustice? Did the communication create a drama for the members to participate in, which served such mythic functions as providing them with an account of the world, the gods, and fate that gave meaning to their community and themselves? How did the rhetoric meet the problems of celebrating the community's values? How well did it initiate and dedicate new generations who inherited the vision to the values of the community? How well did the communicator meet the needs for change within the community? How well did it work to convert new members to the community? How well did the vision aid the people who participated in it to live with people who participated in different rhetorical visions?

Once we participate through criticism in the rhetorical vision of a community or movement, we have come to experience vicariously the inner symbolic world of its participants and to experience a way to life that would otherwise be less accessible to us; we have enlarged our awareness and become more fully human.

KEY IDEAS CHAPTER 6

• In order to evaluate communication, you must learn the basic principles relating to the process involved.

• The basic evaluative process consists of selecting criteria, describing the communication, and applying the criteria.

• Evaluation is important to instruction designed to develop communication skills.

• Evaluation is basic to our role as consumer of communication in a mass media culture.

• One of your purposes in this course should be to become a wise consumer of information, persuasion, and propaganda.

• *Rhetorical criticism* is the technical term for the process of carefully evaluating important messages.

• Rhetorical criticism may function as a way for a person to defend a position in discussion or debate.

• Rhetorical criticism may function as a way for a person to upgrade the general quality of communication in society.

• Rhetorical criticism may function as a way to learn about the way communication works.

• Fantasy theme analysis is a method of rhetorical criticism that explores the social reality of a group of people who share a common vision.

• A *fantasy theme* is a dramatizing message that contains characters in dramatic action within a scene.

• The critic who discovers that a small group or a community has shared fantasies has evidence that the members have created some bonds of community.

• *Fantasy types* are stock scenarios that a community uses over and over again.

• The critic can reconstruct the rhetorical vision of a community from the fantasy types.

• After a critic describes a rhetorical vision, he or she can evaluate it in terms of how well it deals with rhetorical problems.

SUGGESTED PROJECTS

1 • Your instructor will assign an exercise in interpersonal or small-group communication or in public speaking. You select criteria from the appropriate chapters of this book to evaluate the exercise. Using the criteria, you will write a brief communication evaluation of one or more of your classmates.

2 • Select a public issue about which you have strong opinions. Pick some communication relating to the topic and make a rhetorical criticism of it that serves to express your opinion on the controversy. You may select a public figure whose ideas and speaking you particularly like or dislike for the focus of your criticism. Your instructor may have you deliver your criticism orally or may have you write a short paper about it.

3 • Select a number of messages for which you can get good records and which you believe represent a rhetorical community. Make a fantasy theme analysis of the rhetorical vision of the community.

SUGGESTED READINGS

Bormann, Ernest G. "Fantasy and Rhetorical Vision: The Rhetorical Criticism of Social Reality." *Quarterly Journal of Speech* 58 (1972): 396–407.

Bormann, Ernest G. "The Eagleton Affair: A Fantasy Theme Analysis." *Quarterly Journal of Speech* 59 (1973): 143–59.

Campbell, Karlyn Kohrs. "Criticism: Ephemeral and Enduring." *Speech Teacher* 23 (1974): 9–14.

Cathcart, Robert. *Post Communication: Criticism and Evaluation.* Indianapolis: Bobbs-Merrill, 1966.

Kidd, Virginia: "Happily Ever After and Other Relationship Styles: Advice on Interpersonal Relations in Popular Magazines, 1951–1973." *Quarterly Journal of Speech* 59 (1973): 31–39.

Scott, Robert L., and Bernard L. Brock. *Methods of Rhetorical Criticism: A Twentieth Century Perspective.* Detroit: Wayne State University Press, 1980.

Turner, Kathleen J. "Comic Strips: A Rhetorical Perspective." *Central States Speech Journal* 28 (1977): 24–35.

PART TWO

INTERPERSONAL AND
SMALL-GROUP COMMUNICATION

SELF-CONCEPT, PERCEPTION, AND
INTERPERSONAL COMMUNICATION
CHAPTER 7

THE NATURE OF THE SELF-CONCEPT

Everyone has a sense of self. Our image of ourselves is important to our mental and emotional health and a basic feature of our interpersonal communication. Your self-concept is essentially the answer you give to the question "Who am I?" Over the years, usually by the process of communication, you begin to define who you are. You define such things as your basic nature, your personality, your roles in life, your hopes and dreams. You may see yourself as a good or poor student, as a survivor or a loser, as a worthwhile person or as "no damned good."

Much of your self-definition came through talking with others in face-to-face situations where nonverbal communication played an important part in telling you how others thought about you and reacted to you. You also got information to help define yourself from feedback, direct or indirect, about what others said of you.

The basic process of naming we discussed in Chapter 3 plays an important role in persuading us about what kind of person we are. The child's mother and a neighbor are having coffee when the child laughs at something the dog does. The mother remarks to the neighbor, "She always was a happy child." The child overhears the comment, hears the pleasure in her mother's voice, and discovers that she is a happy person and that, apparently, it pleases her mother. As she grows up she may hear other members of her family echo this comment that she is a happy person. Gradually she defines herself as a happy person. The family might have named her *moody, sullen, stubborn, competitive, shy, selfish, bashful, unpredictable, responsible.*

Many times we dramatize who we are in terms of some character in our lives such as a family member or some television or film idol or some teacher or older person we know who becomes the object of our hero worship. "I would like to be like her" becomes "I will be like her" and sometimes "I am like her."

In our fantasies and daydreams we see ourselves acting out scripts that become part of our self-concept either in terms of self-fulfilling prophecies as we work hard to achieve our dreams or as the basis for "I'm no damned good" images when we define our dreams as beyond our reach because of some inner flaws.

Others may also succeed in characterizing us in their communication, so we begin to shape our self-concept along the lines of a person we know personally or have heard a lot about. The father says of the child who has been caught in some mischief, "He's just like his Uncle Harry. We better watch that one or he'll end up in jail." As the child grows up the family members become more and more on the lookout for indications that little Joe is like Uncle Harry, and gradually Joe begins to have an identity and a self-concept modeled partly on his impressions of Uncle Harry. Of course the child may be dramatized as reminding family members of Granddad

Flimmerfiddle who was a paragon of talent, social wisdom, and good humor and was a pillar of the community. Our examples may seem far-fetched, but if you think about your own growing-up years you can undoubtedly find various instances where you were labeled as being "like" someone else in your family. How accurate were these labels?

The unfolding process of communication gradually builds up a self-image, and you currently have a self-concept. Although change is possible and sometimes desirable, it is unlikely to happen rapidly. When rapid change does take place, we often say that the person has an "identity crisis." We say that the person doesn't seem to know who she is any more. The labels she gave herself previously no longer seem appropriate to her. Sometimes, and it appears to occur more frequently during the teenage years and the middle years, people feel they are getting competing messages, conflicting nonverbal cues, about themselves, and they find themselves in a crisis period when their self-identity is less stable and comfortable. During this time they try to redefine themselves in some ways, and even after they become more comfortable within themselves about what kind of people they are, they find it quite a job to communicate their "current" selves to the others in their lives. Since your perception of self is built through the process of communication, it is never totally set, definite. As you interact with others, your self-concept is being confirmed, attacked, changed, supported through verbal and nonverbal communication.

SELF-CONCEPT AND INTERPERSONAL COMMUNICATION

The concept you now have of yourself plays an important part in your interpersonal communication. We all search messages to determine what they mean in terms of our self-image. Because of this natural protective response, when interpreting a message the listener often reads into the words meanings that have to do with herself as a person. Is the other person saying or implying something about me? Is she saying that she likes me? Is he saying that he dislikes me? That he respects me? Values my work? Thinks my work is mediocre? Thinks that I'm attractive? Wants to know me better? A lot of questions about me as a person and my self-concept intrude in my interpretation of the other person's words.

The communicator is often as preoccupied with himself as the listener is with herself, and therefore the speaker puts his own excuses, explanations, interests, biases, and prejudices into the message. The speaker may be wondering about the impression his communication is making. Does the listener find me attractive, interesting, and competent? Does she see the depth of my feeling? The great humor in my personality? Little wonder that the moments of glimpsing the other person's inner self in the course of our conversations come as seldom as they do. Learning to be meaning-centered is a first step beyond the natural self-centeredness we all bring to communication interaction. Learning further to be listener-centered is an art requiring constant awareness and practice on the part of any person.

THE EIGHT IMAGES IN A TWO-PERSON CONVERSATION

In a given communication event involving two people, the way they perceive each other is as important in their conversation as the way they see themselves. Let us take a situation in which John is talking with Mary. John has an image of himself, which influences his manner and approach to the communication; John also has an image of Mary; John further has a dream image of the way he wishes Mary would see him; and finally, John has an estimate of the way Mary really does view him. Mary, likewise, has a set of images, which mirror those of John. She has a self-image; an image of John; an image of herself that she wishes John to have, and an estimate of the way John does view her. Each person, thus, has four images of important selves involved in the conversation. If the four images of John, and the four of Mary are more or less alike, they can talk in a relaxed and trustful way. You might call this an ideal basis for good two-person communication.

Much communication takes place, however, with one or more of the images in conflict. We will illustrate several possibilities leading to conflict—there are many more, of course—and suggest that you try to see what other images might be out of phase and what other communication difficulties are likely to follow. When John's self-image is much less attractive than the impression he wants Mary to have of him, he may overdo everything because he feels inadequate. He may talk too much, drive his car too fast, and generally come across as overbearing. If John thinks Mary has an attractive image of him as a handsome, brilliant, witty fellow, whereas she really thinks he is plain, dumb, and boring, John will have trouble talking with Mary. Mary's internal response may be, "Brother, does he think *he's* God's gift to women!"

According to one thoughtful student who, back in the era of the Vietnam War, returned to school as a war veteran, most freshmen and sophomores in college are at about the worst time of life in regard to knowing who they are, what kind of a person they hope to be, what their self-image really is. "When I was 16 I had all the answers," he went on to say. "When I was 18 I had a different bunch of answers. Now I've been around the world and back, I'm 21 years old, and I know less now than I used to, about me, other people, life; you name it." To ask you, particularly if you are in the usual age group of college freshmen and sophomores, to try to figure out what your self-image is and to keep it in mind when communicating with others, is a big order. Learning to know yourself is a lifetime job, but there is no better place than college to start a more sophisticated, systematic examination of yourself and the way you respond. Many college courses have the examination of one's self as the not-so-hidden item on their agenda. Certainly any course in communication must include this probing of one's own basic reactions to life, to situations, and most of all, to people.

SELF-DISCLOSURE

The way to improve the agreement among the various images involved in a conversation is to open oneself up to the other person. We call the revealing of self the process of *self-disclosure*. We know certain things about ourselves, and sometimes we disclose some of these things to another, and sometimes we decide to hide them. Often we hide the unpleasant truths about ourselves to protect the image we want the other person to have of us. We fear the truth will keep us from gaining the liking and respect of the listener. Oddly enough, there are some things about ourselves that we do not know. We may not know, for example, about our little nonverbal mannerisms that disturb other people when we speak. We often do not know what someone else may have told the listener about us.

When two people talk with each other, therefore, each knows some things about the other. When they share much the same information about themselves and each other, their communication is easier and their talk tends to be free and less protective. Communication becomes protective and less open when one person knows something about the other that is unknown to him, or when one person knows something about himself that is unknown to the other. Take the first instance: Bill knows that Harry has damaged his knee cartilage to the extent that he will never be able to play football again, but Harry does not know his injury is permanent and will partly disable him for life. What Bill knows and Harry does not know makes it difficult for the two of them to have a free and open talk about Harry's future as a professional athlete. Take the second instance: Mary knows something about herself that Ann does not know. Mary knows she is an alcoholic who has controlled her drinking problem through membership in Alcoholics Anonymous. As Mary and Ann discuss plans for a party, the hidden fact of Mary's alcoholism means her communication is always to some extent protective.

When a high level of communication is desirable between two people, the goal of both should be the widening of the area of what they know about one another. Self-disclosure is the technique for such widening or sharing of inner experiences.

SUPPORTIVENESS

How does one go about creating a communication climate in which self-disclosure is possible, even encouraged? Psychologist Carl Rogers, working as a clinical therapist with patients who had mental and emotional problems, used a technique of counseling that he called nondirective. He did not lead or direct the patients in their conversations with him, rather, he encouraged them to pour out things in a free, uncritical, nonjudgmental atmosphere. He learned how to build trust between the patient and himself so that the patient came to know he could say anything he wished and not be punished for saying it. What Rogers began as a therapy technique, he and others have now modified into a general technique for working with normal people to improve communication. The heart of the humanistic approach in psychology is to release the human potential within individuals by eliminating the threatening, critical, evaluative communication that brings out a listener's protective filters and produces defensive or counter-threatening messages, and by using, instead, supportive comments to encourage honest discussion.

Because of the manner in which many Americans have come to communicate with one another, we can say that most of us need to develop skills in being consciously supportive of others in those moments of deep and serious talk that are so important to us. We tend to leave things unsaid, to drift through our conversations leaving many loose ends. Through sheer bad habit we often knock the props out from under one another without meaning to do so and sometimes without even knowing that we have done so. One of our friends who lived in the Middle East for a decade commented, upon returning to live in the United States, that she was more than ever impressed with the coldness and reserve with which we interact socially. "We touch so seldom," she said. "We seem to fear getting personal when people don't want us to, so we stop talking just when people in the Middle East would begin to open up and really help one another. When something really bothers Americans, we tend to clam up." Her comments apply more to the Scandinavian, North European heritage of many people in the Upper Midwest, where the authors now live, than in many other groups of people in our complex, pluralistic society; nevertheless, what she said is true of many subcultures in our country.

The feeling of estrangement that our neighbor found inhibiting upon her return to the United States is sometimes called *alienation*. Today many people feel alienated. All of us are handling more sensory stimuli—the form of messages, sounds, and emotional assaults—every single day than our ancestors had to handle in a week or more. Much of our interaction grows impersonal because we simply cannot devote our full attention to every new person we meet, every conversation we take part in, and every message we hear on radio or see on television.

Our feeling of alienation is increased by the impersonality of urban life. When several generations of a large family live together or nearby, as they may in a small town and as they did a generation ago in the inner-city ethnic communities, there is a feeling of belonging, of having many people who care how you are, how you behave, what you do, and what happens to you. Today, our mobility from place to place, class to class, group to group has resulted in a loss of the feeling of community. The burden of providing the feeling of closeness and belonging has been placed on the nuclear family. One father and one mother are supposed to give each other and their children all the warmth, support, love, and care each needs. The rising divorce rate is one result. When, for any number of reasons, the family is not able to fill our need for close and important human relationships, we go out into the world somewhat crippled in our ability to interact and communicate with others. We fail to be warm and supportive; others, in turn, fail to be warm and supportive to us. People close emotional doors, begin to turn away, and do not care about one another.

Mutually supportive communication between two people is extremely difficult; certainly the degree of maturity each has attained influences its success. The strain caused by the demand that all the supportive human interaction each of us craves must come from just one other person has led to the development of lifestyles other than the traditional nuclear family. These experimental communes, trial marriages, and multimarriages attest to the difficulties involved when two people interact; many of these experimental lifestyles are attempts to broaden the bases for supportive communication, or in the case of the trial marriage, to acknowledge the possible difficulty of developing a continuing relationship and to give both parties an option to stop it without the legal proceedings of divorce. Despite the development of these new lifestyles, the majority of Americans plan to marry, and the requirements for sustaining a supportive dyadic (two-person) relationship are important for most of us. And to a lesser degree than is necessary in marriage, all of us are involved in two-person relationships with family members, good friends, and coworkers.

If we can learn to communicate accurately and meaningfully with those around us, we will find that our skill in human relations is greatly improved. Much of what people feel about us is related to the way we communicate with them. People who make us feel good, we tend to like. People who make us angry or depressed, we tend to avoid. The more genuinely supportive communication we learn to give to others, the more we are liked. If we remember that the other fellow wants to be talked to as a worthwhile person, we are more likely to be successful communicators. Even if the other person misunderstands us, if we have made clear, verbally and nonverbally, that he is a person we value, he is more likely to mention his confusion, to voice his doubts, and generally to disclose his real response to us, often leading to better understanding. Once trust has been established, even unpleasant communication can take place—not without discomfort, of course, but with a feeling of mutual respect.

We believe that good interpersonal communication must be based on trust—which is not necessarily to be confused with liking. Initially we all learn basic communication habits from our own families. If the early examples we use as communication models are good, our chances of being effective communicators are increased. If our parents relate well verbally with each other, they also probably communicated pretty well with us. When the person you should be able to trust most of all, your parent, or if you are married, your wife or husband, lets you down, the experience is a terrible instance of taking an important risk and being punished because of it. If for no other reason than to learn what is considered supportive and what is damaging generally, you can begin to view the interpersonal communication within your immediate family and circle of friends with a better degree of objectivity. Learning what healthy communication is, you can work to build good interpersonal relationships with free and open discussions. In his play *Hamlet,* Shakespeare urged his actors to suit their actions to the words in a play. The advice is good for real-life interpersonal communication as well. If you say one thing and do another, you set up contradictory responses that cause misunderstandings. If you say yes and then do as you say you will, you build trust. If you say "love" and act "hate," you set up discord. In Chapter 4 we saw the potential for psychological damage in the two-edged message.

THE NATURE OF PERCEPTION

We are all bombarded with a continual stream of stimuli. If we attended to all the messages and signals that hit our sense organs we would be overwhelmed by the buzzing, roaring, snapping, stinking, musky, sweet, sour, flashing, colorshifting confusion. We respond to this overload by selecting out some things to attend to and ignoring the others by pushing them into the background. We can shift our attention so that we bring some of the background into focus, or a sudden movement or loud noise may cause us to do so. We learn to filter out anything that we do not want to see, hear, touch, taste, and feel and ignore it if we can, although some impressions are rudely forced on our attention.

People who suffer from gradual hearing loss often lose the ability to filter out the sounds they want to attend to from the general flow of noise. Because their hearing loss eliminates much of the sound they previously had to push into the background, they no longer need to bother, and they forget how to do it. When they first use electronic hearing aids they often find the rush of many different sounds nerve-racking. Many people cease to wear their hearing aids because all that unfiltered sound is so disturbing.

If they try to focus on what another person is saying while a radio is playing, the wind is whistling around the house, and there are traffic noises in the street outside, they cannot filter out the sounds they want to hear and push the rest into the background.

Because we differ in the things we attend to, we differ in our filters and how we perceive the world around us. Look at the vase in Figure 5. Do you perceive it as an attractive or unattractive form for a piece of pottery? When we perceive the world around us we often make sense out of it by fitting the pieces together into recognizable shapes and forms. We may see a pattern in a series of dots and decide that they fall along a circle, as in Figure 6. We may hear a part of a verse and expect the missing word to complete the proper form of rhyme schemes. For example, if someone says, "Roses are red, violets are blue; I'm all wet and so are . . . ," pausing, we will tend to supply a word which rhymes with *blue*. If the person finishes the thought by saying, instead, ". . . all of us who are running through the sprinkler," the form would seem somehow wrong. We might even have to ask her to repeat the final phrase. In our eagerness to make communication "make sense" (to *us*), we perceive not so much what *is* as

FIGURE 5: FORM AND PERCEPTION

| 4 points | 8 points | 16 points |

FIGURE 6: PATTERN PERCEPTION

what we can understand and utilize. We attempt to organize the often chaotic stimuli into units of information we can use.

Look at the two people in face-to-face conversation in Figure 5. Are they having a friendly talk or are they arguing? Figure 5, like much of our experience of the world, presents several faces, depending on how we look at it and what we expect to see. The angle or slant from which we view something influences what we see. From one angle we see the half-dollar coin as a thin rectangle; from another, as a circle. Equally important is what we expect to see and what we hope to see. When we first mentioned Figure 5, we suggested that you would see a vase. You probably expected to see the vase and that is what you saw.

Over the years, all of us gradually build up expectations about what we will see and hear under certain circumstances, and we often perceive what we expect or hope to perceive.

In Chapter 5 we discussed how people change the story in the process of retelling it as they pass on rumors. One principle controlling such distortion is that we try to make the story fit our hopes and expectations. People who were certain that Dallas, Texas, was a center of ultraconservatism in the 1960s often had a first immediate perception of the assassination of President Kennedy as a result of a conspiracy of the radical right.

The way we develop obsessions about certain classes of people or events illustrates how we gradually build filters that help us structure and give meanings to our experiences. An *obsession* is when one idea or thought takes over a person's perception of a number of events or people. While obsessions tend to be extreme, sometimes the extreme case makes the point more clearly than a more average example.

Suppose a man has a near accident with a car driven by a woman. Shaking and angry as he drives on, he tries to make sense out of what happened. An observer, from a different and more neutral vantage point, might say neither driver was at fault, or that the man was more responsible because he made a last-minute turn without signaling. The man, however, might try to explain the occurrence in a way that protects his self-concept as a good driver. He finally decides that the woman was driving recklessly. Still very upset, he notices another car delaying traffic because the driver is timid about changing lanes. "Probably another woman driver," he mutters.

For the next several days the man finds himself watching traffic for further evidence of poor driving by women. (Poor driving by men does not seem to attract his attention.) The harder he searches for poor women drivers, the more he seems to find. Soon he feels confirmed in his judgment that women are lousy drivers and he becomes obsessed with "collecting further evidence."

One evening at a party when he gets off on his obsession, a woman challenges him by noting that she has often ridden in a car driven by his wife and that she finds his wife an excellent driver.

"Yes," he says triumphantly, "but she drives like a man."

Gradually we develop our self-concepts and our perceptual filters—and we *all* have them—by experiencing our world and communicating with others about it. As our filters develop they, in turn, influence the way we communicate. Our perceptions, our self-images, go hand in hand with our interpersonal communication, each influencing and being influenced by the others. As we continue living, filtering our experiences, testing our perceptions through communication with others, we develop patterns of interpretation and denotative and connotative meanings for the words we use. We become islands of meanings trying the best we can to build communicative bridges to and from those around us.

PERCEPTION AND INTERPERSONAL COMMUNICATION

Perception and meaning

Perception is closely tied to meaning. As you listen to a message unfold, you do not simply absorb the other's meanings. You interpret the message by calling up meanings from your experiences—experiences that have shaped and been shaped in turn by your perceptions—fitting them into the forms suggested by the structure of the message. We come, therefore, to the important question "What are *meanings?*" Philosophers, psychologists, linguists, and communication scholars have puzzled about the meaning of meanings and discovered that the definition is much more difficult than might at first be supposed. For the student of communication who wishes to improve his or her daily conversations with other people, the basic question has to be answered, since communication *is* some exchange of meaning.

In two-person conversation, the source encodes a message in words and nonverbal codes. As she talks she can watch for the response of the other person. The receiver provides the speaker with continuous feedback as the message unfolds. Since the channels in a face-to-face conversation include both sight and hearing, the speaker can get a reading on her listener's response throughout, *at the same time* she is speaking, from the nonverbal feedback cues of the listener. We cannot stress too strongly that two-person communication provides ideal conditions for close-range continuous feedback. In many communication situations, such as when you are writing a letter, memorandum, or report, or are watching television or listening to the radio, such efficient feedback is missing. The opportunity for high-fidelity communication is greatest in the two-person situation. Our next chapter explores this in more detail.

When two people talk to each other, the meanings aroused by their interaction are within them. When you talk with another person, what you derive from the talk is something within your consciousness and what the other person derives from the talk is something individual and personal for him. We are islands of consciousness and cannot break out of the boundaries of self to experience directly another person's interior life. For example, when you see a color and call it "red," you have learned from experience that when other people talk with you about flowers of that hue, they call them red. You thus come to call flowers of a similar color red. When a man gives his date flowers and says, "These red roses mean something special," she accepts his characterization of the roses as red; whereas had he labeled roses everyone has learned to name *yellow* with the word *red,* she would have corrected him. You know what the word *red* means, in the sense that you agree with others in the presence of a particular flower that it has the property "red." Such agreement is the basis for much common-meaning when we communicate with one another.

However, even after you agree with another person that a rose is red, you have no way of knowing if the red you see is anything at all like the red the other person sees. Logically we have no evidence that when Mr. A talks with Mr. B. they may not have radically different worlds of color, sound, taste, and feeling. Mr. A's world may be full of bright and garish colors, while Mr. B's is full of muted tones. Mr. A's world may be a noisy, raucous one, full of violent and clashing sounds, while Mr. B's world is muffled and quiet. Mr. A and Mr. B may agree that the rose is red or that the musician is playing a Beethoven sonata, but in an important sense, neither one can know what the color red means to the other or what the music sounds like or means to the other. The point is made by an old unanswerable question, "How do you tell a color-blind person what 'red' means?"

ENCODING MEANING

Within his island of meanings, the source discovers a desire to tell another person about something. He encodes a verbal message and supports the *meaning* with nonverbal intonations and body language. Quite often the speaker finds that for what he wants to say, his tools are clumsy. He struggles to find the right names and right properties and relations. He casts about to form the words into the right kinds of sentences. Still he cannot put everything he wishes into his message. His island of meanings is too complicated; the ideas are so complex. He tries to pattern a message that reflects the complexity and the subtle richness of his ideas. The task is difficult. The world within the message source is changing, shifting, dynamic; the language he encodes is frozen once it leaves his lips. The sentences are set, static. He resembles the painter who tries to put a great idea and deep feeling into a series of static forms on a flat canvas. How can he catch the motion, the shifting relationships? The answer is, of course, that he cannot do so completely. The source approximates his ideas and meanings in the form of the verbal and nonverbal message codes.

Some sources encode messages better than others. The encoding of messages is an art that can be learned. Language is limited, but most natural languages are flexible and have great communicative power when handled by a well-trained and talented speaker. The source's language facility, the size of his vocabulary, the rules of his dialect, his creative ability to combine words into novel patterns and to associate ideas and make new meanings by coining figures of speech all affect the kind of verbal message he encodes. Also, some people use nonverbal communication better than others. The source who has a flexible voice and an expressive face and who uses appropriate gestures enhances the effectiveness of his communication.

All of us when talking with another encode our messages from within our islands of meanings. We have perceptions, obsessions, biases, interests, prejudices, needs, and wants, all of which affect the way we encode messages. If we are trained as policemen or medical doctors or legal secretaries or automobile mechanics, our training and the kind of work we do begin to enlarge certain areas of our vocabulary and that part of our internal world likewise grows in size and complexity, while the areas we seldom think about or discuss gradually dwindle in our perception. Our ability to talk technically and with understanding and complexity about the things we do most often increases, as our ability to talk about those things we seldom do or think about decreases.

All of us have to accept our ignorance as we communicate with someone else. I know little or nothing of you until you tell me. You are ignorant about me, also. Ignorance is simply what we do not yet know. You are bound to know a great deal about something I know nothing about. If I pretend I am not ignorant about something, I mislead you. We can expect communication problems. We have to learn to broadcast our ignorance on occasion and not try to conceal it. Only when we admit ignorance can someone else begin to tell us about what we do not know. Admitting ignorance is a vital key to providing feedback to improve communication.

INTERPRETING MEANING

The source's problems of finding the right message to communicate his meanings are mirrored to some extent in the receiver. The receiver of any message also has a personal island of meanings. The receiver has a certain language facility, a certain dialect, certain biases, interests, and prejudices. The listener tends to read into the messages those meanings associated with her personal biases and interests.

The receiver finds some parts of the message easy to associate with a denotative meaning. Generally, if a name is specific, such as, "My dog, Rover, sitting over there by the chair," the listener associates a part of her perceptual world quickly and easily, and both the speaker and the listener know what is being discussed. The receiver feels confident that she understands the message, and she may nod her head to indicate understanding. Problems arise because some words are abstract and difficult to associate with a denotative meaning, and, as we explained in Chapter 3, with connotative meanings. Messages that are not firmly anchored to clear denotative meanings may trigger a large pool of meanings and their emotional associations in the listener.

Just as the speaker finds his verbal and nonverbal codes clumsy for the task of encoding messages, so the receiver finds the interpretation of messages difficult, but it is through this interpretation that human understanding can come about. Perhaps the listener interprets a nonverbal gesture as a clue to some deep and important idea within the consciousness of the speaker. The excitement of discovery regarding a fellow human being begins. The listener strains to find a verbal key to the idea. She asks for more messages. She strives to interpret these and seeks additional comments. She thinks she sees the shape of the idea; she gets a glimmer of the feeling within the source. Somehow she manages some contact through the self-protective walls of biases, dialect, background, interests, and motives. The interchange has proceeded until the two people feel they have achieved genuine understanding. Both are excited, moved, touched by the experience. They have glimpsed the interior island of another person's meanings.

Such moments of high-fidelity transmission of meaning come too seldom for most of us, and little wonder, considering the difficulty of the task and the fact that we often take the skills required for granted. When they come, they provide some of the most rewarding of all human social experiences.

KEY IDEAS CHAPTER 7

• **Our image of ourselves is important to our mental and emotional health and a basic feature of our interpersonal communication.**

• A person's self-concept is the answer he or she gives to the question "Who am I?"

• Self-definition often comes through talking with others in face-to-face situations.

• The basic processes of naming and labeling play an important part in telling us who we are.

• Our personal fantasies in which we play leading roles and the stories that others tell about us contribute to our self-concept.

• Participants in a conversation are often worried about their images of themselves and of one another.

• The way two people see each other is as important to their conversation as the way they see themselves.

• One way to improve the agreement among the various self-images involved in a conversation is the process of self-disclosure.

• Self-disclosure is encouraged by supportive communication.

• Good interpersonal communication is based on trust.

• We respond to the overload of stimuli by selectively perceiving part of them.

• Because we differ in the things we attend to, we differ in our filters and how they perceive the world around us.

• Over the years we build up expectations about what we will see, and we often perceive what we expect or hope to perceive.

• Perception is closely tied to meaning.

• When two people talk to each other, the meanings aroused by their interaction are within each of them.

• We are islands of consciousness and cannot break out of the boundaries of self to experience directly another person's meanings.

• Our interior world is changing, shifting, dynamic; the language we use to encode our meanings is static and therefore never fully adequate.

• The encoding of messages is an art that can be learned.

• The source's problems of finding the right message are mirrored to some extent by the receiver's problems of supplying the right meanings for the message.

SUGGESTED PROJECTS

1 • Write twenty brief statements in answer to the question "Who am I?" Analyze your answers and prepare a short message, to be given either orally or as a paper, in which you discuss what your answers mean in terms of your communication.

2 • Your instructor will divide the class into pairs and give you a brief period of time for a get-acquainted conversation with another member of the class. Write a short paper in which you describe the image of yourself that you tried to project and the image of yourself that you think the other person, in fact, has of you after the conversation.

3 • Recall an important conversation you had with a close friend or family member in which there was a disagreement resulting in part from different perceptions of what happened. Analyze the way differing perceptions influenced the communication.

SUGGESTED READINGS

Austin-Lett, Genelle, and Jan Sprague. *Talk to Yourself: Experiencing Intrapersonal Communication.* Boston: Houghton Mifflin, 1976.

Johnson, David W. *Reaching Out: Interpersonal Effectiveness and Self-Actualization.* Englewood Cliffs, N.J.: Prentice-Hall, 1972.

Jourard, Sidney M. *The Transparent Self.* 2d ed. New York: Van Nostrand, 1971.

Rogers, Carl. *On Becoming a Person.* Boston: Houghton Mifflin, 1961.

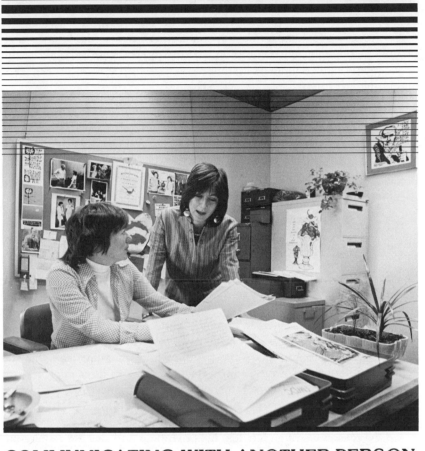

COMMUNICATING WITH ANOTHER PERSON
CHAPTER 8

We may talk with another person for many different purposes, including to fulfill social conventions, to escape boredom, to warn of impending disaster, and to get acquainted. We can also talk just for the fun of it. In this chapter we limit our consideration to the more common and important situations in which two people meet with an agreed-upon purpose. The first is the task-oriented, two-person conference that includes interviewing, planning, briefing, and coordinating meetings. The second is the relationship-oriented intimate communication, which establishes, sustains, and terminates interpersonal relationships.

COMMUNICATION WITH ANOTHER PERSON TO DO A JOB

Much face-to-face business and professional communication takes place between two people. Arranging for a small group of busy people to take part in a meeting is difficult and time-consuming. Arranging contacts between two people is often an efficient way to do business. Supervisors in organizations of all kinds do much of their managing in formal and informal two-person conversations.

Busy people often dash from one conference to another. A doctor may see a steady stream of patients during his office hours. A teacher may have counseling sessions with a number of students during the course of a day. A manager may move from a conference with her boss to a telephone conversation with a salesperson from another company to a discussion of a work-related problem with a subordinate to a briefing conference with her administrative assistant. Often, the person under pressure feels that the communication events are coming so fast, all she can do is improvise on the spot. She may try to keep up by relying on her instincts and mentioning topics as they pop into her mind. Often the off-the-top-of-the-head communication causes misunderstandings and mistakes.

One reason we often feel that little planning and skill are required to talk to another person about a job-related matter is that such meetings resemble the social interactions of passing the time of day. You can chat with a fellow worker about the movie you both saw the evening before while having morning coffee; why not talk about a job-related matter of considerable importance in the same informal, aimless, and casual way? The answer is that even the most casual conversation is a complicated communication situation, as we saw in Chapter 7. To create misunderstanding in a discussion of a movie may not be important, but to fail to communicate on important business or professional matters is often serious.

We could illustrate the basic principles of communicating with another person to do a job with several different types of interviews. We could use the situation where a person is interviewing another for information, such as when a newspaper reporter is preparing a story. We could concentrate on a person interviewing another to sell a product or service. We could use a situation where a supervisor is explaining to a subordinate what needs to be done to accomplish an organizational task.

We will use the job interview to illustrate how to communicate in two-person, task-oriented conferences, because it includes elements from all the above situations. If you are interviewing for a job you will want to find out important information relating to the nature of the work, the salary, and the fringe benefits. You will also need to persuade the interviewer that you can provide important services for the organization. Often the interviewer will determine the time and place of the meeting and you will have to adapt to the way the interviewer has planned the session. Many of the principles of communication that relate to the job interview can be adapted easily to other interviews.

THE JOB INTERVIEW

The function of the job interview

The job interview is not an isolated communication event. The interview takes place in a context of a hiring organization. While the interviewer and interviewee may be meeting for the first time, the fact that the meeting may result in a future association of the prospective employee with the organization over a period of time influences the importance and conduct of the conference. The interview must thus be examined in terms of the long-range effects it may have. The person applying for the job may feel anxious because of the future implications of success or failure. The person conducting the interview may feel some tension and take much more care because she wants to hire a person who will not only do the work required but who will also be able to get along with the others with whom she will be working. A successful job interview is one in which the "right person is hired for the right job." If the right person is hired, then the interview is often the beginning of some sort of relationship between the person hired and the person who hired him.

The interviewer will usually have some information about the applicant's background before the interview begins. She may know about the applicant's educational background, his age, and his previous work experience and may even have some evaluation of his personality strengths and weaknesses if the applicant has furnished her with recommendations from previous employees or associates prior to the interview. Nonetheless, the interviewer usually will want to check out any information she has prior to the interview with the applicant himself; many a face-to-face interview has made the difference between someone getting hired or being rejected. "He looked good on paper, but . . ." Particularly if the interviewer knows that the applicant has the professional skills required (has successfully completed the necessary courses or apprenticeship and so forth), the paralinguistic and other nonverbal skills of the interviewee become more important. The interviewer is trying to assess such things as: will this person be dependable and show some loyalty to the job, or is he self-centered, immature, only looking out for himself, and likely to take off at the slightest provocation? Does this person really want *this* particular job, and if so, why? Is an association between this applicant and the firm likely to be mutually beneficial and satisfying? Call these the hidden agenda of every job interview. Sometimes a direct question regarding these matters will surface, but more often it is a subtle matter of messages sent and received nonverbally.

Planning the job interview

Both participants in a job interview can benefit from making some plans before the meeting. Many large companies have people who do nothing but conduct job interviews all day. Personnel departments of large corporations develop highly specialized methods of trying to find and keep good employees. Smaller businesses, however, may have someone who is actually very inexperienced and awkward in such a situation doing their job interviewing; on such occasions the interview can be unsatisfactory, even a painful chore for both parties. As in all other human interactions, the skills of interviewers vary greatly. The student should understand that a "bad interview" can be as much the fault of the interviewer as the applicant, and it never hurts to request a second interview if things did not go well the first time.

Both participants should determine their *objectives* prior to the interview. What, for each, would be the most desirable outcome? The least desirable? The minimum acceptable outcome? Would pushing for the most desirable outcome force a decision that might bring about the least desirable? (If, as applicant, you want the job, and you push the prospective employer for an immediate decision, might that result in a negative decision? Would leaving the outcome for sometime in the future be more in your favor?)

Here are some ideas that both might keep in mind beforehand:

Considerations for the Interviewer
How can I begin the meeting to develop rapport and create a climate in which the applicant will be at ease and be most natural?
Do we have common ground that can serve as a starting place?
What do I know about this person's motives, and interests, knowledge, expertise, habits, and attitudes already?
What major information do I need to get from him during the interview itself?
What is the best order in which to take up the main topics?
How is the applicant likely to respond to the main objective that I have for the meeting?
What resistance can I anticipate?

Considerations for the Applicant

What can I do to help create a comfortable social climate to aid in getting the information I need?

Do we have common ground that can serve as a topic for opening conversation?

What should my approach be? Should I be serious, solemn, wary, friendly, lighthearted, jolly?

What major points about my background, education, desires, hopes, abilities in working with people, do I hope to make?

What major information about the job, working conditions, pay, fringe benefits, and so forth, do I need to know?

If the interviewer gives me a chance to play the role of message source, what is the best order for me to take up the main topics I want to discuss?

How is the employer likely to respond to the main objective I have for the meeting? What resistance can I anticipate?

Conducting the job interview

The person conducting the job interview can select one of two general strategies, the directive or the nondirective approach. The *directive* strategy is one in which the interviewer assumes the role of message source and takes control of the channels of communication in order to achieve her goal. The interviewer decides what topics to introduce and in what order, and attempts to keep the interview going pretty much according to her plan. She wants certain information from the applicant and plans the interview to cover the matters she considers important.

The *nondirective* strategy finds the interviewer making only minimal moves to assume the role of message source. Instead, the interviewer is alert for cues from the interviewee as to what role he, as applicant, would like to assume. The nondirective strategy calls for an emphasis on listening and encouraging, being permissive and supportive, and actively seeking the role of receiver whenever appropriate. The nondirective approach is appropriate whenever the employer wishes to learn a lot about the applicant's hopes and fears, personality, attitudes, and general level of articulateness.

For most job interviewing situations, some balance between non-directive and directive interviewing techniques is usually advisable. Even if the interview seems to be largely directive, however, an interviewer aware of good communication will allow the applicant to be the source of communication in appropriate subparts of the interview; even if time limits force an interviewer to stick largely to a prescribed list of questions that her organization always requires, she should build in several opportunities for the applicant to volunteer information or ask questions about matters he wants to know.

Skill in asking open-ended questions that cannot be answered by a brief "yes" or "no" comes with practice. The job interview is almost always face-to-face communication, and nonverbal aspects are very important. Feedback is crucial, verbally and nonverbally, and must be consciously built into the interview. Be aware of your nonverbal communication as well as your verbal remarks; shaking the head, nodding, frowning, smiling, looking puzzled, making questioning sounds, sounds of agreement, enthusiasm—all communicate a great deal about both participants. The amount of comfortable eye contact must be decided throughout the interview. Instantaneous appraisals are being made by both parties, and many people feel the nonverbal messages are more important to the outcome than the verbal exchanges, much as when you decide to vote for one candidate rather than another. "I can't put my finger on it; I just didn't get a good feeling about her. It wasn't her ideas so much as the way she expressed them, I think."

When any two people interact, each is projecting his or her self-image, certainly, but it is the applicant in a job interview who is, literally, selling himself as someone of value to the interviewer and to the organization she represents. With our cultural bias against bragging, against selling oneself, the competitive aura of a job interview sometimes inhibits an applicant. Much of the popularity of assertiveness training courses in recent years has come about because of people who walked away from some situation feeling, "Darn; I could have done that better than she did. Why didn't I speak up and give my ideas?" or, "I have to tell people what I can do, tell them my talents; I just get so frustrated all the time because I never speak up in time and someone else always gets the job, or the credit." As assertiveness training developed, it was found that you can learn to stand up for yourself with practice, and the job interview is certainly one such place. If you do not communicate your ability and potential as a job applicant, you really cannot blame the interviewer for not having a magic crystal ball that enables her to read through your blank, inarticulate projection of yourself.

A good interviewer has something to sell, too, of course; the interviewer is selling the organization and the position. The applicant is selling his skills and personality.

COMMUNICATING WITH ANOTHER PERSON
ABOUT RELATIONSHIPS

How many times have you heard someone mutter when he is called to by another person, "what does he want *now*?" The tone indicates that previous messages from that particular source have been unpleasant and that the intended listener is not willing to enter into a communicating relationship because of too many bad experiences. Homeostasis is the tendency to preserve things as they are if we are comfortable, and to struggle to get things back into a comfortable state when we are uncomfortable. If you irritate a person, he usually tries to get away from the irritation. All communication is potentially irritating, and sometimes punishing. Communication often upsets the status quo, asks us to rethink our pet ideas and prejudices, challenges our self-image and questions our habits.

Defensiveness

To some extent, all of us adopt a self-protective, wary attitude as we begin to talk with other people. We develop a protective filter through which we hear what is said to us and which strains out meanings that would be too painful for us to admit to our inner selves. The thickness and complexity of the protective filter varies from person to person. Someone who has a good, comfortable feeling about her worth as a person has a relatively large screen filter. A person whose self-image has been damaged by the problems of life has a fine-screen filter. Rarely is a person so mature and clear-eyed in his self-awareness that he is able to tell you what all his filters are. Most of us have some degree of self-knowledge, but most of us need to work at becoming more aware of the way we distort our interpretations of messages because of such protective devices. As instructors in colleges and universities who try to tell students about their various inadequacies in communication skills so that they can begin to improve themselves, we have had abundant opportunities to watch the fascinating operation of protective filters and the defensive communication that results. An instructor criticizes a student's speech by first pointing out that certain aspects were good. The student accepts this praise without flinching. Next the instructor criticizes the content and organization of the speech and the articulation of the student. The student immediately says he was nervous, that he was well prepared and had much good information but forgot it because he was nervous.

If the student was well prepared, he should not have forgotten, the instructor persists. The student then says he is working 20 hours a week, had to stay up until three o'clock in the morning to get the speech ready, and was therefore tired and could not do a good job. No matter how the instructor tries to cover the idea that the student has certain inadequacies in his ability to communicate that can be overcome by coaching and practice, the student meets each attempt with an excuse or an explanation that blames the problem on something other than his own inabilities. More than likely, as he leaves the conference, the student thinks to himself, "That instructor just does not like me. Why do I always end up with instructors who pick on me because they do not like me?"

Strange to report, on those occasions when students dared to point out where our teaching was poor and to recommend changes in course procedures, we felt a strong impulse to excuse, explain, and defend what we were doing and how we were doing it.

The hidden agenda

Some communication problems come about simply because people avoid talking about what really bothers them. In these instances, people often pretend that when they talk with one another, they are primarily interested in discussing facts, events, and "business." Suppose a teacher and a student have arranged a conference to talk over the student's courses for the coming term. The stated object of the talk is to find out about hours, requirements, and scheduling. To be sure, the topics are important and of concern to both teacher and student. Of equal importance to both, however, are some questions about *self,* and these questions have not been stated. The student may feel isolated and alone in the new environment of the college. He may have liked the teacher's course he took the previous term, and he may have found the teacher an interesting, reassuring person. A personal problem is troubling him greatly. His father has always wanted him to become a lawyer, and he has now decided he does not want to study law. He would like to talk to the teacher about this.

The instructor also has some personal interests she would like to talk about with the student. She has taught the course the student has just completed in a different way, and she would like to have the student's opinion of the course. She has some new projects in mind and would like to ask the student's opinion about them.

Because the stated object of the meeting is to talk about the student's next-term courses, both the student and the instructor feel a certain pressure to stick to the stated business. The conference could very well end with neither of them discussing their more important concerns. We speak of the stated business of a conference, interview, meeting, committee session as the *agenda.* The agenda of the student and teacher we have been discussing concerns what courses the student should take next term. When people talk, they often have hidden items on their agendas. In this example, the student's hidden item was his career problem, and the instructor's hidden item was the student's reaction to the course just finished. Often, bringing what we call the *hidden agenda* into the open through the process of self-disclosure is a good way to improve communication. The responsibility of centering communication interaction on the subject you really want to talk about is *yours.* If you wonder why the other person is acting and talking in unexpected ways, and you sense some hidden agenda item, our advice is simple: *Ask.*

Feedback

Much talking that passes for communication is merely people talking *at* other people, because the speaker and the listener demand neither feedback nor clarification. One of the surprising discoveries of people who study relationship communication is that so many people are so poor at providing and interpreting feedback to aid understanding.

Several important factors operate in two-person communication to keep people from providing the essential feedback. One is the mistaken notion that talking with another person is a simple matter. After all, we reason, we have probably spent more of our total communication time in such two-person talks than in any other form of communication. We ought to be good at it by now, we tell ourselves. Besides the fact that we take such interaction for granted, the situation itself is often informal and relaxed and makes talking seem much less difficult than giving a good formal speech to an auditorium full of people. When we do misunderstand something in an informal conversation, we often blame our failure to find out more on some inherent trait of the other person or some factor beyond our control: "I guess George didn't hear me," or "We were interrupted about then, and I guess it wasn't clear." or, "I don't know what it is about Lorraine, but she just never can get anything straight."

Another factor that operates to prevent feedback is our assumption that our first attempt to tell another person something has succeeded. We often interpret silence as understanding and acceptance. We even interpret mumbling or other unclear answers as acceptance. Actually, our first attempt to communicate is *likely to fail*. The more completely we have failed, the more likely it is that the listener will greet the communication with silence. Silence itself often should be interpreted as feedback indicating not that the other person understands or agrees with you, but rather that he is confused. If you give a directive to someone else, particularly if you are in a position of authority, you should be as suspicious of a simple yes answer as you are of silence. When a policeman has been called to an apartment because of a domestic argument and he "lays down the law" to the couple and then demands of them, "Now, is that clear," what can their answer be but "Yes." As one young policeman said in class, "And then I had to go back five nights later and spell it out again." He was disgusted, until he realized that he had left little opening for the couple to express their real failure to understand his advice and their refusal to appreciate the need for working out their problems in some way that would not disturb their neighbors at four o'clock in the morning.

An additional factor in poor feedback is concern for protecting the self. We have discussed protective and defensive communication at length. One of the important effects of the need to defend self is unwillingness to reveal lack of information, knowhow, understanding, or skill by providing feedback. We have to learn to be comfortable admitting what we do not know in any situation.

A final factor in poor feedback is lack of skill. Watch a television play or go to the theater and watch the actors who are *not* speaking at any given moment. The good performers are acting every minute, reacting to what the speaker is saying, responding nonverbally, *communicating* to the audience what they understand and how they feel about what another character is saying or doing. A good communicator does much the same thing when listening to another person; she responds in such a way that the speaker can see and hear and understand her response.

The importance of privacy

We have stressed the need for self-disclosure to build trust because too often the importance of the *relationship* between two people trying to talk with one another is overlooked. The need for openness and trust is without question, great. We do not want to leave the impression, however, that maximum self-disclosure, honesty, and openness are desirable at all times and under all circumstances in *every* communication situation. The thrust toward instant trust is, we feel, being misunderstood and misused by many people. There *are* limits to what we need to tell others about ourselves. Psychiatrists trying to help mentally ill people rebuild a good enough self-image to get by in the world day by day find themselves not only allowing people to keep certain inhibitions, certain established ways of responding to life, but encouraging them to rebuild many of the defenses they found fairly useful before becoming ill. While not all the defenses these people had constructed could be considered good or even desirable, some of the defenses enabled the people to get along. To some extent, all of us have built into our personality structure defenses that enable us to face life. These defenses are there for a reason, and anyone working to break them down had best be prepared to provide replacements or face trouble.

Many people do not care to go about belaboring the world with their innermost thoughts and feelings, and these people should have the right to keep whatever they want to themselves. Few of us who have passed through adolescence do not remember at least one painful truth session with "a good friend," who after telling us all our faults, assured us that "it was for our own good," and left us hanging emotionally, wondering if that was what all our friends thought of us?

Good communication about relationships, we feel, requires restraints and respect, as well as on occasion, self-disclosure. Part of the trust needed in supportive communication comes from knowing that when we are interacting with a person, he will *stop short of hitting below the belt*. He knows the limits of privacy set by me, and he respects them. The woman who tells her husband's secret worry to outsiders is headed for real trouble; so is the husband who repeatedly reminds his wife about her worst habit. This sort of communication hurts and is extremely destructive to the relationship between two people. There are limits in good interpersonal communication, and they are drawn just at that point where we take a swipe at the underpinnings of the personality of the other person.

Differences must be talked out, and verbal battles are useful when they serve the purpose of clearing the air. Verbal battles fought within agreed-upon limits can be useful, even fun, when they help dissipate the natural hostilities generated in any close relationship. Nonetheless, when two people want to maintain good communication, they both have to know where to draw the line. Naturally, as a relationship deepens, each can push the line back a little from time to time, but no matter how close any two people become, each has privacy limits across which no other human should ever intrude.

Airing grievances

Within a personal relationship with any other person, however, while respecting the limits that he or she places on inner privacy it is still important to express your feelings openly, to be honest about the times when you are hurt or angry. When even the smallest grievance is swallowed, one swallowed word may be added to another, until after a while the load becomes too heavy. Then, when you simply cannot carry those unsaid words around any longer, you will find them tumbling out for almost no reason whatsoever, accusation upon accusation, explosive emotional charges that will strain any relationship. Keeping things to oneself causes inner tension and when things are left unsaid between two people, at least one of those people is aware of it, if not both. Moreover, the person who is the object of a grudge often fears unspoken words far more than he or she should, imagining them to be far worse than they actually are.

When one of your authors was teaching interpersonal communication for the first time, one of our teenagers picked up the textbook she was using. She seized the notion of "gunnysacking" (carrying all your grudges around with you until you unload them on someone inappropriately) and delighted in accusing her mother of doing just that "all the time!" "But that's the point," her mother said, "Since I do it all the time, that's not gunnysacking." "Yeah," our daughter replied, momentarily resigned, since there had just been one of those mother-daughter "and another thing . . ." sessions; "I guess what you always do to me is more like sandbagging."

Relationship communication must be based on openness, trust, a sharing of authentic selves, enough empathy so that you withhold judgments when another person is expressing his feelings, even if they upset you, and an ability to allow other people to grow and mature even if you feel them slipping ahead of you. We wear the lightest reins most easily. If you have sufficient maturity to let those with whom you communicate in close relationships grow, then you will grow with them. Respecting the self you also want respected, you work all the time to keep the channels of communication open between you and those you care most about.

Some years ago there was a movie with a line that was often repeated, it upset us that it seemed to catch the fancy of so many. It was "Love means never having to say you're sorry." We would rewrite that line in terms of relationship communications, which is, at many different levels, a close and loving, supportive bond: "Love means always being able to say, and mean, 'I'm sorry.'" Better yet, a truly supportive communication relation between two people can tolerate success and share joy. If the best thing life has to offer is a truly delightful relationship with another human being—and we believe it is—relationship communication skills are very worthwhile indeed.

KEY IDEAS CHAPTER 8

• **Much business and professional communication takes place face to face in two-person meetings.**

• **Both participants in a job interview can benefit from making plans before the meeting.**

• **Both participants should determine their objectives prior to the interview.**

• **The person conducting the interview can select a directive strategy, in which she assumes control of the meeting.**

• **The person conducting an interview can select a nondirective strategy, which puts an emphasis on listening, being supportive, and seeking the role of receiver whenever appropriate.**

• **The nonverbal aspects of a job interview are important in terms of the impression that the interviewee makes.**

• **The applicant's communication will project a self-image, which is important in getting the job.**

• **We tend to adopt a wary attitude when we begin to talk with other people, because we want to protect our self-image.**

• **Some communication problems come about simply because people avoid talking about what really bothers them.**

• **Often bringing the hidden agenda of a conference into the open through self-disclosure is a good way to improve communication.**

• Many people are unskilled at providing or interpreting feedback in interpersonal communication about relationships.

• Our first attempt to communicate with another person is likely to fail.

• Silence should usually be interpreted as feedback telling the speaker the other person is confused.

• Maximum self-disclosure, honesty, and openness are not desirable at all times and under all circumstances.

• Each of us has limits of privacy, which no other human being should ever cross.

SUGGESTED PROJECTS

1 • This is a job interview exercise. The instructor may have interviewers from companies conduct the simulated interviews. If no outside interviewers are available, the class can be divided into pairs, with one student playing the role of job applicant and the other the role of interviewer. Each pair conducts a brief job interview in front of the class or on audiotape or videotape. You are to review your performance and write a short paper of self-evaluation.

2 • Recall an incident when you had a conflict with a good friend or family member resulting from a hidden agenda and failure to air grievances. Analyze the influence of the hidden agenda on your communication in that instance.

3 • Write a brief paper describing an instance when you became thoroughly angry with someone and could not communicate your anger to him or her? What happened? Why couldn't you communicate it? Do you think that if you could have communicated your anger and brought it out into the open, it would have helped? How?

SUGGESTED READINGS

Brooks, William D., and Philip Emmert. *Interpersonal Communication*. Dubuque, Iowa: Brown, 1976.

Knapp, Mark L. *Social Intercourse: From Greeting to Goodbye*. Boston: Allyn & Bacon, 1978.

Stewart, Charles J., and William B. Cash. *Interviewing: Principles and Practice*. Dubuque, Iowa: Brown, 1974.

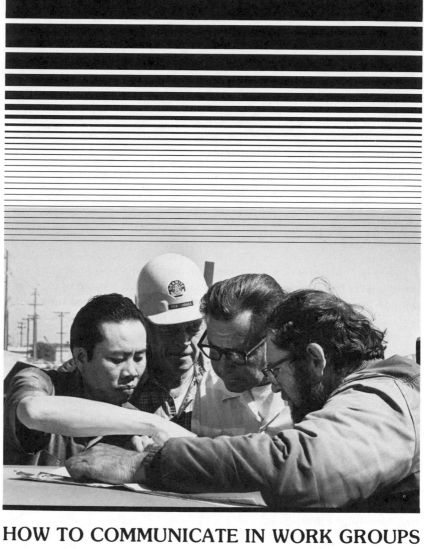

HOW TO COMMUNICATE IN WORK GROUPS
CHAPTER 9

Our emphasis in this chapter and the next will be upon the task-oriented small group. As a student, you probably attend many group meetings in our society. A student may be a member of an athletic team or club, a neighborhood or street gang, a fraternity or sorority, a political club, a special interest group, a departmental association, or a student cooperative. A student may attend meetings or committees for student government, dormitory groups, student unions, religious foundations, and increasingly, of special groups to prepare projects for class.

In addition to performing duties for an immediate work group on the job, a person who works for a store, a factory, a service industry, or a government agency such as a police force or fire department attends committee meetings, union meetings, and work group sessions. Off the job, a typical citizen takes part in religious groups, political organizations, or groups for other community and voluntary purposes.

Every project to get things done requires working with small groups. If we wish to change our neighborhoods and organize for community power or political power at another level, we must work productively with others in groups.

Despite the importance of working with small groups, most of us take our role in a discussion for granted. Few people have a chance to study group discussion or drill in the techniques of group work in order to become professional communicators in the small-group setting. However, one of the best-ways to ensure that the group meetings you attend in the future will be useful and that you will feel satisfied about your contribution to them is to study small-group communication and evaluate critically the dynamics of the meetings you attend.

FUNCTIONS OF WORK GROUPS

A discussion group in our culture is a special form of the work group. Work groups use several different sorts of meetings. If the members come to the meeting with the wrong idea about what the meeting is for and what it will be like, they may be frustrated. For example, if the meeting is just a ceremony to rubberstamp decisions already made and a member comes expecting to change the decision, she feels cheated.

Every organization has some meetings that are rituals. A ritual is a set ceremony that has come to be expected at certain times to celebrate an organization or group. In a meeting that is a ritual, people may say one thing and mean another. Some religious rituals contain prayers that the worshipers repeat over and over again, and the meaning of the prayers as expressed in the words is not as important to the worshipers or to the ritual as the act of saying the words over and over again. The ritual meetings of an organization may aid its cohesiveness or ability to stick together, and ensure that people in authority are recognized. For example, the department heads of a business organization may make an oral presentation of their yearly budgets at a meeting of all the vice-presidents. The meeting is really meant only to rubberstamp decisions already made. Yet the meeting is important to the others in the business. The newcomer who says that the meeting accomplishes nothing and is therefore a waste of time is judging it on the wrong grounds.

Another kind of meeting is the briefing session, used to give members information they need to carry through on plans already made. The objective of the group is clear: the members know what they want to do and need only find out who is to do what, when, and where.

A group discussion may also have the purpose of instructing participants in some concepts or skills they can use in the future. Teachers may use small discussion groups to teach a course in English literature, for example, by dividing up the class and having each group discuss a novel.

A small discussion group may meet to advise the person or persons empowered to make decisions. The person in charge consults or asks the advice of the people in the meeting. A department head at a college or university might ask a committee of students and faculty about changes in course requirements. If the meeting is consultative, the department head does not promise to abide by their advice but does ask for and consider it. The danger in an advice-giving discussion is that if the people who attend may not understand its purposes, they may expect their advice to be accepted, and may feel cheated when it is not. "We spent all that time making that decision, and then they ignored it."

Finally, an extremely important kind of meeting is one called actually to make the decision. Members of decision-making groups often are more fully committed to their decisions and usually work harder to implement them than do the participants in other kinds of groups. One of the most important functions of small groups in many organizations is to provide a way for people to participate in management decisions and to exercise some of the power relating to the use of the organization's resources.

CHARACTERISTICS OF A GOOD WORK GROUP

The work group is a social event. When several people share ideas or produce a product, a social dimension emerges. The first question in the mind of every person in a new work group is "How do I relate to these other people as a human being?" Every member wants this question answered, and he wants it answered early. Even after he has been in the group for months, or years, he wants the answer repeated from time to time.

If a person feels that the others like, admire, and respect her, enjoy her company, and consider her ideas important, she can relax and turn her full attention to doing the job. Such an atmosphere of trust and understanding should be the goal of every participant, and *particularly* of every manager, chairperson, moderator, or leader of a work group.

We are discussing only those groups that have a job to do. Inevitably, the members expect, and usually want, to concentrate on the job. If the group is a discussion meeting or conference, they want to start talking about the agenda. If the group is working in an office, the members want to start reading the mail, filing papers, drafting letters, holding conferences. If it is a production group, the workers need to get the machines rolling. The family too is a working group, its job is to maintain the living arrangements of its members and manage their day-to-day existence. Many studies have been made on "the family as a group." The group's work is hampered by poor plans, misunderstandings, faulty reasoning, inadequate concepts, bad information, and most important, the way directions and orders are given and received. *A whole book could be devoted to the subject of giving and receiving orders.* Orders must be given, but when you give another person an order, the social and task dimensions of your interaction may come into conflict. If the group member thinks the direction indicates that the leader feels superior to him or is using the group for his own purposes, the order may be misunderstood or disobeyed even though it is a good order.

Morale and productivity

A good work group has high morale. The members are happy with the group; they enjoy working with the others on the job and are pleased with their place in the group. They receive a sense of belonging and a feeling of personal satisfaction from their roles.

A good group gets things done. It reaches its goals with a minimum of wasted motion. It turns out a large quantity of a high-quality product, wins games, solves problems, or makes good decisions.

Some people think productivity is all that counts, but the individual should gain a sense of satisfaction and worth from his participation in the group. We do not believe that the individual exists solely for the group. The group has certain duties and responsibilities to the individual.

Cohesiveness

Cohesiveness is the key to successful work groups. *Cohesiveness* refers to the ability of the group to stick together. Another term for the same quality is *group loyalty*. A highly cohesive group is one in which the members work for the good of the group. They form a tightly knit unit, and they help one another. They exhibit team spirit. They reflect the motto of Alexander Dumas's *Three Musketeers:* "All for one and one for all."

Cohesiveness encourages increased and improved communication, morale, and productivity. Cohesive groups do more work, because members take the *initiative* and help one another. They distribute the workload among themselves and take up the slack in times of stress. People in groups with little cohesiveness tend to stand around and wait for assignments. They do what they are told to do and no more. They do not care about the work of others. While members of cohesive groups volunteer to help one another, people in groups with little cohesiveness look out primarily for themselves.

The more cohesive the group, the more efficient the communication within the group. Cohesiveness encourages disagreement and questions. Both are necessary to communication. Highly cohesive groups disagree among themselves. A member of such a group cannot stand by and watch the others do a shoddy job or make a wrong decision. Her group is at stake. She must speak up and do what she can to assure its success. Such disagreements improve the quality and quantity of the work by assuring a high level of communication. Cohesiveness encourages questions, because in the cohesive group all the members know their places and are secure. Their position is not threatened if they admit they do not know something. Indeed, the welfare of the group requires that each member have adequate information. The group rewards questions that help it achieve its goals. Likewise, the important member does not feel insulted when people demand more information. She is more interested in the welfare of the group than in her own personal feelings. Since the success or failure of a group depends largely on the efficiency of its communication, the cohesive group encourages its members to work cooperatively to achieve understanding.

To build cohesiveness in your group, you need to know some of the dynamics of group process. Every member of the work group is constantly experiencing pushes into and pulls away from the group. The cohesiveness of the group changes from day to day. A unit that is highly cohesive this year—an effective, hard-hitting group—may next year suffer a series of reverses or a change of personnel that causes it to lose cohesiveness and be less effective. If the group comes into competition with similar groups, cohesiveness is usually increased. Athletic teams develop high levels of team spirit and will to win because they compete with other teams in a win or lose situation. Coaches know the importance of cohesiveness and how to build it.

On the other hand, a *competing* group may try to lure a member away from his group and thus decrease his feelings of commitment. If you wish to examine the cohesiveness of your group, you must look to the other groups that are competing for the loyalty of the members. The attractiveness of his group for a given member is partly dependent on the character of the other groups he could join. If another group becomes more attractive, a person may leave his original group.

If you want to know how attractive your group is to a member, total the rewards it furnishes her and subtract the costs; the remainder is an index of group attractiveness. At any given moment, an individual feels the pull of her group because it satisfies one or more of her basic needs.

If you understand how a group can satisfy the needs of its members, you are well on the way to understanding how to make a group more cohesive. A group can provide its members with material rewards such as money, with social rewards such as the sense of belonging, with prestige rewards that come from being part of a respected group, with an opportunity to do good work and to achieve, with the chance to fight for a good cause, and with a sense of individual significance and worth. Think of a group you are working with and ask yourself of each member: "What is this person getting out of the group? Run down the list. Does the group give the person material rewards, or does it cost him money to belong? Does the group give the person social rewards? If you wish to improve the group, the next step is to see if changes can increase the rewards the group furnishes for the individuals who are not committed to the group.

BUILDING A POSITIVE SOCIAL CLIMATE

One way to increase the attractiveness of a group is to build a social climate that is rewarding and fun for all members. When the members of a new work group meet for the first time, they begin to interact socially. They nod or talk to one another. They smile, frown, and laugh. All those things help build a climate that is pleasant, congenial, and relaxed, or one that is stiff and tense. A positive social climate makes the group attractive, builds cohesiveness, and encourages people to speak up and say what they really mean.

Investigations of the social dimension of groups indicate three kinds of verbal and nonverbal communication that build good social feelings among group members and three that build a stiff and negative social setting. The positive communications are shows of solidarity, of tension release, and of agreement. The negative messages are shows of antagonism, of tension, and of disagreement.

Any action or statement you make that indicates to the others that the new group is important to you is a show of solidarity. Raising another's status, offering to help do something for the group, volunteering, or indicating that you are willing to make a personal sacrifice for the group shows solidarity.

The opposite of showing solidarity is showing antagonism to the group or to another person. While shows of solidarity build a pleasant spirit and rapport, shows of antagonism make the others uncomfortable.

People in new groups always feel a certain amount of tension. Embarrassment, shyness, and uneasiness when meeting with strangers are shows of social tension. When a discussion group first meets, everyone experiences *primary* tensions. They feel ill at ease. They do not know what to say or how to begin. The first meeting is tense and cold and must be warmed up. When groups experience primary tension, the people speak softly, they sigh, and they are polite. They seem bored and uninterested. No person is really bored when he has an opportunity to speak up and make a name for himself. Every individual, however, gambles a great deal by plunging into the meeting, by taking an active part and trying to make a good showing. A person who has had success in similar situations in the past may be more willing than others to take this chance. The others may be impressed by her ability and decide they like her as a person; on the other hand, they may be irritated by her, decide she is stupid and uninformed, reject her. This gamble makes a person feel nervous and tense, and she may take flight from the situation by pretending she is not interested. Do not be misled. The person who seems bored and uninterested is really tense and most interested, particularly in the social setting of the group. If the meeting never releases primary tension, the whole style of future meetings may be set in this uncomfortable mold. It is vital that the primary tension be released early! Tension is released through indications of pleasure, such as smiles, chuckles, and laughs. Members of a new group should spend some time joking and socializing before getting down to business. Judiciously used, socializing is time wisely spent. Once the primary tension is released, however, the group should go to work.

Once people relax and get down to work, new and different social tensions are generated by disagreements over ideas and by personality conflicts. *Secondary* tensions are louder than primary ones. People speak rapidly, interrupt one another, act impatient to get the floor and have their say; they may get up and pace the room or pound the table. When secondary tensions reach a certain level, the group finds it difficult to concentrate on its job. When that point is reached, the tensions should be released by humor, direct comment, conciliation, or confrontation and working through to a satisfactory conclusion. Secondary tensions are more difficult to bleed off than primary ones. There are no easy solutions, but the tensions should not be ignored. They should be brought out into the open and talked over.

Agreement is one of the basic social rewards. When the group members agree with a person, they say, "We value you." When others agree with us, we lose our primary tension, we loosen up, we get excited, we take a more active part in the meeting. The more people agree, the more they communicate with one another.

Disagreements serve as negative-climate builders. When people disagree, they grow cautious and tense. *Disagreements are socially punishing but absolutely essential to good group work.* They are double-edged. They are necessary to sound thinking. Yet disagreements always contain an element of personal attack. The person who finds his ideas subjected to rigorous testing and disagreement feels as though he is being shot down.

One of the reasons that the number of disagreements increases with a rise in cohesiveness is that groups must develop enough cohesiveness to afford disagreements and still not break up. The rate of disagreements is often highest in the family—the most cohesive unit in our society. How often someone complains, "You're so much nicer with strangers than with the members of your own family!"

Some people try to cushion the hurt in a disagreement by saying things such as, "That's a good idea, *but* . . . ." or "That's right, I agree with you, *but* . . . ." Eventually the others discover that these prefatory agreements or compliments are just ways of setting them up for the knife. They begin to cringe as the ". . . *but* I think we ought to look at the other side of it" hits them. The fact is, disagreements must be understood to mean, "Stop, this will not do." When they are thus understood, no amount of kind words of introduction serves to sugar-coat them.

An important way to resolve conflicts is to build group cohesiveness. It helps to do things to knit the group back together after a period of heavy disagreement. Often disagreements increase as a group moves toward a decision. Good groups use positive-climate builders after the decision is reached. They joke and laugh. They show solidarity. They say, "It was a good meeting." "It accomplished something." "Let's all get behind this decision." They compliment the people who advocated the rejected plan. They tell them they are needed, that the group cannot succeed without their help.

Another technique sometimes used by successful work groups is to allow one person to become the "disagreer." He tests most of the ideas, and the group expects him to do so. Whenever they feel the need for disagreements, they turn to him. They reward him by giving him a nickname or by joshing him about how disagreeable he is. Since he plays the role of critical thinker, other members are less hurt by his criticisms, because, "After all, he disagrees with everybody."

GROUP ROLES

The first important discovery from research into newly formed (zero-history) groups is that after several hours the members begin to specialize. That is, not every member does an equal amount of the same thing. If we analyze the content of the typical group's communication, we find that some members talk more than others and that members tend to say different kinds of things. Some give more information, some talk more about personal characteristics and social relationships, some make more suggestions about doing the work of the group.

When it becomes clear to a person that she is specializing and when the group discovers that she is doing so, she takes a *place* in the group. She has her particular *role*. Individuals change "personality" as they go from group to group. The college woman who has such a sparkling personality in class and enjoys flirting with the men may be quiet, devout, and reserved with her church circle. She may be ill-tempered and bossy with her family. Think of yourself. In one group you may be a take-charge person who gets things rolling. In another you may be likable, joshing, and fun-loving, but not a leader at all. In a third group, you may be quiet, steady, and a responsible worker.

Principles of role emergence

A member's role is worked out jointly by the person and the group. This is the basic principle. We should not blame the group's problems on innate unchangeable personality traits inherent in a troublesome person. Groups can be more neurotic than individuals, and they love to blame their troubles on one member—make him the scapegoat for their failure. If we understand the nature of roles, we will no longer make that mistake. Instead of wishing we could get rid of Bill so we could have a productive group, we ask what the group may be doing to Bill to make him act as he does.

Once everyone has found a place, a second important thing happens. The group judges the relative worth of each role. It gives the roles it judges more valuable a higher status that the others. After a group has been working together for several hours, a trained observer can arrange a status ladder by watching the way the members talk and act. They talk directly and more often to the people they consider important. High-status people talk more to the entire group. The high-status people receive more consideration from the others: The others listen to what a high-status individual says; they often stop what they are doing to come to her; they stop talking to hear her, and they agree more, and more emphatically with her. The group tends to ignore and cut off comments by low-status members.

Since rewards of much esteem and prestige are given to high-status members, several people usually compete for the top positions. In this competition they come into conflict; there are disagreements. The group's energy is directed to the question of who will win, and attention is drawn away from the work. In extreme cases the struggles become heated, and the group gets bogged down. Every new group must go through a "shakedown cruise," during which the members test roles and find out who is top dog, who is best liked, and so forth. During the shakedown cruise, secondary tensions mount, and people who are contending for leadership come into conflict.

Each contender for a high-status role is led to specialize through both his own efforts and the group's encouragement. The group agrees with him when he does what it wants him to and disagrees when he does not; it thus discourages him from a role it considers unnecessary or unacceptable. A given person does not have a monopoly on the role assigned him in this way, but he fulfills most of that role's functions in the group.

Group stability and communication increase side by side. When a group achieves a stable role structure and a high level of cohesiveness, an increase in feedback usually follows. A person who is strongly attracted to the group and wishes it well, wants to maximize communication. She knows the group will do a better job if each member is thoroughly briefed. Therefore, if she does not know something, she is likely to ask. In addition, if she has a stable place in the group, admitting her ignorance does not hurt her reputation. Sometimes bad habits that developed during role struggles carry over, and groups continue to function without adequate feedback. The group should make periodic evaluations of the level of feedback and make conscious plans to encourage it as needed.

Just as the need to appear more knowledgeable disappears with stable structure, so does the need to show off. A person can relax and be honest in a group with a high level of cohesivness, and the change in attitude allows greater concentration on listening to messages. When roles stabilize, the members no longer feel the need to view each message in personal terms. They no longer think, "Does this message mean so-and-so is leadership material? that he likes me? that he doesn't like me?" Members can become more message-centered, which is the first step to improved listening.

The members of an organization vary in their communication skills. Some may have trouble holding long chains of argument in mind. Achieving effective communication takes considerable time and tension-producing effort. Communication is hard work. Groups should establish the rule that enough time will be allocated and spent (not wasted) to ensure that the proper level of understanding is reached during the meeting.

The presence in a meeting of a person with high formal status in a community or organization immediately inhibits the free flow of communication and feedback. People wait for the high-status person to take the lead; they wait for cues from her about the proper tone of response. They tend to tell the high-status person only what they think she would like to hear. If a feeling of cohesiveness is generated within the work group, the dampening effect of the high-status person can be overcome to some extent. If the others discover she is sincerely interested in the good of the group, tolerates disagreements, and recognizes the necessity of sound communication, a productive meeting should follow.

The leadership role

Of all the roles that emerge in a work group, none has fascinated the philosophers, writers, social scientists, and the average person more than the high-status, influential role of leadership.

In our country we are of two minds about leadership. If a member of a new group suggests that another person would be a good leader, that person's response typically is, "Oh, no! Not me. Someone else could do a better job." Despite such protests, nearly every member of every group would like to lead. We would like right now to dispel that old saying that some people are born leaders and others born followers. This just is not so. All people would like to be leaders and usually are, if not in one group, in some other group. Some people have more skills in the leadership area and become leaders in more groups. But never underestimate the desire of every member of any group to take over the leadership role. Publicly, people sometimes do not admit this, but privately they usually do.

Why this ambivalence? On the one hand, our democratic traditions suggest that all people are created equal and that nobody is better than anybody else. We maintain a belief in a classless society. Many groups in the 1960s made a strong commitment to not striving for leadership and tried hard to do away with the leadership concept in their group work because they found it distasteful. They preferred the idea of working in a commune or cooperative rather than in a corporation and tried to arrange their groups so there would be no "leaders." But even the people dedicated to denying leadership—because it meant power, which they viewed as evil—discovered that their groups needed structure to survive and that structure implied leadership.

The most satisfactory explanation of leadership is that it is a result of the individual's traits (inherited characteristics plus training), the purposes of the group, the pressures put on the group from the outside, and the way the people in the group talk, work, and relate with one another.

Such a contextual explanation provides a more complete view of leadership than other approaches. It includes the idea that leaders are to some extent "born." but it also suggests that potential leaders can achieve skills and improve talents. The contextual approach (the consideration of the total context, or all components, of each group) explains why someone who emerges as leader in one group may fail to emerge as the leader of a second apparently similar group.

The members of a group spend time and energy on selecting

leadership because it is so important to the success of the group. We are touchy about the people who boss us around. We do not like to take orders. If we have to, we prefer a leader who gives wise orders in a way we can tolerate. The leader makes crucial suggestions and decisions about the way the work will be divided and the way the material resources of the group will be distributed. In the end, the group rejects potential leaders until they are left with the person who seems best able to lead *for the good of all.*

Sometimes the struggle for leadership is never resolved. Groups in which this happens become invalids. The members spend their time in backbiting and getting back at internal enemies. If, after working together for some time, a group is left with two or three potential leaders, each having substantial handicaps, the leadership question may not be resolved.

CENTRAL PERSONS

Some people are so dominant in their verbal and nonverbal communications in a new work group that they fascinate the others. They may be positive or negative people; we shall call them *central* persons. A central person may be a *star:* He may be usually capable and a potential asset to the group's productivity, or he may be exceptionally skillful at human relations and unusually charming. A central person may be one who seems extremely hostile to the group and its purposes, who downgrades the work, or who makes it plain he feels the other members are incapable. Such a person is a potential threat to the group. A central person may even be someone who is unusually apathetic and uninvolved and simply refuses to take part in the group. All these people are central because they distract the group's attention from its tasks.

A common threatening central person is the *manipulator.* She comes to the group with the intention of exploiting it for her own ends. She intends to take it over and run it. Manipulators tend to be either *hard sell* or *soft sell.* The hard-sell manipulator usually comes on strong. He talks a great deal and takes charge immediately with a strong hand, "Let's get down to business. Now here's what we will do." When the group resists his leadership, he tries to argue and browbeat the others into line. When someone resists him, the others swing to support the contender, and the hard-sell manipulator then stands alone against the group, trying hard to talk everyone down. Sometimes, the hard-sell manipulator is not immediately challenged and is then certain he has succeeded in taking over. When he gives orders, however, they are not followed. People continually misunderstand or fail to follow through. He decides he has not been working hard enough at his leading, so he begins to give his orders slowly, carefully, in simple English, as though he were talking to morons. This arouses even greater resentment and goldbricking. He decides the group members are all lazy and irresponsible. Inevitably, another contender emerges and becomes leader. The manipulator is now extremely frustrated. His self-image is badly dented. He came into the group confident of his superiority and his ability to run the group his way, and the group has rejected him. He seldom examines where he has failed. Usually he turns on the group members. They are ignorant and stupid. If he remains in the group, he is often a troublemaker. Finding him an acceptable role takes ingenuity.

The soft-sell manipulator is often much more successful in his second phase. He often emerges for a time as the leader. He has many tricks and formulas of human relations at his command. He is friendly and congenial. He seems less bossy and more democratic. He sizes up the group to see who can be conned and who will be troublesome. He does more work outside the group's formal meetings, such as chatting with this or that member over coffee. He is a politician. After several weeks of working with him, however, the others find him out. They discover that he is getting his way and that under his apparently congenial and democratic facade, he is using the group for his personal ends. When the soft-sell manipulator is found out, a challenger comes forward, and the group reshuffles roles until a new leader emerges.

CHANGING MEMBERSHIP

A change in group personnel is always unsettling. If a new person is added, this person brings with her certain skills and talents, and a role has to be found for her. All the roles have to be reshuffled to free enough duties to provide the new woman with a job. When a member is removed, a role struggle again results. The remaining members must take on the tasks that the former member used to do. If he had important duties, the members who stand to gain by climbing upward on the status ladder may come into conflict. When a member is replaced, the new man does not simply take over his predecessor's role; reshuffling of all roles is necessary. The importance of realizing that any change in a group's personnel causes problems cannot be overstated. This knowledge will help you to help any group in which you are a member through the inevitable reshuffling of roles.

The effect of changing personnel by adding, removing, or replacing individuals is a repeat of the shakedown cruise. The typical result is a period of role instability and struggle that surprises and frustrates the members. People often do not understand what is going on and why it must go on. They respond by blaming the new member. "Everything was fine until he came." Or they bemoan the loss of a member. "Before Joan left, everything went along fine; we sure miss Joan."

FORMAL LEADERSHIP

Many groups are not composed completely of peers, and everyone does not start out equal. Many work groups function within a *formal* organization. The salesperson works *under* a sales manager within a corporation. The teacher supervises a group within the framework of the class. The executive committee of the fraternity chapter functions within the larger organization. People come to such work groups with different status. Sometimes the status is internal to the organization, as when the dean meets with a group of students. Although status differences introduce complications, the basic process of group development can be adjusted to take these into account.

In our consulting with many real-life organizations and businesses, we have found that the principles of role emergence in leaderless group discussions transfer readily and facilitate understanding of the working of so-called structured, as well as unstructured, groups. To illustrate, we will show how leadership is related to the management of organizational work groups.

The formal structure of an organization is static. The organization's informal work groups, which develop and change with a turnover in personnel and with fluctuating working conditions, are dynamic. They change constantly, a little or a lot. Frequently the power structure of the informal organization differs from what the formal organization would indicate. The organizational chart no longer reflects the realities. You cannot figure out a person's power and esteem by finding out whether he or she is a supervisor, a vice-president, or an engineer. The real boss may not be the person with the title. What then?

Power struggles within an organization

The role-struggle between a person with the power of a formal position (the formal leader) and a person with the esteem and power furnished by his or her standing with the members (the natural leader) can be long and bloody. Let us say that a person in a position of formal leadership leaves the organization and a new person takes her place. Assume that the replacement is a stranger to the members in the work group. The entire group is subjected to a shakedown. The new manager must assume certain leadership functions for the work group because the formal position guide says she must. She is expected by top management and by the organization to lead her group immediately. She is not, however, accepted as the natural leader of the group without a period of testing. She must find her role in the informal groups within her department according to the basic principles of group process. When she finally assumes her role, it is slightly different from that of the former manager, and the whole group experiences a reshuffling of roles.

The new manager does have certain standard levers furnished her by the organization to help her emerge as leader. These may include the right to increase salaries, give bonuses, promote, assign jobs and vacations, and punish tardiness, malingering, and poor work. You may think these levers give the new manager an insurmountable advantage. Wisely used by a person who understands the dynamics of small groups, they may. Sometimes, however, the authority to punish and reward members turns out to be a handicap rather than a help.

Here is how this might happen. The new manager, whoever she is, is a marked woman! Her boss is watching her closely to see how she will work out. She tries to do an exceptionally good job. The members of the group watch her carefully. Will she turn out to be a woman they can follow? If she begins with strong and decisive leadership moves, she can expect some resistance. She may find she is misunderstood. Misunderstanding directions is a common way of resisting an order. To a woman on trial, eager to prove her efficiency, such a response may lead to frustration and anger.

If so, the new manager has come to a crucial point. If she controls her anger and asks, "What have I done wrong?," she may be able to mend her fences and start to build a role of leadership within the group. If she understands the way people emerge as natural leaders, she may win the power and esteem that the authority and prestige of her job deserve, and without which she must remain ineffective and unsatisfied to some extent. If she lashes back and pulls the levers by which she can force members to obey, she will start a spiral that results in malingering, more crises, less production, and trouble with upper management. If she panics and decides she has not been firm enough, she may wildly put pressures on the people in her department. She will lay down the law, read off the lazy workers, make sure her directions are crystal clear, and supervise the most minute details of the work. The members of her unit will then reject her as their leader, and someone else will emerge as the natural leader—the one to whom they all go with their gripes. Such groups disturb their members. Morale declines. Members have difficulty talking about anything but their troubles. They vent their spleen on "her" and on any members who have sold out to "her." They plot and plan ways to get back at "her."

Although our example applies the knowledge about the work group to a hypothetical business organization, the same principles apply to the newly elected club, sorority, or fraternity president, or to the Student

Union Board members, the Black Student Union officers, the American Indian Movement, the YMCA board members, or any of the dozens of organizations, large or small, to which you belong now and to which you will belong in your lifetime.

KEY IDEAS CHAPTER 9

• When people must work together, a social dimension results from their communication.

• When someone structures a group's work, the social and task dimensions come into conflict, because giving and taking orders causes social tensions.

• Good work groups have good morale and get things done.

• A highly cohesive group is one in which the members work for the good of the group.

• The more cohesive the group, the better the communication, because cohesiveness encourages disagreements and questions.

• At any given moment a person feels attracted to a group if it satisfies one or more of his or her basic needs.

• People in new groups always feel some social tension, because they are unsure how the others will react to them as people.

• The person who seems bored and uninterested at a first meeting of a group is probably tense and most interested, particularly in how the others would view him if he spoke up.

• Agreement is one of the basic social rewards in our society. Disagreements are socially punishing but absolutely necessary to good group work.

• One important fact of group dynamics is that members tend to specialize in doing certain tasks over a period of time.

• When all members have a common expectation about how a person will behave, that individual has a *role* in the group.

• A member's role is worked out jointly by the person and the group.

• Members award a higher status to those roles they judge more valuable to the group.

• Feedback is related to role stability and cohesiveness because a person can ask questions with less fear of losing status in a cohesive and stable group.

- The presence in a meeting of a person with formal status within a community or an organization poses a barrier to successful communication.
- The leadership role is the one most fascinating to both the general public and the experts.
- In our culture we both deplore leadership as an undesirable feature of a classless democracy and applaud the successful person who rises to a position of power.
- The members of a group spend much time and energy on the leadership question because it is so important to the successful achievement of group goals.
- A change in group personnel is always unsettling.
- Many work groups function within a formal organization, which in turn exercises a controlling influence on certain factors of communication.
- When the power structure of the informal organization differs from the formal structure, one can predict communication problems.

SUGGESTED PROJECTS

1 • Think through your own philosophy of group leadership. Outline on paper its main points and think through how you have been guided in your small-group communication by this philosophy in the past.

2 • Students are placed in leaderless groups of five or six. Each group is furnished with a tape recorder and spends one or two class meetings, which the group records, preparing a panel discussion program on some important public issue to present to the class. The group selects a moderator for the program and, after discussing the topic in front of the class for 30 minutes, throws the discussion open for audience participation. Each member of the group listens to one of the tapes taken during the planning meetings and writes a short paper evaluating the role emergence that takes place during the planning sessions and the actual presentation.

3 • Select a small group that you work with on a regular basis. This group could be part of an office or business organization, a committee of students working on a long-term project, a church or social action group—any task-oriented small group. Keep a journal of your experiences in the group. Describe the group's cohesiveness, role structure, and leadership. Where do you fit into the group's role structure.

SUGGESTED READINGS

Bormann, Ernest G. *Discussion and Group Methods,* 2d ed. New York: Harper & Row, 1975.

Bormann, Ernest G. and Nancy C. Bormann. *Effective Small Group Communication.* 3d ed. Minneapolis: Burgess, 1980.

Brilhart, John K. *Effective Group Discussion.* 3d ed. Dubuque, Iowa: Brown, 1978.

Philips, Gerald M. *Communication and the Small Group.* 2d ed. Indianapolis: Bobbs-Merrill, 1973.

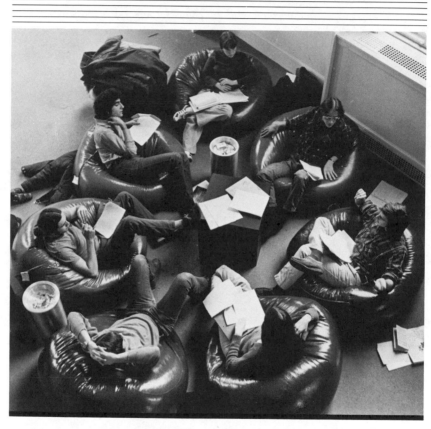

HOW TO COMMUNICATE IN GROUP
DISCUSSIONS
CHAPTER 10

GROUP DISCUSSION

Group discussion refers to one or more meetings of a small number of people who communicate face to face in order to fulfill a common purpose and achieve a common goal.

The small group is an identifiable entity. Authorities differ on details relating to the size of a small group, but the general features are agreed upon. The communication networks and personal relationships that develop while people hold a discussion change when the size of a group is increased, and these changes can be used to describe the "small" group. When a third person is added to a two-person interview, the nature of the working relationships and the flow of communication change, thus a small group is composed of at least three people. The upper size limit of the small group is more difficult to specify. However, when the group becomes so large that it begins to change its patterns of communication, it should no longer be considered a small group. In groups of five or fewer, all members speak to one another. Even those who speak little talk to all the others. In groups of seven or more, the quiet members often cease to talk to any but the top people in the group. As groups become even larger, the talk centralizes more and more around a few people; group interaction falls off. In groups of thirteen or more, from five to seven people hold the discussion while the others watch and listen.

The best size for a group discussion is probably five. Members of groups with fewer than five people complain that their groups are too small and suffer from a lack of diversity of opinion and skill. Groups composed of even numbers of people tend to be less stable and rewarding than groups of odd numbers. A group of five or seven works better than a group of four, six, or eight. On learning this, many people have said when analyzing unproductive groups they have been in, "Well, that was our first mistake! There were ten of us."

CHARACTERISTICS OF THE ONE-TIME MEETING

Students of small-group communications must understand not only that a discussion meeting may serve different functions but also that groups differ in other significant ways. In a group that meets only once, the dynamics of the communication are quite different from those that operate in a group that meets several times. Groups also differ depending on how closely they relate to an organization. A group of students from a speech communication class is different from a standing committee of an academic department composed of students, teaching assistants, and faculty members.

The one-time discussion group is such an important communication event that it deserves some special attention. The people in a one-time discussion group have not worked together before and are not likely to do so again for the purposes under discussion. Some may have worked with others in similar groups and some may know one another socially, but the particular grouping of these five or six people for this particular purpose has not happened before.

CONTRASTS BETWEEN ONE-TIME AND AD HOC GROUPS

The one-time discussion meeting is different from an ad hoc committee. *Ad hoc* is a Latin term meaning "for this special purpose." An ad hoc committee thus is formed for a special purpose important enough to cause the group to meet for several sessions over a period of weeks or months before it makes its final report. An ad hoc committee is also different from the standing permanent committees of an organization which continue for as long as the organization exists. For example, if a political action group has a standing committee for public education, that committee will function as long as the group continues. However, if a group of people organize a committee to meet and work for several months for the specific purpose of getting a city ordinance passed, that committee is ad hoc.

The one-time meeting is held by people who expect to achieve their purposes in a single meeting. Since its composition is unique, the discussion group has no history, and the people who come to the meeting cannot be guided by past experience with one another in such a discussion. The group holding a one-time meeting has no team spirit, no usual way of doing things, no idea about how the communication and social interaction will proceed.

The first meeting of an ad hoc committee is like the one-time meeting in that its members have not previously met together for this particular purpose. But although the ad hoc committee has no history, it does have a future. The members will be meeting together for a considerable period of time, and the influence of the future expectations produces some important differences between the first session of an ad hoc committee, and a one-time meeting.

As we saw in Chapter 9, the group without a history but with a future is under pressure to test potential leaders and other possibly important members to develop a common way of doing things, to take nothing at face value, and to check reputations, formal status, and assigned structures before accepting them.

One of the most important things about the one-time meeting is the willingness of the participants to accept leadership. Whether the person calling the meeting is a self-appointed moderator or has been assigned to lead the meeting by some organizational unit, the members are likely to accept and appreciate guidance from that individual. The group needs quick help in getting started. Members realize they have little time to waste and tend to accept with little argument the leader's description of goals and his or her methods of getting on with the meeting.

Participants in one-time meetings tend to use any information they have to help form an impression of their fellow committee members. If students in a speech-communication class meet to plan something and discover that one member is majoring in elementary education, another is the president of the freshman class, a third was a beauty contest winner, and so on, they use such information to help them structure their meeting.

Once the discussion is under way, those members who do not hold positions of stature, or who are not known by reputation, tend to be quickly stereotyped. The stereotyping that takes place in the one-time meeting comes from first impressions. Each person makes a quick judgment about every other member and, thus, a person who does not speak for 15 or 20 minutes may be stereotyped as quiet, shy, apathetic, or uninterested and be dismissed as unimportant. Another, who speaks loudly, expresses strong opinions, and makes flat judgments, may be stereotyped as bossy or pushy.

The people in a one-time meeting take shortcuts to structure their group into a pecking order, so they can get on with the business at hand. They are willing to risk getting a wrong impression because they are pressed for time and often because they think the purpose of the one-time meeting is less important than that of a discussion group that meets repeatedly.

Members of one-time meetings tend to accept a stereotyped picture of how a meeting should be run. A newly formed group that plans to meet for many sessions works out its own unique ways of getting the job done, but the one-time meeting does not allow enough time to do this. The accepted picture of how a small-group meeting should be conducted—the norms that most North Americans come to accept by the time they reach college—includes the idea that there should be a moderator, leader, or chairperson (depending upon how authoritarian the leadership style is to be) and a secretary or recorder.

The moderator, leader, or presiding officer of a one-time meeting is expected to attend to the administrative details of setting up the meeting place, planning the agenda, sending out preliminary information, and scheduling the meeting.

PLANNING THE ONE-TIME MEETING

If you are assigned the duty of moderating, leading, or chairing a one-time meeting, you ought to do the following things in the planning stage:

1 Determine the purpose of the meeting. Every one-time meeting should have a clear and specific purpose. Make sure the other members know the purpose of the meeting either before it starts or early in the session. You should also make the type of meeting clear to the members: Is the meeting for briefing, instructing, consulting, or decision making?

2 Plan the meeting to achieve the purpose. You should ask such questions as: Where is the best place to hold the meeting? What format will best achieve the purpose? Who should take part in the meeting? Should people with special knowledge be invited? Should some high-status people be invited?

3 Plan the little details. A successful one-time meeting requires time and effort in the planning stages. Do not neglect the small details. If you do, you may save a bit of your own time, but wasting the time of your colleagues in a useless meeting is not wise. Little things such as providing pads and pencils, refreshments, properly arranged and enough seating all contribute to the success of the meeting. When minor details or administration are handled smoothly, people feel the meeting is important and is going to do significant work.

4 Specify the outcomes of the meeting. Making the outcomes clear is not the same as deciding on the purposes. If plans are to be made, how will they be developed? In detail? In general outline? Decide what decisions can be made in such a meeting, and in what form they should be made.

5 Utilize the results of the meeting. What can be done to follow up and apply the results? Do not let important leads drop at the end of the meeting.

LEADING THE ONE-TIME MEETING

During the course of the meeting the assigned (or elected) chairperson is expected to lead the discussion. The chairperson's duties are commonly understood to include the following:

A. Chairperson's duties in regard to the task
  1. Start the meeting
  2. Act as pilot to keep the group on course, remind members of the discussion outline, cut short those who wander too far from the outline
  3. Help the group arrive at decisions (take votes when necessary)
  4. Provide transitions from topic to topic
  5. Summarize what the group has accomplished
  6. Control the channels of communication to ensure that everybody has a chance to talk and that all sides get a fair hearing; encourage the quiet member to take part and discourage the too-talkative ones

B. Chairperson's duties in regard to human relations
  1. Introduce members to one another
  2. Help break the ice at the start and relax people so they can get down to business
  3. Release tensions and bad feelings that come from disagreements and conflicts of personality or opinion

Techniques for leading the one-time meeting

Assuming the willingness of participants to follow his or her direction, the leader still needs certain basic skills to conduct an efficient meeting. The three basic techniques for this purpose are the question, the summary, and the directive. Summaries are always useful to indicate progress and to orient the group. The democratic style requires more questions than directives; the authoritarian style, more directives than questions.

The first task is to get the group down to business. A certain amount of time should be devoted to getting acquainted, but then the group must go to work. Questions are useful, especially open-ended questions asked in such a way that they cannot be answered with a simple yes or no. An open-ended question can get things started. Early in the meeting, the leader should set the mood for short, to-the-point comments. If the first comment runs too long, the leader may have to interrupt with a question directed to someone else.

The leader needs to watch carefully and make running choices about the drift of the discussion. Is it part of the necessary kicking around of an idea? He or she should not take the easy way out and make the choice strictly according to the agenda. When the leader decides the discussion is wasting time, he or she should bring the meeting back to the agenda. Questions are useful for this: "Can we tie this in with the point about rules in the student union?" "Just a minute, how does this relate to grading procedures?" Summaries can give an overview of the past few minutes of the meeting and bring the group back to the agenda. Finally, a leader may simply assert that the discussion is off the track and direct that the group get back: "We seem to be getting off the subject. Let's get back to Bill's point."

The moderator should not push the group too fast; on the other hand, devoting 20 minutes to material that deserves only 5 produces restlessness and frustration. The leader should watch for signs that a topic has been exhausted. If members begin to repeat themselves, fidget, or pause for lack of something to say, the leader should move to the next item. The summary is the best way to do so. A summary rounds off the discussion of one point and leads naturally to a new one. It also gives the group a feeling of accomplishment.

From time to time, the group needs to make decisions. The leader can help by stepping in at those times and asking, "Are we in substantial agreement on this point?" If the question is important, he or she may call for a vote.

Often some tension-producing behavior creates an awkward moment for the leader and the participants. What we offer here are some hints about how to handle the awkward situation immediately when it crops up in a meeting. One common difficulty for the moderator is the member who talks too much. The leader may break into a long comment by an overtalkative person with a yes-no question and then quickly direct another question to someone else.

Leader: **Just a minute, Joe; would you be willing to drop that course from the requirements for a major?**

Joe: **Now, I didn't say . . .**

Leader: **I just want to be clear on this. Would you be in favor of that?**

Joe: **Well, no, but . . .**

Leader: **Bill, I wonder how you feel about this?**

Sometimes the leader can stop the talkative member by asking for specific information. Interrupting him for a summary is another technique. The leader can then conclude the summary by directing a question to someone else. People usually sit back for a summary. Sometimes the leader simply has to say, "I'm going to ask you to stop there for a minute and hold your next comment. Everyone has not had a chance to be heard on this point."

The member who is too quiet also poses problems. The leader should use questions to draw out the quiet members, asking the nonparticipating person a direct open-ended question, addressing him by name, so that only that person can answer. Do not ask a question that can be answered with a yes or no, and, of course, do not ask a question that the person might be unable to answer for lack of information. Once the quiet member answers, encourage some elaboration on the answer.

PARTICIPATING IN THE ONE-TIME MEETING

The norms of a one-time meeting do not assign specific roles to any group member except the leader. All leadership functions are assigned to the moderator, and other members are expected to follow the moderator's lead and accept his or her directions. When the chairperson recognizes a person, the others are supposed to respect that decision and not interrupt. When the chairperson cuts off discussion on a topic, the others are supposed to accept that decision.

The duties of the participant include the following:

A. Participant's duties in regard to the task
  1. Enter into the discussion with enthusiasm
  2. Have an open-minded, objective attitude
  3. Keep contributions short and to the point
  4. Talk enough but not too much
  5. Speak clearly and listen carefully
B. Participant's duties in regard to social and human relations
  1. Respect the other person
  2. Be well mannered
  3. Try to understand the other person's position
  4. Do not manipulate or exploit the other person

Of course, the model of how a good one-time meeting should proceed differs considerably from the realities of even a short session. Participants do not all willingly follow the assigned moderator even when they know they should. They are, however, much more likely to do so in a one-time meeting than in the first session of a group that will meet a number of times. People in the more permanent group move strongly in the first meeting to test the assigned leader's abilities.

Even in a short meeting, role differences become apparent. A few people speak more than the others, despite the best efforts of the moderator. Some people are silent. Others are humorous and friendly. The generalized picture of a meeting composed of a leader and a group of indistinguishable followers soon changes under the pressure of discussion with a common purpose.

The group discussion, even a short one-time meeting, is an extremely complicated event. The addition of a third person (or several more) to the two-person communication situation adds a good deal more than one-third in additional complexity. The general discussion above of how to prepare for, moderate, and participate in the discussion should be viewed in terms of our knowledge of group dynamics.

If, indeed, a small group meeting is such a complicated thing, why do most people think it is easy to assemble a few people, and, in the course of an hour or two, discuss a series of important topics, make a couple of vital decisions, and adjourn in time for the next class?

The main reason for our too-simple approach to groups is that we have a rather clear idea of what we think a meeting ought to be like, and this clouds our perception of what a group, in fact, can be like. Many people think a business or committee meeting should be an efficient, no-nonsense affair. The meeting should be well planned. The discussion should follow the agenda. Everybody should say about the same amount, and everything they say should be to the point and helpful. The members ought to be involved, eager to participate, good listeners and speakers.

The ideal discussion is largely a fiction seldom encountered in real life. Lest you think that our treatment of the one-time discussion reflects only the common stereotype of an ideal discussion, we hasten below to set the record straight. What we have described above are the expectations people commonly have about what moderators and participants should do in preparation for and during a discussion. Below, we describe what, in fact, tends to happen in a discussion.

A REALISTIC PICTURE OF SMALL-GROUP COMMUNICATION

What is a realistic picture of how a good group communicates? Good group communication takes time. Given the complicated communication network that must be developed in a work meeting, we should not expect a group to cover more topics in a two-hour meeting than one person could study and decide about in an hour if that person were working alone. Yet we often expect a group to cover as much work in a few hours as one person would be hard put to accomplish in a day. When we ask a group to do more than it can, it either gets bogged down on the first part of the agenda and leaves some business undone or races through the meeting without dealing adequately with anything. As a result, the people who attend come away feeling the meeting was a failure.

The limited attention span of a group

Also unrealistic is the notion that a group can organize its discussion so it keeps to the main ideas and moves in a logical, step-by-step way through a series of topics. Individuals have attention spans measured in minutes, and sometimes in seconds. When we listen, read or think about something in a logical, step-by-step way, we often find our attention wandering. You may read a paragraph and understand it quite well, then halfway down the next page you realize that while your eyes are moving, your thoughts are on getting a drink of water or on the date you are going out with later. Even when people puzzle about an important problem or decision, they often find their attention shifting to other subjects.

Groups, like individuals, have short attention spans. Most groups cannot talk about a topic for much more than a minute before someone changes the subject. Sometimes the group wants to change the subject, because it has finished talking about one topic, and should move on to another, but quite often the person who changes the topic does so while others still want to consider the original subject. Sometimes the new topic is not relevant to the matter under discussion. A short attention span for a group meeting is natural and inevitable, and we must work within the limitations it imposes.

Most of what we have said about a group's short attention span comes from research on what members say during meetings. Investigators have studied a group's communication and noted when the group changed topics. Of course, during any given period of time during the meeting, people may or may not be listening to what is being said. Thus the job of holding everybody's attention is probably even more difficult than the evidence, gathered by looking at the content of the messages, indicates.

Clearly, people in small groups have difficulty keeping their attention on an idea so they all can understand it and give their opinions about it. Yet if the meeting has work to do, they feel pressure to get on with the job. Participants in a discussion with a purpose do not like the aimless skipping from idea to idea that is common in social conversations. If the group has an outline or an agenda for the meeting, the members will keep looking at the plan, using it to measure how well they are doing. When the discussion leaves the agenda, they often comment that the group is getting off the topic or that much still should be done.

Balancing freedom and structure

People vary as to how much fooling around they can stand in a meeting. Some are uncomfortable unless the point of the meeting is clear and the outline of topics is specific. They want the group to stick to business. Others feel hemmed in by a sticking-to-business approach. They have what seems to them an important or exciting comment, and they want to say it even if it does not relate directly to the topic under discussion.

How does a person organize a discussion in a realistic and yet productive way? At times participants want and need the freedom to suggest ideas and mull them over without worrying too much about how they hang together or how they fit into the agenda. At other times, a group needs and wants to get on with the job and to get things organized. At this point, group members seem to feel they know what they want to do and they are tired of rehashing things that are clear or decided. A leader should be alert to the alternate needs for freewheeling and for structure. Most groups develop a rhythm in regard to when they want to be loose and easy and when they want to get things organized. Careful attention to verbal and nonverbal cues can help the leader decide about any given group. For example, members of a group may display frustration when the chair reminds them that their discussion is off the topic. A person may accept the suggestion that the comment is out of order in a grumpy fashion, sitting back in his chair and frowning. Another person may say, "I don't want to make a motion or ask for a decision, but I would like to throw out a few ideas and see what you think of them before we get down to business." When, as a leader, you see gestures or hear comments expressing the desire for less concern with the agenda or with structure, you should go along with the group members and give them a chance to kick ideas around.

Other verbal and nonverbal cues indicate that the group wants more structure. A member may look at her watch, shift in her seat, and let her attention wander. When several people seem to be saying, "Let's cut out the talk and get down to business," or "What should we do to get rolling?" the chair, or someone else in the meeting may suggest that they follow an outline, and the group will accept the suggestion and stay with an outline. When they wish to have a more tightly organized meeting, their attention span will continue to be short, but they will welcome attempts to get them back to the business at hand and willingly follow such suggestions.

A realistic picture of how groups work includes the notion that groups do not systematically pick the best solution from a carefully drawn list of possible solutions; rather, they tend to throw out the worst, the not so good, and the fair, until they are left with several good answers, which they mull over until the final decision emerges. The group circles problems, rather than dealing with them in a straight line. Thus, a sensible agenda might well suggest running over topics A, B, and C in about 30 minutes and then returning to the total agenda for a more penetrating discussion. The group needs to find the areas of quick agreement and the points of minor or serious conflict.

Groups tend to approach the real problem, grabbing hold of it almost anywhere in order to get started. Their first pass at the topic results in a rather simple approach. They return again, dig more deeply, and begin to cut closer to the important difficulties. When people start to argue and disagree, they feel social tension and become uncomfortable, so they pull back and turn to less painful matters. After a time they return to the central issue and drive still closer to the solution. The approach-withdrawal action is typical of groups making tough decisions.

A group often appreciates a relatively free and unstructured period early in the meeting to allow a quick survey of all the business and to get some idea of how people feel about things. Some members will need to prod the others to get down to the important arguments, because groups do not like to discuss touchy subjects. If you watch for the tendency to take flight, you as leader can often help the group by pushing for a discussion of the tough issues.

Once a decision has emerged, the group ought to state formally, confirm, and plan details to implement the decision. At the point of getting things in order to carry out a decision, the members are usually pleased to have an outline or an agenda, and they work through these items with fewer digressions during the last stages of the problem-solving process.

KEY IDEAS CHAPTER 10

• **Every organized attempt to get things done in our society requires working with discussion groups.**

• **The small group is an identifiable social entity with its own patterns of interaction.**

• **The best size for a group discussion is probably five members.**

• **Groups composed of even numbers of people tend to be less stable and rewarding than groups of odd numbers.**

• **Every organization has some meetings that are rituals.**

• **Discussions may be used to brief or instruct the participants.**

• Some group meetings advise the person or persons with the authority to make decisions.

• An extremely important kind of meeting is one called actually to make a decision.

• People in a group that has no history but is expected to meet again size each other up very carefully.

• The participants in a one-time meeting, with no history and no future, are generally willing to accept assigned leadership.

• The people in a one-time meeting take shortcuts to structure their group so they can get on with business.

• The moderator of a one-time meeting is expected to attend to the administrative details of setting up the discussion.

• During the course of a one-time discussion, the moderator is expected to start the meeting, make transitions, summarize, take votes, and generally guide the group.

• The participant in a one-time discussion is expected to follow the moderator's lead, enter into the discussion with enthusiasm, and stick to the point.

• The main reason many people get upset with meetings is that they have a clear, simple, and impossible ideal for a good discussion.

• The ideal discussion is seldom encountered in real life.

• Groups, like individuals, have short attention spans.

• When several people are fighting for control of the channels of communication, they often do not listen to one another.

• Members in discussions have trouble chaining ideas together and getting an overall picture of the topic they are discussing.

• People vary as to how much fooling around they can tolerate in a meeting.

• At times, particularly early in a discussion, participants want and need the freedom to introduce ideas and mull them over without worrying too much about sticking to an agenda.

• Later in a discussion, participants want some structure to organize their work.

• Decisions tend to emerge from group discussions rather than being carefully discussed and voted upon.

SUGGESTED PROJECTS

1 • The class is divided into one-time-meeting discussion groups of five or six, and the instructor provides each group with a timely community or campus topic to discuss. A moderator is appointed, and the group plans a brief agenda. The group tries to have a good discussion and, at the same time, to let everybody participate equally. To aid in this equal participation, each group member is given the same number of poker chips or tokens of some sort. Each time a member speaks, he has to "spend" a token. When all his tokens are spent, he can no longer participate. Each group should devote 10 minutes after the discussion to evaluating the effect of striving for absolutely equal participation during the meetings.

2 • Attend a one-time meeting of a real-life campus group. Write a short paper describing and evaluating the leadership of the meeting. List the specific techniques used by the leader to keep the discussion moving, on the track, with maximum involvement of the group members.

3 • Find three real examples that have occurred in the last month in your community of each of the following kinds of group discussion meetings: (1) ritualistic, (2) briefing sessions, (3) instructional meeting, (4) consultative meeting, (5) decision-making meeting.

SUGGESTED READINGS

Bormann, Ernest G. and Nancy C. Bormann. *Effective Small Group Communication.* 3d ed. Minneapolis, Burgess, 1980.

Brilhart, John K. *Effective Group Discussion.* 3d ed. Dubuque, Iowa: Brown, 1978.

Phillips, Gerald M. *Communication and the Small Group.* 2d ed. Indianapolis: Bobbs-Merrill, 1972.

PART THREE: PUBLIC SPEAKING

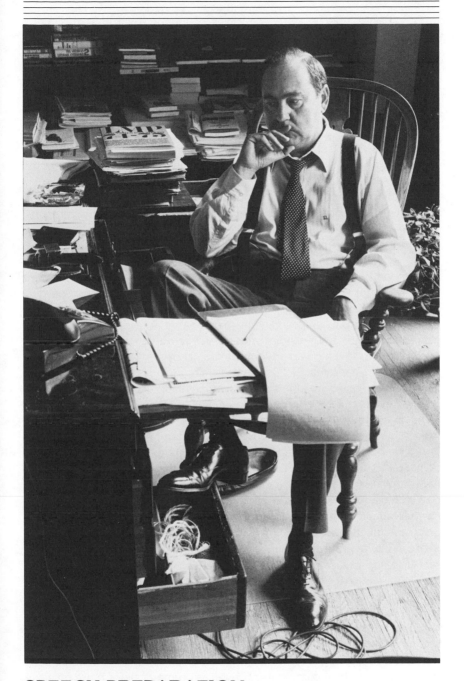

SPEECH PREPARATION
CHAPTER 11

In Part Two we discussed the principles of interpersonal and small-group communication as they applied to the casual, informal conversations and business meetings of our day-to-day living. In Part Three we consider the less frequent but important form of communication in which one person delivers a speech to an audience.

THE NATURE OF PUBLIC SPEAKING

The public speech is a formal communication event, a showcase where the speaker becomes the center of attention and has a chance to star or to fail in the eyes of a number of people. We usually spend more time in preparing our public speeches than we do in planning our interpersonal and small-group communication.

Our speech preparation is aided by the fact that in our culture the public speech is an established communication occasion with well-understood patterns of how we ought to behave and communicate. Once we know what kind of speech occasion it is, we also know a good deal about what is expected of us as a speaker or as an audience member.

For many public speeches the participants anticipate that one individual will deliver an extended message. The audience comes to hear a certain person speak on an advertised subject or title. The public-speaking transaction has a definite format that usually includes a time at which the audience is to gather and the speech is supposed to begin, and quite often a time when the speech is to close. Americans are time-conscious and pay a great deal of attention to the length of a speech. If the speech draws out longer than they have anticipated, audience members often grow restless.

For many public speeches the audience expects and appreciates activities that set the stage for the speaker. A simple format for a speech is to have a local dignitary call the meeting to order and introduce the speaker by identifying his background and experience. The speaker then delivers his message, and the person who introduced him thanks the speaker and closes the meeting. The basic format is often elaborated so that the speaker is preceded by music, group singing, or performances, by lesser personalities, to increase the audience's susceptibility to the main speaker. Big revival meetings, for instance, often have prayers, announcements, songs, and introductions before the evangelist delivers the main message of the evening. Political rallies generally have music, introductions, and some enthusiastic partisan comments before the main speaker comes to the podium.

After the speech, the audience may participate in questioning the speaker or in making comments. The occasion may call for more music or some additional comments by other people.

Generally, the people planning the public speech arrange things so the audience has some place to sit or stand, so distractions are minimized, and so the speaker is provided with a public-address system in good working order that allows everyone present to hear him.

The variety of specific expectations aroused by such situations as the after-dinner speech, the revival speech, the agitator's speech at a political demonstration, and the funeral eulogy praising someone who has died can be identified by questions such as: Does the audience expect and enjoy humor? Does the audience listen quietly to the speaker? Does the audience interrupt and heckle? Does the audience interrupt to reinforce the speaker with shouts such as "Hallelujah! Praise the Lord!" or "Right on!" or "You tell 'em, George!" Does the audience expect the speaker to read a carefully prepared message? Does the audience expect the speaker to deliver an extemporaneous speech with high feeling and vigorous nonverbal communication? To some extent, of course, expectations of audiences are culturebound; more than likely a black rural southern congregation will expect a different funeral eulogy than will a small-town Scandinavian Lutheran congregation in Minnesota.

An adept speaker may sometimes break one or two of the expected conventions that relate to a certain speech occasion and even benefit from the novelty of the violation—people usually enjoy a mild surprise—but if he violates a number of the conventions surrounding a public speech, the audience will often be confused, indignant, bored, or even angry. If a minister, for example, introduces some humor into an ordinarily serious religious meeting, most of the audience will respond as the speaker hopes. If the minister violates other expectations in addition—for example, in the way she is dressed, her style of language, her dialect, her use of profanity, her use of bald humor, or her appearance of drunkenness while delivering the sermon, the audience's responsiveness will be seriously disturbed.

If the audience comes to a public-speaking situation expecting to hear a fire-breathing politician, a hellfire-and-damnation revival preacher, or a violent revolutionary, the members are often predisposed to respond with high feeling. The planners of the meeting, trying to fulfill these expectations, may precede the main speaker with music and warmup speeches, as we mentioned earlier. By the time the speaker begins, the audience may be quite excited, and if he is skillful, the orator will soon have focused the attention of the listeners upon his speech.

We have, admittedly, taken the above examples from that group of public-speaking situations that conventionally arouse expectations of emotional excitement. The same principles of audience behavior, however, apply to other situations. The audience attending a lecture by a Nobel prize winner, for instance, places equally strong pressures to conform on individual members of the audience. If the speaker is wearing an evening dress, if the ushers whisper as though loud and boisterous talk were out of order, if the audience sits upright and with great dignity, the pressure is strong on all audience members to do likewise. If members of the audience begin to cough, grow restless, and look at their watches, all these behaviors put pressure on the speaker and other audience members alike.

Because of the general cultural expectations that govern public speeches, we need to adapt the communication model from Chapter 1 to fit the specific context of speaking occasions. The *S M C R* model can be applied if we use more specific terms for the basic concepts. The more specific term for source is *speaker;* for encoding is *speech preparation;* for message is *public speech;* for channels is *sight* and *sound;* for decoding is *listening;* and for receiver is *audience members.* Feedback in the public-speaking situation consists of the audience response and the interplay between audience and speaker as the audience responds, the speaker adapts to the response, and the audience responds again.

In addition to the basic parts of speaker, speech, and audience, the public speech is delivered on a specific *occasion,* and that becomes an important part of the communication model. The last important part of the more specific model of public-speaking communication is the *topic* of the speech. The planners of a public speech usually clearly specify what the speech will be about and announce it ahead of time for those who are invited or encouraged to attend.

The speaker should take the occasion into account in planning the speech. The audience is also an important consideration in planning. The speaker may be free to select the topic, or the topic may be assigned by the people asking the person to speak. In any case, the focus is on the speaker, center stage, who has thoroughly prepared material on the topic, carefully studied the audience, and skillfully adapted the topic and the supporting material to the audience and the occasion.

The audience is not passive. Even listener apathy or disinterest is an important response to a speech. Often the audience members will be interested and respond either positively or negatively to what they hear. Audience responses may cause the speaker problems. If the audience is uninterested the speaker is expected to use examples, strong delivery, compelling language, and other communication skills to arouse and maintain its interest. If members of the audience are hostile to the speaker or the topic or both at the beginning of the speech, the suspense is heightened. Not only that, but we often evaluate a speech that succeeds against high odds as a better speech than one that achieves the speaker's objective with little trouble.

The ideal model of a public speech is one in which a skillful speaker, with a clear purpose, analyzes the audience and occasion wisely, selects a suitable topic, gathers and analyzes material relating to the topic, audience, and occasion, preplans the organization and content of the speech, delivers the speech with appropriate nonverbal gestures and vocal intonations, phrases the ideas in language suitable to the hearers, carefully reads the audience's response as the speech unfolds, accommodates the ideas to the audience both in the planning and during the delivery, and achieves his or her purpose by gaining the intended response from the audience. The first step to such success as a speaker, therefore, is careful speech preparation.

SELECTING A TOPIC

Your planning begins with the selection of a topic for the speech. Someone may assign you a topic area or even provide a specific title for your speech, but often you can pick your own topic. A student speaker often finds picking a topic a major problem, second only to managing communication tension. The two problems are interrelated. Our recommended treatment for stage fright is to pick the right topic for you and for the audience and to prepare thoroughly before you speak.

We will not provide you with a long list of suggested topics for class speeches. Any list we might prepare now from the headlines, which indicate the current hot news topics, would be out of date by the time you read this chapter. You would find a better guide to topics about business, politics, entertainment, government, religion, and military affairs by skimming the headlines in the most recent copy of your local newspaper or the most recent issue of a national news magazine. More important, lists are no substitute for the ability to meet each new speaking occasion with a creative solution to the problem of finding the right topic *for you.*

In our discussion of speech preparation which follows, we will discuss the creative process and how you can learn to use it in planning your speeches. Thinking up topics for a speech that you could give to your classmates is an excellent drill to improve your creativity. We recommend that you take out a few minutes each day for the next few days and write down ten possible speech topics each day. Try to come up with ten topics in the shortest amount of time you can. Write down anything that comes into your head no matter how silly it may seem. Strive for speed; do not worry about quality. The matter of quality can come up later when you have to pick a topic for a specific assignment.

Our best advice is to pick a speech topic that is of interest to you. If you are already well informed on the subject, fine. Even if you are not well informed, if you are curious and excited about learning more about some subject, it can serve as a good topic for a speech. Once you have an established career, people will usually ask you to give a speech because you have specialized knowledge, training, or experience that makes you a person they want to hear.

Even now you probably know more about some topics than most of your classmates. You may know more than they do about hang gliding, or making men's ties, or the workings of an automobile engine. Your special knowledge equips you to make a speech whenever you are talking to people who know less about a particular subject than you do. If you are a trained or hobby automotive mechanic, you could make a speech about whether or not efforts to conserve energy by increasing the mileage of American automobiles are likely to succeed—a very timely topic as we write this chapter.

Even if we have not yet had much special training or study in a technical topic area, we are all experts in some fields because of our personal experiences. We are particular experts in the areas of how we *feel* about a topic, what our responses are, and why, on some issue. Did you attend a high school where belonging to, or not being a member of, certain cliques or groups or gangs was an important factor in your enjoyment of school? You can speak about how such groups function to illustrate the principles of small-group communication, as explained in Chapter 9. Did you attend a high school at which busing for integration and racial balance resulted in an improvement or a decline in the quality of your education? You could speak from personal experience on the effects of busing on the quality of education. Do you know from firsthand experience or from observing friends and acquaintances about drug dependency, teenage sex, or the group pressures that encourage or discourage academic excellence? Perhaps you have a hobby or some consuming interest in a sport. Do you collect coins? records? Do you like some particular kind of music? Are you a movie buff? Are you fascinated with computers? Do you find machines "friends" or "foes" as you look ahead in your lifetime? What do you want from life? How do your goals differ from those of your parents, and what are your personal hopes and dreams? What is your response to the media? Do you feel television has enriched or stifled your growth intellectually? Everyone agrees that reading skills are a basic necessity in today's world; tons of material have been written about "why Johnny can't read." Think back over your years in school; you know who had trouble with basic reading skills. Read some of the research; search your own memory of the process of teaching reading in your own school experience. Your speech topic could then be "I Think I Know Why Johnny Can't Read."

Put your mind to it. Use the tips on creativity that follow. Look on topic selection as a challenge rather than a chore. Skills in creative thinking are elements of your education that you will be able to use for the rest of your life.

MAKING A CREATIVE ANALYSIS OF A TOPIC

A creative analysis is important to understand a topic. Once a speaker has decided on a general topic for a speech, the next step is to assemble all the information possible within the time available. At this point your ability to use the library, to interview for information, to assemble and remember all the information that you know from personal experience becomes important. Excellent books devoted to library use and research are readily available in your own library. If you want to learn to use your library more effectively, see if a reference librarian will give you a short tour and explain the main reference tools available to you. You will find the skill of using a library effectively important not only for your career as a student but for the rest of your life. A course in speech communication, particularly one that includes the study of public-speaking, provides a good stimulus and context for you to learn the very important skills of collecting and recording information for further use in writing and speaking. One expert in the use of the library boasted that, given a first class library and two weeks' time, he could become the second-best authority on any topic in the world. Such claims are probably, like the expert, legendary, but there is a good point to the story. An important part of anyone's education involves learning how to gather information quickly and efficiently.

Once you have an assignment to deliver a speech and have selected (or have been given) a general topic, you should assemble all the information you can and begin to analyze it. *Analysis* is the process of dividing the information into parts, examining the parts, and discovering the important questions that relate to understanding the subject. Some of your thinking ought to be systematic and disciplined, and some ought to be freewheeling and creative. You start by being systematic. Collecting and reading the basic information sets the stage for the more creative analysis later.

Preparation

As you begin the creative "mulling over" of the information you will undoubtedly make false starts and run into dead ends. You may find the topic confusing and be unable to see a pattern in all the information you have collected. You are in the first stage of the creative process, the *preparation phase*, which is a warmup period in which you systematically try to make sense out of the material you have available for the speech. Often you seem to be wasting time, getting nowhere. Do not be discouraged by your seeming lack of progress. You must immerse yourself in the material before you can make a sound analysis of it. Often a person becomes frustrated in the preparation stage and stops working on the analysis. If one has really worked for a sufficient period of time, however, putting the topic aside may be exactly what one should do for a while. The key to the successful ongoing creative process is doing each step sufficiently so that the next step can take place. You must prepare thoroughly, gather everything you can find; try to organize it systematically in as many ways as you can. Then, if you have really filled your mind with the material, you are ready for the second stage to happen.

Incubation

As you consciously put the topic of the speech out of your mind for a while and work at other tasks (preferably manual work!), the second phase of the creative process, the *incubation period,* should begin. In the incubation period, although you are not apparently working on your speech, your subconscious is mulling it over. Many people are aware of this process when they suddenly see the solution to a personal problem such as a difficult decision, right in the middle of doing something completely unrelated to the problem itself. But not everyone is aware that this is a natural, creative sequence and that *we can make it happen;* and that the more often we work at it, the more easily it becomes a source of problem solving. In terms of organizing a speech, while you are doing some routine job such as washing dishes, mowing the lawn, or driving the car, you may suddenly find yourself thinking about the speech in a stream-of-consciousness way. Maybe you hear yourself giving parts of the speech. The words sound "right" in your mind. You are not purposely trying to work on the speech, but it just seems to happen as your ideas associate freely, and you combine ideas, seeing yourself give the speech maybe, image following image. At first these ideas and images bubble up to your consciousness in bits and pieces.

Illumination

The bubbling up of ideas signals the beginning of the third part of the creative process, which usually comes after a period of incubation and is a very exciting part of any creative job. When you are thinking of something else, suddenly and unexpectedly you may clearly see the important ideas relating to the topic of your speech and how they fit together. Inspiration seems to strike: you suddenly know what your central theme for the speech will be, and you see how you can best approach it. The answers seem so right and good that you become excited and enthusiastic about the project. The third part of the creative process is this moment of *illumination.*

Verification

The final part of the creative analysis comes after the illumination phase and consists of the careful and conscious checking out of the details of the solution. Sometimes, upon reflection, the moment of illumination will turn out to have been a "flash in the pan"—when you check out the answer for consistency and plausibility, you discover it is not such a good idea after all. Often, however, the moment of illumination turns out to present a good solution to the problem, and your final task then is to verify, check, shape, and fill in minor details. The final part of the creative process of analysis is called the *verification phase.*

Disciplining creativity

The creative process often seems groping and unstructured. Yet there is a method to the creative madness; it is not completely random, nor is it the same as striving at an answer by trial and error. Creativity requires disciplined work habits. The person who waits for inspiration to strike before beginning to prepare a speech is seldom lucky enough to be struck by the divine lightning. Professional writers who must continually stimulate their creativity to meet deadlines often suggest that the best way to learn to write is *to write*. Successful creative people repeat the slogan endlessly that creativity is 10 percent inspiration and 90 percent perspiration. This advice and the slogan about creativity may seem to be simpleminded, if not question-begging, but they contain the important idea that disciplined work habits are essential to the use of creative talent. Good public speakers also advise that the best way to learn the art is by disciplined practice. One popular slogan that catches the spirit is "If anybody is foolish enough to ask you to give a public speech, be foolish enough to accept."

The more creative you are, of course, the more difficulty you will have getting started on a creative task. Talent acts as though it were lazy, and your creativity will think up all sorts of good excuses for not getting to work. You sit down with a blank piece of paper to begin organizing a speech, and suddenly you remember that you need a glass of water. Having gotten the water, you sit down once more and realize that your typewriter needs a new ribbon. Once the new ribbon is in, you realize it is twelve o'clock and time for lunch. Finally you do get down to work, but as you strike the first key and start the first sentence, you remember that you really ought to go the library and look up some more information before you proceed. All too often, the beginning public speaker puts off the analysis of the topic until the very last minute, and in the rush to meet the deadline the creative process never really has time to get under way. Undoubtedly most of you found some of the above "creative" excuses very familiar. On the other hand, if someone asks you how "creative" you are, you may not rate yourself too highly. Most people are more creative than they realize; they have simply never learned to use their creative energy in any controlled and accountable way.

You can discipline your creativity by developing systematic work habits. Set aside certain times during the week to do creative work such as writing papers and preparing speeches. Make it an iron rule to spend that time doing your projects. If possible, pick the same desk, worktable, or corner of the library for your preparation and writing. Gradually you will discover that the familiar surroundings and the habit of regular work sessions will make the warmup period less painful, often shorter. You must be faithful to your schedule, however; you must push ahead even when you feel little inspiration and the work is not going well.

Often, with a little planning, you can allow enough time for your analysis to go through all four stages of the creative process. You cannot make a creative analysis all at once in a period of several hours or by cramming it into an all-night session as you might prepare for a final examination. Begin your preparation early and allow time for the incubation period. Set aside some time each day for contemplation. If you can do some routine activity such as walking, running, jogging, sweeping the floor, mowing a lawn, or gardening, the incubation process will be encouraged. Be careful about reading, though; reading occupies your mind too much and keeps it from moving into the free association of ideas and images that is useful for incubation.

When you are in the creative phase of analysis you need the proper mental set. Welcome far-fetched ideas and elaborate on them. Imagine as many solutions as you can for a given problem. Modify, change, combine the ones you read about. Play with the ideas and do not worry too much about how stupid or crazy they may seem at first glance.

Once the creative process discovers the basic issues in a body of discourse, you can find a suitable central idea for your speech by answering one or more of the basic questions to your satisfaction. Next, you need to find the most important subpoints that fit under your central theme and the logical relationships that hold among them. When the process of analysis reaches its conclusion, you should have a logical arrangement of reasons in support of your idea, something like a lawyer's brief, which lays out the basic points in a case in a tightly ordered and reasoned fashion.

DEVELOPING BASIC MESSAGE UNITS

The basic building block for messages consists of two parts: the point to be made and the material to support it. The ability to construct basic message units with good supporting material that relates clearly to a well-expressed basic idea is a communication skill that you can use in all your communication, but it is essential in giving a public speech.

When a communicator presents only the main points, without supporting or amplifying them, the speech sounds and reads like a telegram or an outline of the major headings for a theme in an English class. Brief comments on points to be made are hard to understand. Telegraphic talking has the advantage of brevity but usually produces confusion.

Stating a point

A point to be made clear should be expressed in a complete, simple, declarative sentence. We use the terms *complete, simple,* and *declarative* in their technical meanings for English grammar. Complete sentences include both subject and predicate, as follows: "You must know black English to teach black students," "The operators of the numbers games pick the winning numbers from common experiences," "The moon's gravity affects the way a person can walk on the moon's surface."

Remember that a simple sentence has but one subject and one predicate. Put another way, the point to be made in a message unit ought to contain only one idea. The following sentence would make a poor point for a message unit: "The operators of the numbers games pick the winning numbers from common experiences and generally pay off the police to keep in business."

A declarative sentence states something in contrast to a question, which asks for information, or a command, which tells somebody to do something. "How do they pick the winning numbers for the numbers game?" is not a good point for a basic message unit. Neither is the command "Stop playing the numbers."

Never underestimate the importance of finding a good, clear way to make the point you want to make. If you can express what you want to say in a good, clear, simple sentence, you have gone a long way toward getting your point across.

Supporting material

After you have found a good statement of the point to clarify, provide supporting material to make the idea clear. Give an example (real or hypothetical), an analogy (literal or figurative), or a narrative that applies directly to the point. (Of course, if the idea is difficult for the receiver to understand, you may give several examples or analogies or stories to clarify one point.) An important mistake of beginning speakers is to use an example that does not have much to do with the point they are trying to make. Here is a hypothetical example of the does-not-apply mistake:

The operators of the numbers game in my neighborhood pick the winning numbers from almost anything. For example, I know one bookie who pays protection money all the time, and he's been working one place for a long time and nobody has bothered him or given him any trouble.

In the above instance, the so-called "example" has nothing to do with the point made before it.

Patterns of forming message units

Basic message units can be formed in several ways. The following four patterns are often used:

Type 1
Point to be made clear
Supporting material (examples, analogies, stories)

Type 2
Supporting material (examples, analogies, stories)
Point to be made clear

Type 3
Supporting material (examples, analogies, stories)
Point to be made clear
Further supporting material

Type 4
Supporting material (several examples, analogies,
stories); The point is never stated in so many words,
but the audience is supposed to be able to figure it out
from the mass of supporting material; the point is made between the lines.

As a general rule, the patterns that state the point to be made clear first or last are the best; certainly you seldom will be wrong using message-building blocks of these first two types. Burying the point in the middle of a message block often hinders the listener's efforts to dig it out and follow your comment. Leaving out the point entirely is quite risky. However, if you are reasonably sure of your listener's ability to identify the point on the basis of your clear examples and analogies, the fourth pattern can be effective, partly because it provides variety and partly because it creates the illusion that the point is the listener's own notion and facilitates his or her willingness to accept it. We recommend, therefore, that you use the basic message unit without a clear statement of the point primarily for persuasive situations and that you stick to types 1 and 2 for most messages.

When we discuss proving a point for an audience, we must remember that we cannot tell whether a given piece of information is proof until we look at it in relation to the point to be proved.

Evidence is material that furnishes grounds for belief or makes evident the truth or falsity, rightness or wrongness, wisdom or folly of a proposition. It is a technical legal term that refers to material supplied by lawyers in support of their arguments in court. Legal evidence may include testimony of witnesses, written documents, or actual items, such as pistols, knives, or clothing.

Proof is the process of gathering together, ordering, and presenting enough evidence to convince the judge or jury (or us, the listener-consumers) to accept a given proposition.

Although we can look at evidence and make some decision about how good or bad it might be in terms of general rules about evidence, we must look at proof in terms of the audience. We can evaluate evidence against some absolute and general standards of excellence, but proof has to convince somebody. A given message unit, consisting of proposition and supporting evidence, may convince one individual but not another. An old folk saying claims that "the proof of the pudding is in the eating." Even though the cook thinks the ingredients are good and his recipe interesting, if the people eating the pudding do not like it, for them anyway, the pudding is no good. No matter how good the speaker thinks his evidence is, no matter how sound his reasoning, if the listener is not persuaded, his proof is no good.

The three major forms of evidence used as proof for persuasive messages are statistical descriptions of facts, real examples, and testimony. A speaker uses evidence for two main functions to describe and to evaluate the facts. The first and most important use of evidence is to describe what is the case. Factual information consists of statistics, real examples, and eyewitness accounts of what happened. The second use of evidence is to present expert opinion about what the facts mean. The testimony of authorities provides expert interpretation.

MAKING A LOGICAL ANALYSIS OF A TOPIC

We have seen that the clear statement of a point to be made and the evidence that supports the point are the basis for logical analysis. We turn now to how the basic message units can be fitted together to form a good description and explanation of human behavior and physical events or a strong case for a particular position.

For our purposes we will define *logic* as the process of drawing a conclusion from one or more points that serve as assumptions or premises or that need to be proved with evidence.

Lawyers call the paper they write that contains the logic of an argument a *brief*. Someone working on an important persuasive project might well outline the main conclusion and the points that support it, much as a lawyer briefs a case. By following an outline, a person can see the connections from reasons to conclusions clearly and decide whether they fit together logically.

Checking logic

When people question our logic, they often ask the short but troublesome question "Why?" When we answer a *why* question, we usually provide a *because* response. One good way to check the logic of a conclusion following from reasons is to write the conclusion clearly at the top of a sheet of paper and list the reasons supporting the conclusion under it, beginning each reason with *because*. If—keeping in mind our common-sense meaning of *because*—the outline makes good sense, the logic is probably all right.

For instance, here is a conclusion with its supporting reasons, using *because* to indicate logical connections:

Black English is a good legitimate language dialect *because* black English is not a substandard dialect *because* black English is not a deprived language.

One can also test the logic of conclusions drawn from a set of reasons by listing first the reasons and then the conclusions introduced by the word *therefore,* as in the following example:

Many businessmen believe that women are by nature not tough enough for top management positions; and many male personnel directors assign women to positions that are traditional women's roles in society; therefore, many women are discriminated against in business and industry.

When checking your own logic, keep in mind that the evidence must relate to the point you want to prove and that the reasons you present must support your conclusion. One of the most difficult things to do when trying to think clearly and logically is to make sure that every step of an argument is to the point. Here is an example of an argument that makes a mistake by trying to fit two related reasons together, as reason and conclusion:

Many women are being discriminated against in business and industry because many women get a psychologically damaging image of their role in society from motion pictures and television.

The point to be proved relates to the discrimination in business and industry, and the reason supplied to prove the point says something about motion pictures and television. Although both ideas are related to the general topic of women's role in society, they do not fit together as main point and supporting reason.

When we prove to someone the wisdom of acting, believing, or thinking in a certain way by means of evidence and logic, we have used one of the most powerful means of persuasion. Often the decision based on facts and careful inferences from evidence is better than the decision made solely on the basis of the advice of a person we like and trust or on the basis of suggestion. Most important, as consumers of persuasion, we need to be skillful in testing messages for their factual content and the soundness of their logic.

Faulty Analysis of Causation

The error of assuming that because one event followed another the first caused the second is a very common one. In general, the entire question of causation is a difficult one for the public speaker. Usually events are interrelated in very complex ways, and when a person assumes that event A caused event B, many factors that contributed to event B are probably ignored. Generally you should be suspicious of any argument that asserts that a single cause brought about a complicated event. Consider the following faulty argument:

Herbert Hoover was elected as a Republican president before the depression of

the 1930s; Dwight Eisenhower was elected as a Republican president before the recession of the 1950s; Richard Nixon was elected as a Republican president before the recession of the 1970s; therefore, Hoover, Eisenhower, and Nixon caused the economic problems.

If we were to indulge in another common fallacy, which is to make a hasty generalization on the basis of too few examples, we could assert that Republicans cause economic depressions and recessions. Both fallacies are present in the next argument:

Woodrow Wilson was elected as a Democratic president before the United States entered World War I; Franklin Roosevelt was a Democratic president when we entered World War II; Harry Truman was a Democratic president when we entered the Korean War; and John F. Kennedy was a Democratic president when we escalated the Vietnam War; therefore, the Democrats always get us into war.

The error of assuming that because one thing preceded another it caused the event that followed is an easy one to make. You ought to be careful in evaluating the arguments you hear as well as those you use yourself to be sure they do not contain the fallacy.

Circular reasoning

The fallacy of arguing in a circle is illustrated by the following assertions:

"The Bormanns are authorities in speech communication because they have written several books."
"Why have they written several books?"
"Because they are authorities in speech communication."
"Liz is in the movies not because she is a good actress but because she is a personality."
"Why is she a personality?"
"Because she is so widely known."
"Why is she so widely known?"
"Because she is in the movies."

The above examples may seem rather trivial, even though they illustrate the fallacy clearly, but the circular argument can crop up in important political and economic discussions as well:

"Detente with the Russians will not work."
"Why?"
"Because you cannot trust the Communists."
"Why?"
"Because the Communists will never keep their treaty obligations."
"Why?"
"Because Communists are untrustworthy."

The contradictory argument

The inconsistent or contradictory argument is probably the most basic logical fallacy. In the study of formal logic, an argument that contradicts itself is always invalid, and on that basis, public speakers should put a premium on logical consistency. The debater who can convincingly point out that the opponent's argument is contradictory carries the issue. In the debates at the Virginia Convention, called to consider approval of the new Constitution of the United States, Patrick Henry argued against Virginia joining the new government, and James Madison argued for the Constitution. During the course of the long debate, Henry presented a great many different arguments against the proposal, and Madison was able to challenge Henry's reasoning on the grounds that he contradicted himself. For example, Madison first pointed out that Henry had argued that the provision that three-fourths of the states would be sufficient to start the new government was a bad one, because this would allow too few states to form the new government. Next, Madison pointed out that Henry had later argued that the stipulation that two-thirds of the states be required to ratify amendments would make it too difficult to change the government. Madison argued that Henry's argument was inconsistent, in that Henry said three-fourths of the states were too few to start the government, but two-thirds were too many to amend it.

THE AUDIENCE-ADAPTATION STEP

After you have made a creative analysis of your topic, you should have a thorough understanding of the material. You will have done your "homework" and will have a firm grasp of the ins and outs of the question. You will not yet be ready to speak to a specific audience, however.

Too often, people untrained in public speaking but very knowledgeable and authoritative in a given profession or field will be called on to give lectures; they do a poor job, because they present their logical analysis of the topic, period—no matter what the audience and the occasion. They act as though there is an ideal lecture on their topic, which has universal appeal to all audiences, and they need only find that lecture.

Another problem is that untrained public speakers often want to present everything that led to their own understanding of the question, and since they do not know where to begin in cutting down the information, they find time limits frustrating. "You just can't do justice to this topic in one hour," they may say.

A good public speech requires that the speaker take the results of an analysis of a topic and skillfully adapt it to a specific audience and occasion. For the study of public speaking, therefore, the second phase of analysis is of utmost importance. In the second stage, you can turn your attention to analyzing the audience according to the recommendations in the next chapter (Chapter 12), and you plan how to adapt and arrange the material for the needs of your particular audience.

KEY IDEAS CHAPTER 11

• In our culture the public speech is an established communication transaction with well-understood patterns of general usage.

• The model of public speaking consists of the speaker, the audience, the occasion, the topic, and the speech.

• The speech results from the speaker's dynamic adaptation of topic, ideas, and purpose to the audience and occasion.

• The ideal communication event is one in which the speaker skillfully adapts ideas, delivery, and language to the audience to achieve his or her purpose.

• The first step to success as a speaker is careful speech preparation.

• Your planning begins with the selection of a general topic.

• After you have a topic you should gather information relating to it.

• Once you have sufficient information, you should make an analysis of the topic.

• A creative analysis is important to understanding a topic and the result of the four-phase creative process of *preparation, incubation, illumination,* and *verification.*

• You can discipline your creativity by developing systematic work habits, such as working on a regular schedule at a specific time and place.

• The basic building blocks for messages consist of a point to be proved and the material that supports, explains, or illustrates it.

• A message can be too brief, because points that are not explained or illustrated are hard to understand.

• As part of the analysis of the topic, you should fit the message units together to form a coherent account of the topic of your speech.

• Logic is the process of drawing conclusions from one or more points.

• Decisions based on careful inferences from evidence are often better than those made solely on the basis of the persuasive power of personality and suggestion.

• One common logical fallacy is to assume that because one event followed another the first caused the second.

• Other common logical fallacies include arguing in a circle and being inconsistent or contradictory.

• A good speech requires that the speaker take the results of a careful analysis of a topic and skillfully adapt it to a specific audience and occasion.

SUGGESTED PROJECTS

1 • For a five-day period take out a few minutes each day and, aiming only for speed, write down 10 topics that could be used for speeches in your class. When you have a list of 50, go through it critically and check off those that you might be able to use.

2 • Write 10 statements illustrating good points to serve as the topic sentence of a basic message unit. Make sure each statement is phrased as a simple declarative sentence.

3 • Select the best topic from your list for a five- to eight-minute persuasive speech. Gather information relating to the topic and make an analysis of the material in which you discover a central thesis, main subpoints, and how the subpoints relate to one another and to the central idea.

SUGGESTED READINGS

Bettinghaus, Erwin P. *Message Preparation: The Nature of Proof.* Indianapolis: Bobbs-Merrill, 1966.

Mills, Glen E. *Message Preparation.* Indianapolis: Bobbs-Merrill, 1966.

Walter, Otis M., and Robert L. Scott. *Thinking and Speaking.* 4th ed. New York: Macmillan, 1979.

AUDIENCE ANALYSIS
CHAPTER 12

A substantial portion of your planning time for any public speech should be given to an analysis of the audience and the situation. A good public speaker is not self-centered or message-centered, but *audience-centered.*

Audience-centered speakers make all their final planning decisions in terms of their analysis of the listeners. Indeed, the art of interpersonal communication as well as the art of public speaking is the adaptation of ideas, world view, information, and arguments to a listener, to several listeners (a small group), or to many listeners (an audience). Let us say that three speakers have essentially the same information to present to an audience. Consider the three ways they might go about preparing the speech. One might be mostly speaker-centered and give a lecture in which his nonverbal cues indicate that he is worried about how he looks, how his voice sounds, and how his gestures are affecting the audience, and seems concerned that his fingernails are clean. His verbal expressions might indicate he is sure of his own intelligence and superiority and feels he has worked up the material of the speech brilliantly, has accomplished many things, knows many great people personally, and is very important indeed. (Doesn't he sound charming?)

A second speaker might be mostly message-centered and give an obviously laboriously prepared lecture filled with difficult-to-follow statistical information and references to events and people unknown to the audience, all put together in language more suitable for a scholarly journal than a busy college audience.

A third speaker might be audience-centered; she delivers essentially the same information as the other two but uses language that is clear to the audience, supports her ideas with examples that tie into the audience's experience, and holds her hearers' attention by showing how what she is saying relates to their wants, hopes, dreams, heroes, and villains. The essential difference between the first two and the last of our hypothetical lecturers is that the last is skillful in the art of communication.

Audience-centered speakers understand that information has to be adapted to the listener and that the techniques discussed throughout this book are tools to use in adapting ideas to people. They know about hypothetical examples and how they can use these examples to arouse the listener's interests. They know what the selection of names for people and things means in terms of suggestion, and they choose their words carefully with the audience in mind. They know about dialect's relation to classes of society, geography, race, and ethnic backgrounds and understand how their own dialect and their own use of standard and nonstandard grammar will affect the people in their audience. They understand the importance of public dramas in which the members of the audience are most likely to participate; they think about their probable heroes and villains and adapt their remarks to all these things. They consider every element of their speech in terms of the people who will be hearing it and the occasion when they will be hearing it. In the parlance of advertising, audience-centered speakers think always in terms of what it (the audience) will or will not *buy*.

GENERAL FEATURES
OF AN AUDIENCE
FOR A PUBLIC SPEECH

People gathered in a large group to hear a public speech respond differently than they would in two-person conversations or even small discussion groups. Because one person is the center of attention and the primary source of messages, and because a large group of people play the role of receiver, the dynamics of the situation are changed in several important ways.

The social pressure of 4 or 5 people is strong, but the power of 50 or 100 is much greater, and when thousands of assembled people stand up or shout, the influence of the crowd upon any individual is immense. Have you ever been part of a large audience at a football game, a student demonstration, a religious revival, when the crowd began to groan or shout or chant, and felt the emotional impact of thousands of voices moved by a common feeling or emotion?

The audience responds to various details of communication in a fashion that differs in some regards from the more casual and informal interpersonal speech-communication situations. The larger the audience, the more likely it is to expect an elevated style of language from the speaker. The keynote speaker at a political convention generally uses a more careful and formal speech style (and is expected to do so by the audience) than the same politician uses when she is talking over a strategy move with five of her staff members in her hotel room.

The larger the audience, the more it expects and demands that the speaker appeal to the so-called "higher" motives of human beings. The new president of the United States giving an inaugural address is expected to appeal to the better nature and the more unselfish motives of the American people. President John F. Kennedy said in his inaugural address, "Ask not what your country can do for you—ask what you can do for your country." His statement was in line with the expectations for the occasion as well as for the vast size of the television audience. If the president were to express similar sentiments in the same lofty style in a meeting with an assistant and three leaders of an antipoverty group lobbying for legislation to guarantee an annual income for everybody, he might well get, and deserve, a scornful laugh. On the other hand, the speaker at a high school commencement would receive an outraged reaction from much of his audience if he said he knew the seniors were not interested in a lot of pious baloney from him, that all they wanted was to get out of the auditorium, out of their robes, and into their cars to head for the nearest pot party or beer bust to get stoned out of their heads in celebration of the end of their four miserable years in high school, and that he, for one, thought they had the right idea.

The larger audience enjoys a rosy picture of the world and humanity, whereas the same message in a group of one or two people in a casual setting causes embarrassment or laughter. By the same token, the toughheaded recognition of basic desires that is appropriate to small groups of people sounds crude and disgusting in large assemblies.

One of the reasons we predict the continued importance of public speeches to large groups is that such speeches provide one of the few experiences in our culture in which people expect and get messages about heroes with high motives and where they are appealed to on the basis of their better nature. No matter how shoddy the community or how crude the general mode of conduct, people require some sense of worth and significance. The appeal to the better nature of the audience is a high form of flattery and is a source of pride and significance. Aside from the speech to a large audience, the only other major source of mass communication is television, and it does not provide many rosy depictions of life and of the community. The predominant style of the newscast and the television documentary, with few exceptions, is the style of the inside dopester (a person who has all the inside information). Television journalists tend to cut all public figures down to size and point out that important people are not larger than life, but ordinary people just like the rest of us, maybe even a little worse in some regards. The general tone of the story presented on television is factual, and what the tone presents as fact is tinged with skepticism about high motivations; the reporters appear to be continually searching for shoddy or unethical behavior. Saints are not dramatic; sinners, on the other hand, make good news copy.

ANALYZING A SPECIFIC AUDIENCE

While the audiences of public speeches share many similarities, each audience is also unique. The first question a skilled public speaker asks about a given audience is: How much alike are the audience members in terms of background, experience, interests, and attitudes? If all the audience members at least resemble the typical member on important features related to the speaker, the topic of the speech, and the occasion, the problem for the speaker is clear and can be handled directly. If the audience members are greatly diverse, the problem becomes much more difficult, and the speaker may have to seek some broad and abstract common ground or some overriding goal that can in some way unite such a varied group.

A speaker may start by finding out the composition of the audience in terms of such obvious, but often important, qualities as age, sex, socioeconomic class, race, ethnic background, religion, and occupation. Not all factors are always important. For many speeches, the audience's age may be irrelevant, but for other situations, it may be crucial. We noted in Chapter 3 that dialects reflect social structure, and so a speaker planning to adapt language and grammar to his or her audience would need to know if the members were primarily from the working class in an inner city or from an upper-middle-class suburb, if they were predominantly Mexican-American, black, Native American, or white.

A speaker often adapts to an audience by selecting an appropriate example or analogy to clarify a point, and if the audience is composed of farmers and their families, he selects different example than he would if the listeners are members of the American Medical Association.

More important, often, than the general information about age, sex, and social economic background are the audience's attitudes and interests. A person planning a persuasive speech in behalf of more funds for state-supported community colleges would like to know if the audience is generally in agreement that community colleges ought to be supported, or hostile to paying more taxes for colleges, or interested but undecided, or apathetic to the whole question. Likewise, she would benefit from knowing how many of the audience members hold attitudes toward her position that are friendly, hostile, undecided, or apathetic.

A speaker making a thorough analysis of his audience finds that specific details are vital; the general features of the audience provide only hints that help when making a more complete study. The speaker with the time and opportunity to study the audience and the occasion would do well to explore their rhetorical visions of the issue.

As we saw in Chapter 6, a *rhetorical vision* is an angle on events that makes sense out of them. It consists of a cluster of interpretative scripts in which human beings, fictitious characters, and supernatural or other forces are personified and proceed to enact a series of actions that explain why things happened as they did. Events are often complicated and chaotic. People dislike a senseless world, so they try to find an explanatory pattern within the chaos. One way to provide an explanation is to portray the events in terms of human dramatic action; you look for the "good guys" and the "bad guys."

As we write this there are American hostages in the embassy in Iran. Undoubtedly much of what happened in Iran when the hostages were taken and in the subsequent developments was accidental, unplanned, and confusing to those involved as well as to the American public. What people did was to select characters such as the Shah, the Ayatollah Ruhollah Khomeini, Bani-Sadr, President Carter, and United Nations Secretary-General Kurt Waldheim and have them act out dramatic stories that explained what happened and why. They explained certain incidents as happening because President Carter did this, or did that, or the Ayatollah decided in this fashion, or that manner, or because the Shah had committed certain deeds, or because the Secretary-General had acted in order to accomplish some purpose. Depending on who you are, of course, certain of these people are heroes and others villains—same events, same people, but differing dramas: different rhetorical visions.

It is truly amazing how imaginative we can be when we write our interpretative scripts. It is equally unfortunate how quickly we assume that *our* rhetorical visions are the right, true, only valid ones. An interesting feature of our interpretative scripts is that different people can provide equally plausible stories that make sense out of the very same events but put a different slant on them. Recall the discussions on the highly individualized nature of one's perceptions in Chapter 7. You can usually find others who share your perceptions to some degree, however, and when several or many share an interpretative script about events, we say they are sharing a rhetorical vision; they agree about who the heroes are and who the villains are. Until you understand the individual nature of one's rhetorical visions, however, you will have difficulty trying to analyze your audience.

Assume that two students, one male, one female, meet in college and decide to begin living together. Some months later, they are involved in an automobile accident; the man is tagged for drunken driving. Only in the course of the investigation of the accident do the parents of both students learn they have been living together. The parents of the male develop an interpretative script in which he is the innocent victim and the woman is the corrupting influence. She has seduced their son, who left home for college as an upstanding, decent, admittedly somewhat gullible boy. The parents of the female student have an interpretative script that reverses the roles. As they see it, their daughter fell in with bad company, as personified by the no-good delinquent who moved in with her and introduced her to alcohol, dope, and who-knows-what-all. Undoubtedly the students involved, if asked, would come up with scripts differing from both their parents' and, in some ways, from each other's as well.

Suppose that the Russians invade a neighboring country such as Afghanistan or Yugoslavia. The mass-media stories suddenly focus the attention of the American people on these events. Why did the Russians do it? What does it mean for the United States? What does it mean for me? Will I have to register for a draft? go to war? be killed? We want to make sense out of events, and we listen to the various interpretative scripts provided by the President, by newscasters, by our family, and by our friends. There are some old familiar stories still around, which have been used by Americans to explain similar events; we recall these; they form a rhetorical vision that can be thought of as a cold war view of the events. In line with the cold war stories we could explain the invasion in terms of Russian communism out to foment international communism and conquer the world. The only way to stop such aggression is to be militarily strong and mentally tough. The invasion means that somebody must have failed either in strength or toughness. We could further explain the invasion in terms of a failure of nerve on the part of our president. Another way we could explain things would be in terms of a drama in which the leaders of the Russian government had fallen to fighting among themselves for power and a group of fanatical zealots, paranoid about bordering countries' allegiance, had gained control. Despite the best efforts of our wise and resolute president, these fanatical Russian leaders were causing the international difficulty. Which script would be that of the members of your class? Does some other script fit the audience better?

In addition to the rhetorical visions we form about events, we also have interpretative scripts to explain our own hopes and dreams and many times the hopes and dreams of groups, whole communities of people. Much has been made of the "American dream." The American dream is the drama in which a poor but talented, deserving, hard-working person can climb to success, no matter how humble his or her beginnings. People who believed in the American dream often came from foreign countries to the United States at great sacrifice and hardship and when they arrived in the new country worked hard, often under miserable conditions, to achieve success. Individuals may have personal scripts today much like the widely held American dream of the nineteenth century. You may day-dream that you are playing a hero's part and doing interesting and exciting things. All of us want our lives to matter. We want to be appreciated for what we are, for what we can do. The boy who dreams of being a big-league pitcher and sees himself striking out the opponents in an all-star game may practice long hours and live only to achieve his dream. The girl who wants to be a professional basketball player may spend hours shooting baskets in her driveway.

How can you make an audience analysis of the members' rhetorical vision as it relates to a topic for a speech? To illustrate, we will take the most difficult audience situation—one in which most members are hostile to your point of view. How would you go about making a script analysis in preparation for a persuasive speech to a hostile audience?

Suppose a classmate has made a speech against registering women for the military draft. The response of the class has been strongly supportive. You decide that although you may be the only person in the class who feels that way, your next speech will try to persuade the class members to sign a petition in favor of universal registration for women as well as men.

Start by asking, What is their level of understanding of the whole situation? Do they know the current status? Do they know what has already happened? Do they know what is being planned? Do they understand the machinery of registration? Do they know how other countries handle problems of defense and security? Do they understand how various governmental groups must approve a program before it can go into effect?

The preliminaries out of the way, you can raise the most important query regarding the nature of their vision, What is the source of their hostility? Generally, hostility is associated with change. As time goes by, circumstances alter, accidents happen, power shifts, crops fail, people fall ill, things go badly for individuals and groups. They experience a time of troubles. When people have troubles they grow upset, and if their problems continue, they may become frustrated. One response to the troubles and frustrations is to seek change.

As those seeking change gain publicity and apparent power, untroubled people may begin to feel threatened, for change is unsettling. In the case of registering women for the draft in the 1980s, the troubles began with developments in the Middle East, which some people interpreted as threatening the United States because the Russians might gain control of the important oil fields in that area. The script portrayed the best answer to such threats to be one in which President Carter was tough and mobilized the military forces of the country. Many who had felt comfortable previously, according to their personal plans to stay out of military service, suddenly could envision themselves drafted.

The hostile members of the audience are those most threatened and frustrated by the change. They are likely to be angry, but before they can funnel their emotions and begin to hate the bad guys they have to explain what is going on and attribute its causes to the behavior of people. We find it hard to hate an abstract idea or concept but easy to hate an individual.

In an interpretative script there is always an account of the forces that control the way things are going. The script may portray the cause of the trouble as being those who bear the brunt of the suffering, oddly enough. Think back: the Puritans who settled New England "wrote" scripts in which they brought their troubles on themselves. When they had difficulties, they assumed it was because they had sinned and God was letting them know that they had. They turned their attention inward at those times to see what they had been doing wrong so they could get right with God. If your female classmates interpreted the registration of women in terms of a drama in which women had brought the trouble on themselves by their demand for equal rights, they probably would not be very hostile to your speech. On the other hand, many times people turn the blame outward and focus their anger and hostility on outsiders. Hostile people are those whose interpretative scripts focus the blame on characters who are creating the trouble for them, often for personal gain or with malice aforethought.

In order to discover the root of the hostility, you can ask the following questions as a guide to an analysis of your audience members' scripts: What are their definitions of the time of troubles? What are the basic story lines of the script? Who or what caused the trouble? Who are the leading good people, the heroes of the scripts? What motivates the good people? Who are the leading bad people of the scripts? Are you or the institutions or agencies that you seem to represent among the villains? What motivates the bad people?

We all have scripts on matters that are important to us, and you have your own rhetorical vision to account for the troubles that brought up the issue of registration for women. As part of your preparation for such a speech, you should examine your own script and ask the same questions about it that you ask about the audience's vision.

Where do you find information that relates to the way individuals and groups in the audience interpret events? You can often find out a good deal about them by reading speeches, pamphlets, newspaper accounts, letters to the editor, and editorials, or by actual interviews with potential audience members. In the case of registering for the draft, those who are hostile to it usually use their interpretative scripts in expressing their hostility. If after the first speech a class member said, "I'd like to see us draft some middle-aged senators," you can begin to figure out the interpretative script of that individual. A person who says, "I will not register until the Equal Rights Amendment is passed" also reveals a lot about her rhetorical vision. On the other hand, if a member of the class said, "Phyllis Schlafly was right. I wonder what Gloria Steinem will say now," you would be alert to several conflicting scripts in your audience. Even though both groups might be against registering women, their rhetorical visions are opposites. Schlafly is a personality who symbolizes the women who are fighting the adoption of the Equal Rights Amendment, whereas Steinem is a symbol of those who are fighting for it. If you praise Steinem, you please one faction but irritate another.

If you take some time to talk to your classmates, if you learn to listen to them carefully, if you ask a few leading questions, you will often bring out their interpretative scripts. We have an emotional attachment to our favorite scripts. Because human beings and other characters are in conflict, we can empathize and identify, love and hate them and watch the outcome of their confrontations with suspenseful, involved interest.

Once you have made some estimate of where your audience members are likely to fall on the continuum, from those who want change immediately to those who are resisting it at all costs, you can make a specific estimate of how best to approach them.

What sort of person will these people be more likely to trust and believe? What can I say to get their confidence? What are the public dramas that excite and move these people? Who are the heroes of their group fantasies and public dreams? Who are their villains? What dramatic actions do they use to build a sense of community and purpose? What attitude do they take toward these lines of action? For example, if all the audience members participate in a public drama that casts the president of the United States into a heroic role, then the speaker who says that the president, whoever he is at the time, is a man of low morals, insincerity, and bad motives will find himself in trouble with that audience. On the other hand, if all the audience members participate in a common drama in which the president is cast as villain, a negative statement about him may draw a strong, positive response from the listeners. If the audience members are strongly divided in terms of their political fantasies so that some see the president as a sympathetic figure fighting villainous forces and others see him as a dark and evil personality, the speaker may well decide not to mention the president at all!

GATHERING INFORMATION ABOUT THE AUDIENCE

Often the experienced speaker knows what sort of information about the audience would be useful to her but does not have the resources to collect it. In those long-range and important campaigns of persuasion where the success or failure of a new product, the election of a candidate to major office, or the organization, recruitment, and administration of a social or political movement is at stake, the campaign planners generally have sufficient resources for elaborate formal surveys of their potential audiences.

Experts in persuasion have brought scientific marketing and polling techniques to a high state of perfection and proved usefulness. Most public-relations firms, advertising agencies, professional fund-raising companies, and experts in political campaigning and revolutionary organization know how to sample the audience, administer attitude tests or questionnaires relating to opinion, and discover what a target audience thinks about a product or an issue or a particular personality. Some of the public-opinion polls publish their results in newspapers, and even speakers with little time or money can find out how various age groups with various educational backgrounds are currently responding to such general questions as "How well do you think the president has been doing?" When money is available, pressure groups often take their own polls to discover audience attitudes.

Sometimes the main themes of a persuasion campaign are pretested by showing samples of the persuasive material to people, who indicate their reactions by pressing buttons on special monitoring machines or answering questionnaires.

We mention these elaborate and expensive techniques of audience analysis mostly to show how far the art has been developed beyond the mere collection of information about age, sex, and geographic origin. Most of us do not have the resources needed to use these sophisticated audience-survey techniques; yet we can often acquire useful information quickly and cheaply. While the following example is hypothetical and exaggerated, it contains elements that resemble the speech situations in which you might find yourself. In this instance we are dealing with a speaker analyzing an audience that is more likely to be bored than hostile.

Professor Gilbert Johnson, our example, teaches at State University. He has been a lifelong student of the process of eutrophication (too much plant food in a lake causing a lush growth of water plants which, in turn, decay in the late summer sucking the oxygen out of the water). When ecology became an important issue, Johnson suddenly found his specialty popular with the general public. He won several awards and then attracted national notice on a television program. Soon he found himself in great demand as a speaker around the country.

Unfortunately, Professor Johnson's previous speaking experience had been in lecturing to classes of students who were already, at least to some degree, interested in the subject and willing to listen to a detailed, solid presentation. He found his public audiences growing restless, coughing, even dozing off. Gradually, over a period of months, and with the help of a fellow faculty member knowledgeable in speech communication, Johnson discovered that his problem was one of audience adaptation. He began to change his approach and in a while was getting standing ovations and receiving more invitations to speak than he could comfortably accept. (And here the authors indulge in some fantasizing about the value of their field, their careers, and this book!)

Back to Professor Johnson. He has just accepted an invitation to give a speech entitled "Eutrophication and What We Can Do About It" for the Sandy Hill City Commercial Club's bimonthly luncheon. He immediately sends his research assistant to the campus library. He brings back a pad of notes about Sandy Hill City and its surrounding county, Goodwin. The assistant found that the main industry includes the gravel pits and stone quarries south of town; a cement factory has the second most important town payroll. Sandy Hill City is one of the oldest settlements in the state and is the site of the Goodwin County Historical Society Museum, which contains, among other things, the personal effects of the town's most famous son, Brigadier General Allan Snyder, World War I ace of aces and leading proponent of the development of air power prior to World War II. Armed with this information and various devices he has learned about audience adaptation, Johnson begins his speech to the Commercial Club as follows:

"Eutrophication and What We Can Do About It." (He smiles.) I guess the first thing we can do about it is define it. (Audience chuckles.) I will define it in a minute, but first I'd like to share some of my thoughts with you as I was flying here over the lush farmlands of the central part of the state. I think far too often those of us living in cities forget the contribution the farmers of counties like Goodwin and the thriving towns like Sandy Hill City make to our economy and our quality of life. The countryside was beautiful, fertile, tilled—productive. I could see this as we landed. And as we taxied up to the Goodwin County airport terminal (which is, I was surprised to discover, a remarkably handsome facility, the newest in the five-county area, I'm told), I was impressed by the thriving bustle at the airport. The growth and power of this nation is made up of the dozens of cities such as Sandy Hill City.

When my taxi drove north toward the downtown area from the airport, I was struck by the immense size of the Terrara gravel pits. I asked the driver to pull in so I could get out and look at them. Producing, as they do, 35 percent of the gravel and crushed rock used in this state, the Terrara gravel pits make a real contribution to the entire state's economy and progress and really put Sandy Hill City on the map.

When we started driving toward town again, we had no sooner gotten under way than we came upon the imposing buildings of the Snyder Cement Works, and I suddenly recalled the name of Allan Snyder, World War I flying ace and far-seeing statesman in the air force—a native son. I had a little time left before I was due at the hotel, so I asked the driver to take me by the Goodwin County Museum. . . .

In the real world, most audiences would consider this much over-done; still, it demonstrates that our professor could find out a great deal about his Commercial Club audience in a short period of time; he combed the public sources of information (libraries, newspapers, and the like) and he allowed some time in the area to talk to the natives themselves before he was to speak.

Often when we are asked to give a speech, we can learn about the audience we will address simply by interviewing the person who contacts us to make the talk. This person will probably be able to tell us about the room or auditorium where we will speak, about who will attend and what they will expect. As we gain experience speaking to various sorts of audiences, we develop an awareness of what is expected from us in various speaking situations. A PTA meeting in a large urban school presents one kind of audience; a PTA meeting in a suburb presents another kind of audience—similar in many ways, different in some others. The luncheon meeting of a businesspeople's service club is a different audience than a social-business dinner of the same group.

Our best advice, therefore, is to remember that there are many sources of information about audiences and you should collect as much information as you can. Further, you should give public speeches whenever and wherever you can if you want to develop skill in audience analysis and adaptation; by so doing you will gain a personal knowledge about varied audiences, how they respond to you, and how you adjust to control their response. If you have the chance to give a speech to your class, set aside enough time to study your classmates as members of an audience. If you focus on them as potential members of an audience, you will find that you know a lot about them simply from interaction with them as you go to and from the classroom, from class participation, and from discussions. Think of them as individuals in a real audience rather than as "Just our speech-communication class." Try to think through their response to you, quite objectively, and plan and rehearse your speech keeping your specific audience in mind. Adapt your examples, analogies, evidence, and positive and negative suggestions to these people—these individuals collected at a particular time to hear you. Pay particular attention to the analysis of their rhetorical visions.

When giving a public speech, you will often have to work with less complete and precise information about the listeners than you can have when you are speaking in an interview or small group situation. As a public speaker, you seldom get as much feedback from the audience about how well your messages are comprehended and how they are evaluated as you can get in less formal communication situations. At the same time, however, you do not need as much specific feedback from larger audiences, because the public speaker can use broader strokes and get the desired response with less carefully adjusted messages. A member of a large audience adjusts her listening to react to someone talking to "us" rather than just to "me". She thus does not expect the same person-to-person adjustment she would demand if you were engaged in a conversation.

While we live in an age of electronic communication, a time in which intimate and informal conversation is prized and common, we also live in a culture that uses the formal public speech for many important occasions and purposes. The complete communicator, in the present age of increased need for quality interpersonal communication, also needs to know about audiences for public speeches and about how to adapt his or her ideas to them.

KEY IDEAS CHAPTER 12

• A good public speaker is audience-centered.

• Excitement and emotional responses are contagious in a large crowd; the audience response affects the individual listener.

• The larger the audience, the more it appreciates an elevated style of speaking and appeals to higher motives.

• Public speeches fill one's need to celebrate the better side of one's nature and community.

- Television, with its emphasis on shoddy and unethical behavior, is a poor medium for building community-sustaining myths.
- An important question for a speaker is "How diverse is the audience in its attitudes toward my position?"
- More important, often, than the general information about age, sex, and socioeconomic background are the audience members' rhetorical visions.
- If you want to adapt your ideas to your audience, it is a great help if you can analyze their rhetorical vision.
- We can most easily understand events if we see them acted out by people who symbolize complex institutions, organizations, and movements.
- An interesting feature of our interpretative scripts is that a number of plausible stories can account for the same events while putting a very different slant on them.
- Script analysis provides an excellent guide to audience adaptation.
- Begin a script analysis by asking about the audience members, "What is their level of understanding? How interested, supportive, or hostile are they to my topic?"
- The script analysis can reveal the heroes and villains of the audience's rhetorical vision as well as their interpretation of who or what is causing things to happen.
- Remember, there are many sources of information about audiences, and you should collect as much as you can.

SUGGESTED PROJECTS

1 • Assume that a visiting speaker asks you to brief him about his probable audience. Analyze students at your school. Identify their heroes, villains, and dreams, as well as their general interests and attitudes.

2 • Pick some city or town within 100 miles of your school and analyze its chamber of commerce as an audience for a speech, to be made by a student, concerning student attitudes today toward business as a career. What sources would you use in informing yourself about this audience?

3 • Select a topic for a persuasive speech suitable for a class assignment. Make a script analysis of the various rhetorical visions that your classmates have in regard to the topic.

SUGGESTED READINGS

Clevenger, Theodore, Jr. *Audience Analysis.* Indianapolis: Bobbs-Merrill, 1966.

Eisenson, Jon, J. Jeffery Auer, and John V. Irwin. *The Psychology of Communication.* New York: Appleton-Century-Crofts, 1963.

Jeffrey, Robert C., and Owen Peterson. *Speech: A Text with Adapted Readings.* 3d ed. New York: Harper & Row, 1980.

ORGANIZATION
CHAPTER 13

QUALITIES OF A WELL-ORGANIZED SPEECH

People who have not studied public speaking are likely to have only a vague notion of what constitutes "organized material" according to the ideal model of that communication process. If they can outline a message when they listen to it, or if a speaker presents a message in the form of an outline, they often assume that it is organized. Indeed, many students keep their notebooks in outline format, and many business and professional people present their material in outline form; it *looks* organized. Unless a speaker is trained, however, his material usually is actually disorganized. All you have to do to outline is to list and number some points. You can list points with numbers and letters even though the ideas do not fit logically together. Sound organization, on the other hand, requires more than just listing and using numbers and letters to label items on the list. A well-organized spoken message must have the qualities of unity, coherence, relevance, conciseness, and comprehensiveness.

A good public speech has *unity*. A critic can tell if the speech is unified by looking for a central idea to which each part of the speech relates. Often a speaker helps unify the speech by stating and highlighting the central theme in a way that makes it stand out clearly for the listener. When this is done well, almost all the listeners can later recall the speaker's main point. If the speaker does not state the central theme in so many words, the speech may still be unified if the subpoints are arranged and presented in such a way that the listener is led to figure out the main conclusion by inference.

A well-organized public speech is *coherent*. Coherence refers to the way the parts of the speech cluster or hang together. Each part of a good speech relates to *every* other part in a way that reveals some clear design. A coherent speech is like a jigsaw puzzle of a picture of, say, a horse; when it is properly put together, the resulting picture is unmistakably a horse. A speech that lacks coherence is like the puzzle when it is only partially put together, with a portion of the head completed but much still missing, and with other parts spread over the table in jumbled fashion.

A well-organized public speech contains main points with supporting information and evidence that clearly and directly *relate to the central theme*. The speaker who feels that something not obviously related to the central idea is nonetheless important and relevant should explain this reasoning to the audience. Speakers who organize a public speech poorly often include much material that is not related to the topic under discussion. When you are first preparing a message you may "free-associate" ideas and list them just as they come to mind. You may daydream along so that one idea follows another, one image triggers another, one story causes you to think of another, one experience reminds you of another. You may be tempted to include these materials in your speech plan because they interest you at the moment. Rambling and disjointed speeches, however, are undesirable. Everything you say should have clearly understood relevance to your central theme.

A well-organized speech is *concise* in the sense that it does not contain a high proportion of repetitiveness. In a good speech the speaker deals with each point in enough detail for the purposes of the situation and occasion and then does not deal with it again except for emphasis in summaries, transitions, introductions, and conclusions. A common fault in the organization of a public speech is for a speaker to deal with a topic, drop it, take up another topic, perhaps a third, and then return to the first point again. The beginner is learning good technique when he or she can cut a poorly organized message into parts and paste it together again so that all statements about a point are put together and unnecessary repetitions are eliminated. Keeping your speech concise for the listener helps the listener come away with your ideas intact, as you hoped to present them.

A well-organized public speech is *comprehensive* in the sense that it deals with the leading topics relating to its central theme. Of course the speech's comprehensiveness must be evaluated in relation to the audience, the occasion, and the amount of time that the speaker has to discuss the central idea. A skillful speaker will restrict the scope of the speech so that the topic can be dealt with in sufficient detail in the time available. A less skilled person often works out a central theme that is vague or too broad and must then deal with the topics in abstract fashion or leave out so many important ideas that the speech, as heard, is sketchy and lacking in completeness. The public speaker who covers the stated topic as thoroughly as the context warrants has produced a speech with sufficient comprehensiveness.

CONSTRUCTING AN ORGANIZED SPEECH

The speaker constructing a message for an audience has to do three main things in order to organize the speech for maximum effect: *select* the material to include, *arrange* the items in some order, and *proportion* the items by deciding how much time to give to each point.

Although the speech construction step involves many concrete problems relating to the details of the nuts-and-bolts aspects of fitting a speech together, a speaker still profits from applying our advice about creativity to these matters. Even though you have a general theme for a speech and have analyzed it, you will need to develop a clearly worded central idea for each specific occasion. The central idea for a persuasive speech should be worded as a positive suggestion: "Buy this Bearcat now!" "Picket City Hall tomorrow!" The central idea for a lecture or an informational presentation should be a simple declarative sentence. A central idea for a lecture might be: "I will explain a good basic model of the communication process."

Vaguely worded central ideas, such as "I will tell you something about communication," are poor guides to use in organizing a speech. Complex sentences that contain several ideas, such as "I will explain a basic model of communication and discuss the nature of communication theory," are likewise troublesome, because they require a speaker to keep *two* main ideas before the audience.

Once the speaker has picked a specific and clear central idea for her speech, she can select material that is appropriate for her audience and fits logically under her central idea.

The next task in organizing a speech is to arrange the material in some order. As a rule, the speaker should stick to the one kind of arrangement only. Later in the chapter we will discuss three important patterns of arrangement in greater detail, and in later chapters, on informative and persuasive speaking, we will provide additional ways to order the points in a speech.

Deciding how much time to give to each point is a matter of judgment, depending on the total amount of time allotted to the speech and on the audience's attitude and knowledge. The speaker has to think carefully about the arguments to be presented, deciding which is the most important, what material is familiar to the audience, and what is unfamiliar and must be more fully developed.

A good speech has a beginning, a middle, and an end. The beginning is called an *introduction*, the middle is called the *body* of the speech, and the end is called the *conclusion*.

A good introduction catches the audience's attention, arouses and holds its interest, and lets it know what the speech is to be about. Because a speech is different from a theme or essay in that the speaker is talking directly to people sitting in front of him, he must spend some time at the beginning of his remarks just getting everybody's attention. The listeners need a chance to size up the speaker as a person, to get acquainted with him.

The body of the speech contains the main points that make up the message proper. If, instead of speaking, you were writing an article about the same material, the bulk of the article would be similar to the information contained in the body of a speech.

The conclusion of a speech is a brief comment that rounds off the message and gives the audience a feeling that you have finished. A conclusion tends to be a summary of the main ideas in a speech, an appeal for action or reaction, or a summary plus an appeal.

A speaker further achieves unity by clearly and logically relating all major subpoints to the central theme and to one another. You can explain the relationship among ideas to your audience by telling them how you will arrange the main subpoints. "I will begin by . . . Next, I will . . . And, finally, I will . . ." "First I will discuss . . . Second, I will deal with . . . Third, I will . . . " "I want to examine two main questions with you this evening. The first question is . . . The second question is . . ." You can also indicate when you have completed your comments on one point and are moving on to a new part of your speech. "So in summary, my answer to the first question is . . . , but remember that I said the answer to the first question is not enough. We must also answer the question . . ." Finally, you can indicate relationships among points by summarizing what you have said and pointing out to your listeners what you have so far accomplished in terms of your overall plan. "We have now seen that, first, . . . and second, . . . With this evidence I have proved what the lawyers call a prima facie case—that is, a case that, unless answered, gives you enough evidence to render a verdict of 'yes.' But I promised you more than a prima facie case. Let's look now at the most important evidence. . . ."

Transitions are brief comments composed of statements or questions or both that lead the hearer from the point just finished to the next point in the speech. Transitions tie the various points of a speech together.

Inexperienced speakers feel the need for transitions but have a tendency to use one or two words over and over again. Novice speakers say "and another thing" and "another point," or overuse the word *next* or *also*. The good speaker has to learn to use varied transitions that summarize the points just made, forecast the point coming next, or better yet, both summarize and forecast.

The speaker who makes comments such as the above helps the listeners see the overall structure of the speech and understand how the details fit together into a meaningful "big picture." The next time you watch a television drama, notice how the director arranges the shots. She will often begin with an establishing shot—that is, a picture of the larger scene—so you can understand how the actors are arranged and how they fit into the larger context. She may then cut to a closer shot of several actors, and cut again to a closeup picture of one actor's face as the scene builds to a dramatic climax. At a transition point, she will often use another longer shot to once again establish context before moving the camera to more detailed closeups. Such "big picture" establishing shots are useful for the speaker as well as the television director. You must verbally and nonverbally unify your speech for your listeners throughout.

PATTERNS FOR ORGANIZING PUBLIC SPEECHES

The three-part division of a speech into an introduction, body, and conclusion is a good standard way to frame your remarks, but it does not help you much in selecting and arranging the main points, supporting ideas, and transitions in the body of the speech. Over the years public speakers have discovered a number of recurring patterns that have proved useful in organizing speeches.

If you learn some of the "tried and true" ways of arranging the points in a speech, you may be able to use them in planning a speech of your own. At least you will have a place to start. You might buy a coat from the rack in a clothing store and wear it immediately. The coat is cut to a standard pattern, and it will fit you more or less well. You might buy a coat cut to a standard pattern but have a tailor alter it, modifying it to fit you better. And finally, you might have a tailor measure you and design a one-of-a-kind coat to your taste, made out of your chosen material. As a speaker, you are in somewhat the same situation as when you buy a coat in that you can use a good standard outline and often end up with a well-organized speech that fits the audience and occasion more or less well; or you can alter a standard outline and make it fit better; or you can design a unique organizational pattern tailored especially for your specific audience and occasion.

We recommend that for important speeches, you try to alter one of the three very basic patterns that follow or that you design a unique outline tailored for your audience alone. An understanding of these three most important and widespread patterns will certainly help you get started in the practice of organizing public speeches.

State your case and prove it

The state-your-case-and-prove-it pattern of organization is the basic, straightforward development where you "tell them what you are going to tell them, tell them, and then tell them what you told them." You begin with an introduction, state your central thesis and the points that you will develop in support of it, take up each point in turn, and end with a summary.

State-Your-Case-and-Prove-It Pattern
I. Introduction.
II. Overview, consisting of central idea and listing of points.
III. Development of each point.
IV. Conclusion, consisting of a summary.

The pattern of stating a case and proving it is a good one for a speaker dealing with a familiar and much-discussed controversial topic. When a person talks on a well-worn issue, the audience members probably know a good deal about the pros and cons of the subject. The speaker dealing with a much-discussed issue does not need to explore the topic comprehensively and go over as much background information as is often necessary with a fresh topic. If you are dealing with such a topic, you might well just state your position and support it in line with the basic pattern.

Because of the elementary nature of the pattern, you can use it in situations where you have little or no time to prepare your remarks. Have you ever received an honor and been in a situation where, to celebrate the occasion, people began to yell at you to give a speech? "Speech, speech" is a familiar call. Often you can shrug off such a request, and people are good-natured about it and let you off the hook, but sometimes you really must respond. Sometime you may be told before you sit down at a banquet, for instance, that after the meal the sponsors of the banquet would like to have you "say a few words." The technical name for the speech you give when you are asked to say a few words on very short notice is an *impromptu speech.* You can remember a variation of the basic pattern, which is ideal for impromptu situations, and by carefully following the directions for each step of the speech, you can end up with a well-organized speech on the spur of the moment.

The impromptu speaking pattern we recommend consists of the following four steps; you will notice they are essentially a version of the basic state-your-case-and-prove-it pattern:

Impromptu Pattern
I. Begin with an illustration.
II. Give an overview consisting of the central idea and listing of points.
III. Follow through (cover each point in turn).
IV. Recap, with a twist (conclusion consisting of summary).

By memorizing the key words *illustrate, overview, follow through,* and *recap,* you can recall the directions for quickly organizing your remarks.

You begin the impromptu pattern with an example, preferably a narrative with human interest that illustrates the central idea you want to make. You do not set the stage for the story or example in any way; you simply begin to tell it:

"In the Old West, when they got civilized and stopped hanging the socially undersirable citizens from the nearest tree, they turned to finding a long, thin fence rail, and they'd tie them to it, and then they'd form a long procession and run 'em out of town on a rail. One such individual gained notoriety by asserting, 'If it wasn't for the honor of the occasion, I'd just as soon walk.'"

If you have some ability to dramatize the story, audience members will become interested. Furthermore, they will become curious as to why you are telling the story and what you are driving at. You catch their attention, arouse their interest, and make them want to continue listening.

The second step of the impromptu pattern consists of a statement that leads easily to the central idea of your speech. You then give an overview (state what you will talk about) by listing the two or three points that you will talk about:

"You really surprised me just now by making me team captain. But I know what it takes to be captain of this team, and I feel a little like the old westerner. Let me tell you why. We can win the title this year, but to do so, we must do two things; first, it's our tradition that the team captain is the leader of the team, not a figurehead, *the leader;* and second, all of us will have to level with one another about any problems we have as a team."

In the third step of the impromptu pattern you take up each point in turn and comment on it, supplying the examples and evidence that come readily to mind.

The fourth step is to conclude the speech with a recap and a twist. The recap is a short reminder of each of the points, phrased in different words than you used when you first made them, and the twist is a surprise ending that makes the speech sound unified and rounded off. A good twist is to refer back to the opening example or story with a tie-in that again shows the relevance of the introduction, thus unifying the speech:

"If we do those two things, we can win the championship this year. If you are willing to do these two things, I will be willing to ride the narrowest, sharpest rail you can find. If you aren't willing to do these things, despite the honor, I would just as soon get off now."

The state-your-case-and-prove-it basic pattern of organizing a speech is simple but effective. It is an adaptable form, including the impromptu speech outline we used, and it is a straightforward, useful pattern for you to consider.

The problem-solving pattern

The problem-solving pattern is one in which the speaker describes a problem, discusses its causes, suggests possible solutions, and recommends a course of action most likely to solve the problem. In its simplest form the pattern consists of (1) a description of the problem, (2) an analysis of its causes, and (3) an explanation of the best solution. A useful variation is a pattern similar to the one that the philosopher-educator John Dewey introduced at the beginning of the twentieth century. Dewey presented an analysis of what he called *reflective thinking* and discussed the way the trained mind studies problems in the scientific laboratory. According to Dewey, reflective thinking is not random stream-of-consciousness thought, nor is it trial-and-error problem solving. When you daydream, your mind moves from image to image and does not focus on any specific problem. When you solve a problem through trial and error, you simply try everything that pops into your head, until finally you reach a solution. Reflective thinking, on the other hand, begins when someone has what Dewey called a *felt difficulty*—a disturbance of the environment or pattern of life that becomes so strong that the individual begins to work to try to do something about it. The person begins to search out the problem and find out what is causing the difficulty. As the individual's vague feeling of puzzlement and difficulty comes under rational analysis, the problem comes into focus and the pattern of reflective thinking begins. As the person gets a clearer picture of the problem, possible solutions come to mind. The individual postpones trying out the solutions, as would be the case in trial and error, and instead *reflects* upon each, weighing the solutions against one another in terms of the causes of the problem. After methodical and reasonable analysis, the individual tries what seems like the best solution, in an effort to relieve the felt difficulty.

Dewey's analysis provides a step-by-step, logical progression that a speaker can use in organizing the materials for a speech. The pattern is as follows:

Problem-Solving Pattern
I.   Introduction.
II. The nature of the problem.
   A. Definition of problem.
   B. Exploration of causes.
III. Listing of representative solutions.
IV. Examination of representative solutions.
V.   Selection of the best solution.

The problem-solving pattern is a particularly good one when the problem is complicated and the audience is hostile to the speaker's proposed solution, or when the problem is complicated and the audience is relatively unfamiliar with the facts of the situation. The pattern gives the listener an easy-to-follow and logical path through what might otherwise be a baffling and chaotic topic.

The problem-solving pattern encourages the listeners to adopt an objective, thoughtful attitude toward the speech, and this can help to disarm them of some of their emotionalism and prejudices. The speaker should adopt an appropriate tone in giving a speech in the problem-solving pattern. When the speaker says, "Let us explore the problem and see if we can decide what is causing it, and let us list all of the good solutions we can think of and compare them to see which is best," the openness of his approach should lead the audience members to follow along thoughtfully. One must be careful, however, when using the pattern, to adopt a scientific, objective manner and not use emotional or "loaded" language or any of the typical persuasive devices. Use matter-of-fact, direct language that conveys objectivity to the listener.

If you make a speech examining a number of possible solutions to a problem, and then eliminate all but the one you recommend, you will be following the natural tendency of much human decision making and problem solving. Research into the problem-solving dynamics of small task-oriented groups indicates that groups use this method in making decisions and solving problems. People tend to eliminate undesirable solutions first and let the decision emerge as the only remaining option.

Often they find it easier to decide which solutions they do *not* want to follow than to decide what they would prefer to do. The pattern of organization that eliminates the undesirable answers until the one best solution is left, is the *method of residues.*

The actuating pattern

The third and final pattern that we will consider in detail is another useful way to organize public speeches. When you organize a speech in this pattern you lead the audience members in a logical progression from arousing their interest to creating understanding to sharing in an interpretative script to acting in line with your recommendations. We call the pattern the actuating sequence. The actuating pattern consists of the following steps: (1) you begin with material that arouses the audience's interest, (2) you next demonstrate that they should be dissatisfied with the way things are going, (3) you move to an explanation of how best to gratify the need you have created in the second step, (4) you dramatize an interpretative script that envisions the way things will be if the audience follows your recommendation, and (5) you move them to action.

The fact that you cannot reverse the parts of a speech that is organized into the steps of the actuated sequence indicates its organic unity. The pattern is based on the psychology of consciousness raising or conversion. When people shift from one rhetorical vision to another, they begin with a feeling that something is not right with their world. They are restless and dissatisfied. At the point of dissatisfaction, communication that breaks up the old vision serves to set the stage for a new and more gratifying consciousness. Persuasive messages that dramatize a new rhetorical vision can provide a new pattern of self-actualization.

An attractive feature of the actuating sequence is that you can remember it easily by committing the five key words (*arouse, dissatisfy, gratify, dramatize, move*) to memory. When you need to develop a persuasive speech, you can think of each key word in turn and begin to draft a section of a speech aimed at that response. The end effect is a speech arranged in a proven effective psychological progression.

You might well want to draft your outline by asking the following questions about your audience: How can I arouse their interest? How can I make them dissatisfied by showing them the things that are wrong with their present situation? How can I show them that my solution will meet the problems and be gratifying to them? How can I dramatize an attractive future for them once they accept my solution? How can I move them to implement the plan?

Another good thing about the actuating pattern is that you can often eliminate some of the early steps if the audience is already highly interested in the topic and very dissatisfied. You can then simply remind them of your common problem and concern and move quickly to the gratification step.

Sometimes, of course, one speech is part of a whole campaign of persuasion. Much contemporary advertising is planned as a campaign. Revivalists often talk of a crusade, a campaign that is designed to create a total persuasive climate through the use of a large number of integrated messages, prayer meetings, public speeches, revival meetings, and sermons. If a speech is part of such an ongoing and elaborate campaign, a given speech might concentrate on arousing interest, and subsequent messages and speeches could take up the other steps in the actuating sequence.

The actuating pattern is best used to bring about change. The pattern is basically a persuasive one and usually includes both logical support and nonlogical support such as dramatizing, which generally arouses audience emotions.

HOW TO OUTLINE A SPEECH

We are going to conclude this chapter with a general sample speech outline that indicates one good way to plan a speech or presentation. Any speech you give is bound to have individual requirements that you will have to work out for yourself. This outline includes a wide column (to the left) in which you can comment about the communication techniques you plan to use to achieve your purposes. This method has proved useful to our public-speaking students over the years. It helps develop some objectivity about why you put a speech together in a particular way, and it helps develop a sense of control over material. Many beginning public speakers can dig out much material on a subject for a speech and can make a fair prediction about the probable response of their audience (the other members of the class), but when it comes to deciding what material to use, what to leave out, and how to order the material once they have decided to include it, they are lost without a model outline to follow.

The outline on the following pages is for a persuasive speech, but the same sort of outline can be used for all other forms of public speaking if you modify the content according to the kind of speech.

No one way to organize a speech guarantees its effectiveness. Everything that you learn in this course—about language usage and structure, audience-centered messages, and the many factors involved in persuasion—are vital factors in public speaking. Outlines can aid structure, but the individual art, the creativity, the fun of speechmaking comes when you make the *choices* of what will go into the outline.

To use the outline, start with the left-hand column. Write out what you plan to do. Put in some detail. Then in the right-hand column write a comprehensive outline of the content of your speech.

Introduction	I will begin by taking the audience into the future
I am starting with a	where they set their alarms at 6:00 A.M., in time to
science fiction	rush out when the gas stations open, so they can join
dramatization of the	the mile-long line to fill their tanks with $3-a-gallon
future, to catch the	gas—if there is any gas left.
attention of the audience	
and also to reveal that my	
speech will be about the	
energy crisis.	
This is my central idea.	Urge your representative and senator to support gas
	rationing.
Body	
Point 1	I. Our current energy crisis, particularly as it relates
	to petroleum products, poses a major problem for
	all of us, for
Supporting material	A. Our current laws allow
	shortsighted waste of gasoline.
	B. Our current laws will result in a
	crisis for our economy in the
	near future.
This is my transition	Clearly our present laws relating to the sale of gasoline
from point 1 to point 2	are intolerable. What is the answer? The best solution
	is gas-rationing legislation with teeth in it.
Point 2	II. Gas rationing is a good solution.
	A. Gas rationing can work,
	because [example of the way
	the new law would work].
	B. Gas rationing is fair, because
	[literal analogy of current
	situation with the plan for gas
	rationing].
This is my transition	Gas rationing is a workable solution to our present
from point 2 to point 3	petroleum energy crisis. What difference does a
	change in the law make to you? How do you stand to
	gain from change?
Point 3	III. Gas rationing will be beneficial to you, for
	A. It will assure you of a fair
	share of the available gasoline
	in the future.
	B. It will enable us to adjust our
	economy to a future of limited
	petroleum resources without a
	depression.

Conclusion

I will summarize the main points of my speech and make an appeal referring back to my example in the introduction of the miserable future without rationing, and I will dramatize a future where, if they accept my plan, they can drive into a station at any time and purchase their just ration of 50-cent-a-gallon gasoline.

KEY IDEAS CHAPTER 13

• People who have not studied public speaking are likely to have only a vague notion about how to organize material for a speech.

• If a public speech is unified, the listeners can usually recall the central idea and the main subpoints.

• In addition to being unified, a good public speech contains only relevant materials, concisely presented in a coherent and comprehensive pattern.

• A good speech has a beginning, a middle, and an end, usually called an *introduction, body* and *conclusion.*

• The body of a speech consists of points supporting a clear central idea, all tied together by good transitions.

• The state-your-case-and-prove-it pattern is the one in which you "Tell them what you are going to tell them, tell them, and then tell them what you told them."

• The problem-solving pattern is the one in which the speaker describes a problem, discusses its causes, examines possible solutions, and suggests a course of action.

• The method of residues is the pattern of organization in which the speaker lists a number of solutions and eliminates the undesirable ones, thus leaving the recommended one as the only remaining alternative.

• The psychological-progression pattern evolved from revival preaching and is well adapted to persuasive speeches.

• The psychological-progression pattern consists of the steps of arousing, dissatisfying, gratifying, dramatizing, and moving to action.

SUGGESTED PROJECTS

1 • Select a topic of some complexity that will require clear explanations in order for your audience to understand it. Develop a carefully planned speech outline for a five-minute informative speech on the topic. Use the model outline in the chapter as a guide.

2 • Select a topic of concern to you and, taking a controversial stand on the matter, develop a five- to eight-minute persuasive speech on the topic. Prepare a carefully planned speech outline to turn in to the instructor prior to giving your speech, as directed in this chapter or as modified by your instructor.

3 • Your instructor will have prepared a number of topics suitable for impromptu speeches. Draw three of the topics, pick any one, and return the other two. You will be allowed to step out of the classroom for five minutes to prepare your speech. Follow the directions for an impromptu speech outline in this chapter in preparing your talk.

SUGGESTED READINGS

Jeffrey, Robert C., and Owen Peterson. *Speech: A Text with Adapted Readings.* 2d ed. New York: Harper & Row, 1980.

Howell, William S., and Ernest G. Bormann. *Presentational Speaking for Business and the Professions.* New York: Harper & Row, 1971.

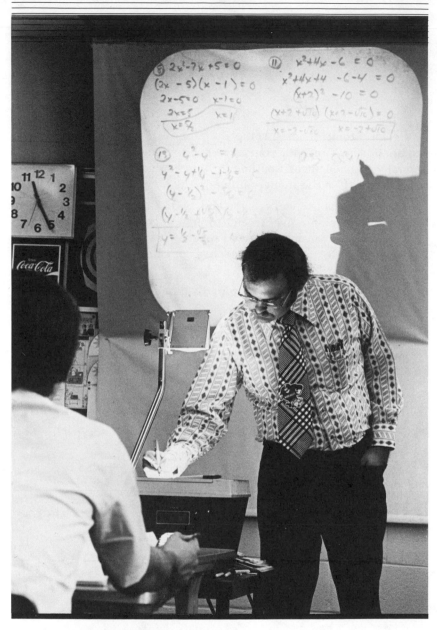

SUPPORTING MATERIAL
CHAPTER 14

Once you have adapted your basic analysis of the topic to a specific audience and occasion and organized an outline for your speech, you still need to amplify and develop your ideas with supporting material. One of the most important basic communication skills is the ability to find, invent, and refine supporting material that clarifies ideas and convinces the audience.

Two speakers can take the same basic speech outline and one can leave the audience confused and bored while the other can have them on the edges of their seats, interested, involved, and informed. While the power of individual personality and delivery would be a factor in such a situation, much of the difference would relate to the differing skills with which the two supported their basic points.

The beginning speaker often thinks of an idea and says it as best he or she can, but if an audience member asks for more information the beginner restates the idea, tries to rephrase it, or falls silent. Someone may ask, "Can you give me an example?" For many the request is confusing. What is an example? How can I find one? Or think of one? Or make one up?

We can learn the basic tools for supporting ideas and drill on their use. Such skills apply to all communication.

One good reason to study public speaking is that preparing messages carefully provides you with an opportunity to think about, try your hand at, and be coached in regard to such skills as using examples, analogies, and statistics to support ideas. These skills then transfer to the interpersonal and small-group setting.

In order to develop skills in supporting ideas, you need to learn the technical terms we use in discussing the rhetorical tools; you need to see some good models of the various devices; you need to try your hand at developing them; and you need some helpful evaluation and coaching of your efforts. In this chapter we provide the technical terms and descriptions of good models to follow.

The main tools you can use to support ideas relate to the high-fidelity transmission of information (the expository supporting material) and convincing the listeners that something is the case (the argumentative supporting material).

EXPOSITORY SUPPORTING MATERIAL

Specialists in communication have long debated the question of whether or not information is different from persuasion. Recall our discussion in Chapter 7 of perception and in Chapter 12 of the way groups of people come to share rhetorical visions, which they then think of as reality. Probably there is no such thing as neutral objective information. Still there are some important differences between understanding an explanation and accepting it. We might understand that someone is explaining an automobile accident as resulting from an evil eye, but we may not be persuaded that the explanation is a good one. At any rate whether you're primarily interested in transmitting information or in getting someone to follow your advice, you often need to get some points across so they are clearly understood.

We define *exposition* as the process of setting forth, spelling out, clearing up, making plain, and shedding light on. The speaker's basic expository tools are examples, analogies, and narratives.

Examples

One of the most important skills you should develop to improve your communication is the ability to recognize and use examples. What we call *examples* are sometimes also called *illustrations.*

An example is one (of a number of things) taken to show (the nature or character of) all. The example illustrates some important points about all the things like it. An example may also be an instance that illustrates the operation of a law or a general principle.

Earlier in the chapter we used examples to clarify abstract ideas. In discussing the notion that beginners often cannot use expository devices, we used the case of a student asked to provide an example. In drawing a distinction between understanding and acceptance of ideas, we used the example of a person understanding the explanation of an automobile accident but not believing it. Both of these examples were hypothetical, but you may also use real examples.

Real and hypothetical examples. When speakers use examples to make points clear, they may select an instance that actually happened, or may invent an example, much as an author makes up a story. When speakers use nonfictional accounts of actual events or people, they are using *real* examples. When they dream up a fictitious incident that might have happened, but in fact did not, they are using a hypothetical example.

Real examples are useful in making a point clear, but they may also be evidence to prove a point in an argument. If a person wants to prove that the smoking of marijuana does not necessarily lead to the use of heroin, he may submit as proof the real examples of a number of people who have smoked marijuana but have not used heroin. Hypothetical examples, on the other hand, are not proof, because if you were in an argument and made up a number of examples to support your side, another person could make up an equal number of examples to support the other side. Suppose one person argues that juvenile delinquency is caused by poverty and miserable living conditions in the inner city. "Take the case of Johnnie," he says, "growing up in the ghetto. Johnnie is much more likely to become delinquent than a child in the suburbs." "Not at all," answers the other person. "Take the case of rich Billy, whose parents have no time for him and who give him every material thing he wants instead of giving him enough love, time, guidance, and discipline." Both parties in such an argument can dream up make-believe characters such as Johnnie and Billy as long as they like and match hypothetical example with hypothetical example. When using real examples, however, the debaters can submit only actual happenings as evidence.

Real examples carry more weight, because they are factual and because the person in a conference, interview, group discussion, or public speech who explains ideas by using real examples gives her listeners the feeling that she is speaking from a firm basis of facts and that she is an expert.

We may have trouble using real examples, however, when we take part in informal talks and do not have notes with us. If a point comes up in a conversation or an interview and we need an example to make the idea clear, we may not remember the details of a real example and may not have time to look them up. Even when we have time to prepare for a public speech, we may search the library in vain for exactly the right example to make a point. We can tailor the hypothetical example to the needs of the audience, the point to be clarified, and the time available. Thus, although hypothetical examples are not evidence, they are a good way to make a point clear.

The artful use of examples. Why are examples so important to basic communication skills, no matter what the setting or the occasion? Examples are concrete and make broad principles and laws easy to hear, smell, see, taste, and feel; when we stop talking about the law of gravity and start using the example of the falling basketball, the listener can visualize the event and see how the law works in actual practice. Examples add interest to a message. A good example makes a difficult idea easier to understand. We enjoy the understanding that comes from seeing how or why something works. We like to be able to understand things, and so an example that brings understanding also brings interest.

People appreciate the skillful use of example. Most of us enjoy watching an expert perform. Even though we may not be good musicians, we probably enjoy watching and hearing a skillful pianist. Although we may not care much for baseball, we may enjoy watching a talented shortstop field ground balls. When a talented and skillful speaker uses a good example—one well suited to the listener, the occasion, and the point under discussion—we get a similar sense of interest and appreciation.

The use of examples is an art that can be acquired through practice. Any speaker can pick an example to clarify a given idea. A good speaker is able to pick an example that interests the listener and is within the listener's experience and level of understanding. By skillful use of examples she can connect even abstract, difficult ideas to the experience of the other person.

When you pick examples to clarify a point, you ought to be listener-oriented. A good speaker has a number of different examples available for illustrating the same point. He invents examples from different situations. The speaker who picks an example that interests the listener helps ensure the success of his attempts to inform. By selecting examples of different lengths, the speaker can make his comments shorter or longer. The speaker who has a good supply of examples can be guided by feedback and supply the listener with additional examples until he is sure he has been understood.

Suppose we wish to clarify the point we made in Chapter 3 that each person should carefully decide whether to learn the standard general American dialect if he does not already speak it. Suppose, too, that we know quite a bit about the people who will hear our speech. We know how old they are, whether they are male or female, what jobs they have, their hobbies, their social and economic class, and whether they are from the South or the North, from the city, the suburbs, or a rural area. We have available the following examples to clarify the point about the decision to learn a new dialect:

An actual person who is a network television announcer and grew up in Tidewater, Virginia

A hypothetical person who is an education major from Brooklyn and plans to teach in Brooklyn

An actual person who is a business major at Louisiana State University and speaks with a Cajun accent

An actual person who is a community-college student with no major as yet and who comes from a suburb in Los Angeles

An actual person who is a black star in the National Basketball Association, attended a Big Ten university, and was originally from a ghetto of New York City

A hypothetical person who is a Chicano from New Mexico and attends a community college there

An actual person who is from an aristocratic old family in North Carolina, is proud of her background, and is studying art

An actual person who is a militant black from an inner-city ghetto in Detroit, studying to be a social worker

Each of the above examples contains a great deal of information in addition to what we have described. Some are quite detailed and take longer to explain than others. Some are humorous, some serious, and some full of conflict. When we prepare to talk to a given group of people, we have to pick the example that seems best for this audience in this setting, at this time. Decide which of the above examples would be best for each of the following occasions:

A meeting of the Parent-Teachers Association in a wealthy suburb of Detroit

A meeting of the Parent-Teachers Association in an inner-city school in New
   York City
A speech-communication class in a Los Angeles College
A group of students at a high-school careers-day convocation in Atlanta
A meeting of the Black Student Union at a Big Ten university

Since examples can add interest and emotional tone to a message,
the speaker must consider the occasion as well as the audience when
selecting which examples to use. If a person plans to discuss a topic in an
informal two-person conversation over coffee in a cafeteria, she might use
a light, humorous example. If she plans to clarify the point in an important
presentation before a large group in a formal setting, she should pick an
example that has a different tone and treatment. One should not use
humorous or sexy examples on solemn occasions, nor should one use
serious, weighty, or complicated examples in an after-dinner speech.

Examples that are factual can also support a point as evidence of its
truth or wisdom. A person trying to find out the truth about a particular
problem must weigh the real examples carefully to be sure they are
factually accurate and typical of the things they are supposed to illustrate or
represent. We can take one or two examples as being representative of a
class of people or events. We imply that the examples are able to stand for
a great many more just like them that we could use if we had the time to
discuss them all. The danger, therefore, is that we may, in the interest of
proving a point, use an extreme example. In the early 1970s, two dramatic
and compelling events caught the imagination of the American public. The
first was a series of bloody murders of Hollywood personalities, for which a
long-haired commune leader named Charles Manson and several of the
women in his "family" were convicted. The second was a war atrocity in
which a number of Vietnamese women and children were killed at a village
called My Lai, for which an infantry lieutenant named Calley was
convicted. Some people argued that the hippy culture was morally
bankrupt and vicious, and they submitted the Manson murders as an
example to prove their point. Other people argued that the military-
industrial complex was morally bankrupt and vicious, and they submitted
the My Lai massacre as an example to prove their point. Both groups were
guilty of using extreme, rather than typical, examples.

The use of extreme examples as proof is characteristic of popular-
magazine articles. A writer in search of an attention-catching device for his
opening paragraph often describes a dramatic but unusual case and
implies that it is typical.

Students of straight thinking have found so many instances of the use
of a few extreme examples to prove points that they call such errors of
thinking the fallacy of *hasty generalization*. If one of your friends did
something your parents thought was out of line, they may have made a
hasty generalization about your whole group of acquaintances. When

someone submits an extreme example to another person in a conversation or discussion and then jumps to the conclusion that the example is typical, both speaker and listener may be misled about the facts of the case. When we make such mistakes, we can usually expect a rude awakening sooner or later.

Analogies

The analogy is another important way to clarify ideas. If you become good at using examples and analogies, you will be able to meet 80 to 90 percent of your needs in making a point clear. An *analogy* is an extended comparison. When a speaker takes two things or two events and points out that they are the same in important respects, he is making a comparison. If he continues to point out several similarities, he makes an analogy. The short comparison is a figure of speech. "She has a neck like a swan's" is a figure of speech, a simile. If we take the figure of speech about the girl's neck and extend the comparison of girl to swan, we may invent an analogy as follows: "She has a neck like a swan's. She swims with the grace of a swan, but when she walks she waddles like a swan. Her voice is a swanlike screech, and her nose looks like a swan's beak."

Analogies are like examples in many respects. Like examples, analogies come in two major types—the literal and the figurative. A *literal* analogy resembles a real example. The literal analogy is a comparison between two things, people, or incidents drawn from the same class or genus. The speaker who compares Metropolitan Community College to North Oaks Community College in regard to size of student body, quality of instruction, courses offered, and extracurricular activities available is using a literal analogy. He can find and verify this information. A *figurative* analogy, on the other hand, resembles a hypothetical example. It is a comparison between two things that, at first glance, do not seem comparable. A girl's neck is not really like a swan's neck. A girl does not have feathers on her neck, nor is a girl's neck as thin and long as a swan's. And yet the listener understands when we say that the girl's neck is like a swan's. Life is not really like a football game, although many a coach has used that figurative analogy in his annual speech for the team.

The literal analogy, like the real example, is an important tool to prove a point as well as to inform or clarify. If you know a great deal about one event, you can often reason about what will happen in a similar situation. Let us say that a student did well in science courses at a small liberal-arts college in the East. In his sophomore year he transfers to a small liberal-arts school nearer his home in the Midwest. We might argue that since he did well in science courses at the first school he will do well in science courses at the second; this argument is based on a literal analogy.

We often think in terms of analogies and try to reason from past experience to the present and future on the basis of literal comparisons.

The literal analogy is an important way to make ideas clear to a listener. The ability to identify literal analogies is basic to better thinking. If we practice inventing analogies and expressing them, we can improve both our thinking and our communication.

The literal analogy can build on the past experience of a listener. A good way to make a new idea or a new situation clear to another person is to compare the new idea to the old. Moving the listener from the familiar to the unfamiliar creates interest and understanding. The listener often finds familiar material dull. If the content of a message is unfamiliar, on the other hand, the listener is often so confused that she rejects the material and makes no attempt to understand it. In a good message the content is familiar enough so the listener can keep her bearings yet is novel enough to create interest. If a recent graduate returns to her high school after her first semester at college, a young friend still in high school might ask, "What is college like?" The college student might answer with a literal analogy comparing the high school they both know to the college only the speaker knows.

Literal analogies, like real examples, usually depend on factual material for their development. You cannot always find a good literal analogy to use in an informal conversation or discussion. When you do find an apt literal analogy, however, you have a powerful tool for making ideas clear.

Figurative analogies resemble hypothetical examples in that they are largely fictitious. Often the message source can express an emotion or an attitude toward some person or event more by comparing two things that might not, on the surface, seem comparable. For example, the president of a large oil company might argue:

> My company is criticized because we have a large share of the market for gasoline. I can't understand the criticism. The oil industry is like the National Football League. If a team wins a large share of its games in the league, everybody thinks it is a great team, because that is what football is all about—winning games. But when we win a large share of the gasoline market, we are criticized for being a monopoly. Yet that is what the oil industry is all about—winning a share of the market.

The comparison of the oil industry to the football league expresses a strong positive attitude toward the industry on the part of the speaker. Try to invent an analogy that would express a different attitude toward the oil industry on the basis of this following hint: "Big oil companies are like octopuses that have their tentacles into every aspect of our lives, including the government!"

Figurative analogies add interest to a comment designed to clarify an idea. They reveal the speaker's basic communicative skill, and we enjoy the artistry of a good comparison, whether it is a short figure of speech or an extended figurative analogy. Figurative analogies can help make complex notions and principles easier to understand.

Narratives

The final important device for making a point clear is the narrative. *Narratives* are stories, either true or fictitious, long or short, that contain characters, situations, and action. Stories are about one central character who draws the audience's interest. Usually the main character has a clear object in view and attempts to achieve his goal; in the process he runs into trouble, and the story tells about his good and bad times as he works for his objective. The old formula for a love story, for example, is boy meets girl, boy falls in love with girl, boy loses girl, boy gets girl. The fun of the story is in the many different ways in which the boy may lose the girl and the unusual ways in which he may win her back. In a good story, the forces that keep the boy from getting the girl ought to be evenly balanced with the chance the hero will get the girl. Conflict and suspense result from the hurdles the character must overcome to win his objectives and the even odds on his success or failure.

Narratives may be factual; among real-life stories, some of the most effective are the speaker's personal experiences. Perhaps it would be appropriate to tell about the time she was supposed to get to school for a big examination but had stayed up late studying and slept through her alarm. When she did wake up she had only a short time to get to school. Racing to make it in time, she was stopped by a policeman, and so forth. The personal-experience story is one of the most common and effective ways to make a point clear. A well-told personal-experience story can amuse, illustrate, clarify, and present the speaker in an attractive light as a person of insight and humor.

The *anecdote* is a short narrative concerning one particular happening of an interesting or amusing nature. When the anecdote is amusing, it also may be called a *joke.* Both serious anecdotes and jokes tend to have a sudden twist at the end, which is called the *punch line.*

We can explain some things by telling a *plausible story* that includes all the facts to be explained and makes them hang together so they sound plausible. In Chapter 12 we discussed the way groups of people come to share interpretative scripts that account for their experience and provide them with a rhetorical vision of their social reality. Speakers often use interpretative scripts to explain and persuade in the hope that the audience will participate in the story.

As we noted at the beginning of this section, it is often difficult to decide whether a given speech or piece of supporting material is primarily an explanation or an argument. We have pointed out in our description of real examples that they can be used as evidence and that the literal analogy is one way to reason from what we know to what we think might happen. Interpretative scripts not only throw light upon the subject but always give events a slant. Nonetheless we find it useful to think of the rhetorical devices in terms of their ability to explain and convince in teaching students how to use them. We have now explored the ways in which examples, analogies, and narratives can be used to clarify ideas. In the next section we emphasize ways to make an argument in behalf of a proposition by use of statistics supplemented with real examples and by use of the testimony of eyewitness observers and experts.

ARGUMENTATIVE SUPPORTING MATERIAL

Statistics

Statistics are numerical comments about facts. A person may comment that Bill is tall. A similar statement may say that Bill is 6 feet 6 inches tall. This last statement includes numbers and is thus a statistical comment. When the statistics are accurate, they give us more precise information about facts than can most other forms of description. When a person wants to talk about many things and has only a short interview or conference in which to make her statement, her use of statistical description enables her to pack a lot of information into a few sentences.

Suppose a student asks the dean, "What are my chances of going on to the university if I enroll at Pleasant Hills Community College?" If the dean answers, "Of every 1000 freshmen who start at Pleasant Hills, 300 go on to the university," she covers a large number of facts (implicit in her answer is the information that while 300 go on, 700 do not), and she has given this information in a short sentence.

However, because the answer provides only a little information about a lot of students, we may get an incomplete picture. How many of the 700 who do not go on for further education wanted to or planned to? Many community-college programs are designed as two-year programs and are complete in themselves. How many of the 300 who go on for more education finish with university or four-year college degrees? In other words, many things are left unsaid by the dean's initial statistical statement. Many persuaders and pressure groups use figures to fool the public as well as to inform people. Even when used carefully and honestly, as in the dean's statement, statistics are abstract and present only a part of a larger picture. In our discussion of statistics, we will particularly look at both the sound use of statistics and the dangers of presenting factual information in the form of figures without explaining exactly what these figures mean or, almost more important, without explaining what the figures do *not* mean.

Numbers suggest precision and accuracy. Most of us think of figures as being factual and scientific. We do not know how to answer a statement such as "Twenty percent of inner-city teenagers use heroin" unless we have some statistical information of our own. We may say, "I find that hard to believe," or, "That figure seems awfully high," but if the other person repeats the statement, the suggestive power of the number itself, "20 percent," is persuasive, making it difficult for us to answer.

Numbers as measures. We all use numbers to talk about such things as our age, height, and weight. We count things like apples, pennies, and oranges, and we know how useful counting and measuring can be. One important way to reason is to count things and then—applying addition, subtraction, multiplication, and division to the numbers we have—compute further answers for ourselves. If I make $100 a week, and $22 is deducted in taxes and insurance, I figure that I will have $78 in my weekly pay check. As long as my basic premises are right (I make $100 and $22 is deducted), then when I make my mathematical computations, my experience will agree with my predicted outcome. I calculate that I will have a $78 paycheck, and when payday arrives, I *do* have a check for $78.

All this seems somewhat obvious to us at this stage in our lives. We have no difficulty counting apples or people, because we can tell one apple from another and we can differentiate people. But the use of numbers becomes much more complicated as soon as we leave individual, single items. Counting the length of a table, for example, is more difficult than counting the number of tables in a room. A table is one long uninterrupted length. We have, then, to make arbitrary divisions or units along the length of the table, so that we can count each division just as we counted the apples. In spite of the complications of measuring and counting, however, we can achieve fairly accurate results when we measure a table or count apples. We can compare lengths of various tables, and we can compare the total number of apples in one box with the total number of apples in another.

Numbers as evaluations. Because numbers are such useful labels, we tend to use numbers for many things that cannot be counted in the simple way apples and inches can. When we do this, the accuracy with which the numbers represent the real world is decreased. You have all taken essay-type tests in which the instructor assigns points for each answer. Question 1, you are told, is worth 25 points. The instructor has the job of deciding whether the answer given by a particular student is worth all 25 points, or only 20 points, or 10, and so on. What can the instructor count to arrive at a conclusion that the answer is worth 20 points? Nothing, really. The number 20 is an evaluation that corresponds to a word evaluation of the answer, such as *good* or *fair,* and the instructor is simply using the convenience of a number to make his general evaluation of the answer.

If you say that Mary is 5 feet tall and weighs 100 pounds, you have made a measurable, accurate statistical statement. Suppose you are told that Mary has an IQ *(intelligence quotient)* of 140. Is this an accurate, dependable statistical statement? Not so much so. We are impressed that Mary's IQ is 140, because we know that this value borders on the genius range of human intelligence, but what have the testers counted to arrive at the number 140? They have certainly not been able to count anything like apples or inches or pounds. Mary has done certain tasks, and the tester has assigned number values to them. He has added up the number values of the tasks Mary completed correctly (her score) and has compared her score with those of others her age who have taken similar tests, in order to determine her mental age. On that basis he has assigned the number 140 as a measure of Mary's intelligence. To say Mary has an IQ of 140 is a less valid statistic than to say Mary is 5 feet tall and weighs 100 pounds.

When we use or listen to statistics, we must make sure we know how the people who observed the facts picked the numbers they assigned to the facts as statistics about them. Did the person gathering the statistics count something that could easily be counted by you or by anyone else, so that several people would come up with the same numbers, or did he use the number as an evaluation or a name? Numbers that come from counting tend to be more useful and accurate than numbers used as names or evaluations.

Many people and organizations are engaged in counting and evaluating things and publishing statistics. Today's student acquires facts and figures from many different sources. In organizing communication messages, we seldom have any trouble finding statistics; the newsstands are full of magazines that are, in turn, full of statistics we can repeat in a communication class. Our trouble comes when we begin to puzzle out what the numbers we find actually mean.

The basic information we need to understand something or to make a wise decision is often a comparison of how two things are similar or how they are different or how they are changing in relation to one another. The things we want to know can often be described by such terms as *enough, too much, on time, gaining, out of reach, leveling off, losing ground, the weakest regions, the strongest area, ahead of schedule, above average,* and *less than we expected.*

Using figures in comparison. One of the most important ways people use figures is to make comparisons. Basically, we compare figures to get a clear indication of *more* or *less.* We can use figures to find out about more or less by looking at two things at about the same point in time (we measure Joe's height and Harry's height and say that Joe is at this moment 2 inches taller than Harry) and by looking at the same thing at different times (Metropolitan College had an enrollment of 1500 in 1965, 2200 in 1970, and currently has 2100).

When we compare figures we must be sure not only that the numbers are a result of counting and not of naming or evaluating, but also that the units counted are comparable in terms of the point we wish to prove. The most common thing people try to count that is not comparable from time to time, is the dollar. Usually the dollar buys less this year than last, although in some periods of American history the reverse was true. Suppose an older person says to a high school student, "When I started my first job I made only $1 an hour and here you are beginning at $4. Are you lucky! You're making four times what I made then." The idea that a student making $4 an hour today is earning four times as much as a man making $1 an hour in 1945 is wrong, because the value of a dollar depends on its buying power—how many hours a person has to work to buy a good dinner in a restaurant, or a car, or a bag of groceries. Someone making $4 an hour today can buy little, if anything, more than a person making $1 an hour in 1945.

Even on the same day in different parts of the country, the dollar is not comparable in terms of buying power. If someone says welfare payments are much higher in New York City than in Jackson, Mississippi, what is he saying? Maybe the dollars paid in New York City buy less than the dollars in Jackson. What you buy for a dollar in one part of the country often costs more, or less, in another part of the country. This is even more true when one compares cities around the world.

Even when the things compared are the same size, or are corrected to make them comparable, the people who compare figures for today with statistics from the past often ignore the effect of the increasing or decreasing numbers of people in a given city or region. For example, the latest figures regarding deaths in automobile accidents, arrests for using illegal drugs, or the occurrence of venereal disease are usually larger than the same statistics from 10 to 20 years ago simply because the population of the United States has increased in the last 20 years. Comparisons of absolute numbers are poor evidence to prove a trend toward better or worse. Comparing the total number of deaths on the highways 10 years ago with the total number this year is not as valid a statistic for proving the increased rate of automobile-related deaths as is the number of deaths per 1000 cars in those years or, better yet, the number of deaths per 100,000 automobile-miles driven in those years. Because some cars are driven so much more every year than others, a comparison of car-miles driven is more meaningful than a comparison of deaths per so many automobiles. Airlines usually present safety statistics in terms of passenger-miles rather than in terms of number of flights or length of flights.

The random sample. To this point we have assumed that the figures under discussion are the result of observing everything we want to know about. That is, if we want to know how many students are enrolled at our college, we find out the number by tabulating every student. Many important statistics are the result of such complete counts. If the counting is complete and no item is overlooked, the numbers that result are the most useful kind of statistics. Much statistical information, however, comes from observing only part of the total and then trying to figure out what the whole picture looks like by making educated guesses about the whole from the part actually counted. The argument is that you do not have to drink the whole glassful to know the milk is sour.

A good way to take a sample is by picking items in such a way that every member of the total population has an equal chance of being selected. The result is a *random sample* that allows statisticians to compute with a specified margin of error the nature of the parent population.

Most polls of public opinion are based on the answers of several hundred or perhaps several thousand people to various questions. Surveys of television viewers also record the responses of a sample of the total viewing audience. Often surveyors report their results in specific figures. One may read that the most recent poll shows that 53 percent of the American people approve the way the president is doing his job. These same polls seldom also indicate that, given the number of people polled and the error that creeps into such sampling, the results are accurate only within 2 or 3 percentage points.

Averages. In addition to describing numerically the whole of a group, statistics can be used to describe the average of a group. For instance, the average student at a state college is 21 years old. We often want to know what is typical, and averages help us find out. But an average can be misleading as well as useful. For example, if all 20 members of a class have part-time or full-time jobs, we may not discover the typical salary if we add all the salaries and divide by 20 because, for one thing, those with full-time jobs probably earn more than those with part-time work. Even if we limit our group to 10 students with part-time jobs, averaging may be misleading. For example, if one student is a highly successful door-to-door salesman who makes $20,000 per year, including this high salary in the averaging gives us a misleading figure. Say the 9 remaining students have salaries between $4000 and $8000 a year, averaging for the 9 people about $6000 per year. Including the single $20,000 salary produces an average of $7400 per year, which is higher than the earnings of most members of the sample and lower than the earnings of only a few.

All numerical statistical evidence must be carefully examined when you use it or hear it as part of a persuasive campaign to prove a point.

DETERMINING WHAT IS TYPICAL

The notion of typicality ties together the use of statistics and examples. An important part of statistical analysis is the discovery of the fact or facts that are the most usual or that are in the middle of a range. We have mentioned the average—the sum of all the numbers divided by the frequency of their occurrence—which is often an appropriate device for indicating what is typical. It is called the *mean*. If we take the weight of each of the 11 players on a football team, add them to find the total weight of all players, and divide by 11, we have the average weight of a player on the team. If the average turns out to be 220 pounds, that statistic gives us a better impression of how heavy the players are than would the extreme example of Harry Potter, a 180-pound quarterback, or William Jones, a 167-pound scatback. As the two lightest-weight players on the team, Harry and William would be poor examples of the weight of the team as a whole. There may not even be a player who weighs the exact average, 220 pounds, but if we use Fred Smith, a 223-pound end, or Elbert Reed, a 217-pound running back, for our example, we have selected an example close to the actual average weight.

Another way statisticians discover the typical is by arranging all of a group of statistics in order from larger to smaller, and then picking the statistic at the middle point and using this to show what is usual. If we made a list of the incomes of all the students in our sample of 10 and arranged the incomes in order from the highest to the lowest, we could count halfway down (or up) and consider the income in the middle of the list to be the typical example of the income. In the case of the 10 students, a midpoint, or *median*, example would give a more accurate indication of what was typical than would a numerical average. The median example is often a good statistic to use when the figures you are discussing range from unusually high to unusually low. These extremes are accounted for when you pick the point in the middle.

Real examples add interest to statistics because they relate the dry figures to the human world. Statistics can express many facts in a short statement, but without examples they often seem dull and boring. Facts presented in terms of people who are heroes or villains, who suffer and have moments of joy and happiness, are more interesting and more understandable.

TESTIMONY

Eyewitness testimony

"When in doubt, go see for yourself" is generally good advice. In other words, if you don't believe someone, go find out with your own two eyes and ears. We depend on the evidence of our senses in deciding many factual questions. If you want to know if it is raining, you go to the window and look outside. Say that a fight breaks out in the hallway. You run to see what is going on. Someone else runs up after the fight is over and asks, "What happened?" You describe the fight. This other person says, "I don't believe you." You shrug your shoulders and say, "Suit yourself. But that is what happened." We believe the evidence of our own senses.

However, many times in our communications with others we want to prove a point about some facts but have not had the time or the chance to see the particular facts for ourselves. Maybe the facts, such as what happened in the fight in the hallway, occurred at only one place in time, so that unless we happened to be there, we have to depend for information on the story of a person who did see the event. Some facts are complicated and occur over a period of time or at a considerable distance, so that we would need much time to observe them all. During the years the United States did not have diplomatic relations with Communist China, the facts about what was going on in China existed but could not be observed by Americans. If we wanted to know how things were going in China during those years, we had to rely on the testimony of people who were there—foreign correspondents from countries that did have diplomatic exchanges with China; we often read reports about China that were written, for example, by Canadians who went there to observe at first hand.

Thus an important source of evidence is the testimony or word of an eyewitness. In a court of law, the only testimony about facts allowed is that of an eyewitness. Sometimes in everyday living, we are willing to depend upon what the law terms *hearsay* (second-hand information, gossip, or rumor; the word of somebody who got a story from someone else), but when we are trying to prove something, rumor is a shaky substitute for eyewitness accounts. Think of several rumors you have heard recently. How many turned out to be entirely accurate?

Many times we quote testimony from a witness who has written up an account of what he saw in a newspaper or magazine. Sometimes we refer to a statement made on radio or television by an alleged eyewitness. When using the testimony of a witness to prove a point, we ought not to assume that just because the person saw the event he is necessarily telling the truth about it or giving a good picture of what happened.

Suppose we ask a friend of Bill's what happened in the hallway fight between Bill and Harry. Bill's friend may well say that Harry did not knock Bill down, that Bill slipped. Another eyewitness who has no stake in the matter, such as friendship with one of the participants, may say that Bill provoked Harry, and Harry hit Bill a solid blow to the jaw and knocked him down. Which eyewitness do you believe? How do you decide which reporter is the more reliable witness to what actually happened?

When trying to decide what happened in any given instance, we have to examine the testimony of eyewitnesses carefully. You should ask yourself such questions as:

What exactly did the witness intend to say?
Was the story a put-on? Was it supposed to be funny?

Was the person able to make a good report? Was he in a position to see? Did he have the training that would make him better able to keep track of what was going on? Is he a reliable person?

Was the person willing and able to tell the truth?

Was there any reason for the witness to lie or distort the truth?

Did the witness have a bias? What did the witness expect to see? (We all have a tendency to see what we expect to see. Each of us has a personal bias built in when we view or hear an event.)

Expert testimony

Speakers frequently use direct quotations from well-known authorities in interpreting facts. Usually we use *expert* witnesses to testify about what the facts mean. If we go to a doctor and he shows us our X rays, we may still ask, "What does it mean?" He could then tell us that the X rays indicate there is a fracture of a small bone in the right foot. Many facts are difficult to interpret, and people who specialize in a given area can often help us decide what the facts mean. An expert in foods may testify that the diet of the poor people in an area is not good enough to keep them healthy; he may testify, further, that studies have shown a direct relationship between diet and intelligence in young children. Another expert on drug usage may testify that the facts indicate that the use of marijuana does not affect a person's physical ability to drive a car as much as does the use of alcohol in comparable amounts. Speakers often quote the interpretation of facts by widely known experts to support their case.

Another way in which we may use testimony is to decide what we ought to do in a given case. We might ask the doctor who told us we have a fractured bone in the foot, "What shall I do?" He might advise us to have the foot put into a cast to keep it immobilized for six weeks while it heals. We often depend upon an expert's advice; in the case of the doctor, his advice is testimony you should consider as you decide what to do about the facts. Obviously, when you want advice, you must ask the right expert. Suppose an unmarried pregnant girl asks her mother, "What should I do?" Suppose she asks her boyfriend, a girlfriend, or her doctor the same question. Her mother might say, "Get married." The boyfriend might say, "Have an abortion." The girlfriend might say, "Keep the baby." The doctor might say, "Take these pills, they're vitamins; don't gain too much weight, and come back to see me in a month." The girl has received testimony from four sources. Whose testimony is more persuasive? Whose testimony ought to be more persuasive? Has the girl perhaps not asked the right expert or the right questions yet? Consider the involved interests of her sources. A speaker may quote or allude to advice from leading authorities who recommend the same proposals as does the speaker.

One widely used propaganda technique features the testimony of glamorous and famous people telling us we ought to buy or do something.

The form of the argument is similar to the legitimate use of the testimony of experts to support a case. However, the persuasive power of the testimony comes from the old propaganda device of nonrational transfer of glamor and prestige of a popular or famous name to a product or proposal. We often see baseball or basketball or football players advising us to buy a certain kind of shaving cream, cologne, or breakfast food. Movie stars advise us what political candidates to vote for. Supposedly, if we admire and value the opinions of a sports or television star, we will transfer our liking to the product he tells us to use and will buy it.

When an expert tells us what to do about a health problem, or getting an education, or voting for or against a tax increase or school bond, or to support an antiwar position or candidate, or to support a disarmament conference or an antipollution effort, we should be sure that the person is an expert *in the field* he is talking about. We should not follow a person's advice just because he is likable or glamorous. If the person talking about facts has a vested interest in how he interprets the facts to us, we must keep that in mind when we consider his testimony. Remember most personalities are paid handsomely when they make commercials advising you to buy a service or a product.

KEY IDEAS CHAPTER 14

• The most important tools for making ideas clear are the example, the analogy, and the narrative.

• The example illustrates some important points about all things like it or provides an instance of the operation of a law or general principle.

• When people use examples, they may select examples that actually happened or ones that are made up.

• Real examples not only clarify points but can be used as evidence in an argument.

• We can tailor hypothetical examples to the needs of the listener, the point we are making, and the time available, but since they are fictitious, we cannot use them as proof, only as clarification.

• A good example makes a difficult idea easier to understand and arouses the interest of the listener.

• The choice and use of examples is an art that can be learned.

• A short comparison is a figure of speech; an extended comparison is an analogy.

• Literal analogies are comparisons between things from the same class or genus.

- The literal analogy can build on the listener's past experience by comparing the thing to be explained to something the listener already knows.

- If we know a good deal about one event, we often use a literal analogy to reason about what will happen in a similar situation.

- Figurative analogies are based on comparisons that are unusual; they add interest to a message because of their novelty.

- In a narrative, conflict and suspense result from the hurdles the main character must overcome to win his or her goal.

- Stories may be factual or fictitious.

- Among the most effective factual narratives for a speaker are those dealing with his or her personal experiences.

- Statistical descriptions of factual material often contain much information in a few words.

- Even when carefully and honestly presented, statistics often give the listener an incomplete picture.

- Numbers that come from counting tend to be more useful in informing about the world than figures used as names or as evaluations.

- Some units, such as the American dollar, are not comparable from time to time.

- The latest figures regarding any vital statistic are usually larger than the same figures for several years ago simply because the population has increased.

- Much statistical information comes from observing a sample of the total population and making an educated guess about the whole on that basis.

- A random sample allows a more precise guess about the total population than most other kinds of samples.

- Extreme examples are poor evidence.

- The fallacy of hasty generalization results from jumping to a conclusion on the basis of a few extreme examples.

- An important part of statistical analysis is the discovery of facts that are usual or typical of a wide range of things.

- Real examples are a good way to add interest to statistics, and statistics provide a good guide to typical examples.

- We depend on the evidence of our senses in deciding many factual questions.

• The testimony of reliable eyewitnesses is an important source of evidence about factual matters.

• In an age of specialization, expert testimony interpreting complicated factual matters is often an important part of persuasion.

• A widely used propaganda technique is to cite the testimonial of a famous and glamorous person in behalf of a product or service.

• If someone testifies that we ought to do or believe something, we should examine that person's authority carefully.

SUGGESTED PROJECTS

1 • This is an oral exercise in making ideas clear. Select a complex concept from one of your other courses, such as the concept of comparative cost advantage in economics, or the concept of valence in chemistry, or the concept of mitosis in biology. State the point to be made clear, and using only one extended real example or one extended hypothetical example, make the point clear to the class. Your example should be two minutes in length. You should announce to the class *before you begin* which form of example you will use.

2 • This is another oral exercise in making ideas clear. Select a concept similar to the one used in project 2 above. State the point to be made clear, and using only one extended figurative analogy or one extended literal analogy, make the point clear to the class. Again your analogy should be two minutes in length, and you should announce which analogy you will use before you begin.

3 • This is a project in proving a point. Select a controversial point, phrase it in suitable form, and then, using only statistical information, support the point for two minutes.

4 • Select an argument presented in a newspaper, magazine, or on television. Note the point to be proved and then analyze the supporting material critically. How could the argument have been better supported, in your estimation?

SUGGESTED READINGS

Huff, Darrel. *How to Lie with Statistics*. New York: Norton, 1954.

Jeffrey, Robert C., and Owen Peterson. *Speech: A Text with Adapted Readings*. 3d ed. New York: Harper & Row, 1980.

Newman, Robert P., and Dale R. Newman. *Evidence.* Boston: Houghton Mifflin, 1969.

Olbricht, Thomas. *Informative Speaking.* Glenview, Ill.: Scott, Foresman, 1968.

Walter, Otis M., and Robert L. Scott. *Thinking and Speaking,* 4th ed. New York: Macmillan, 1979.

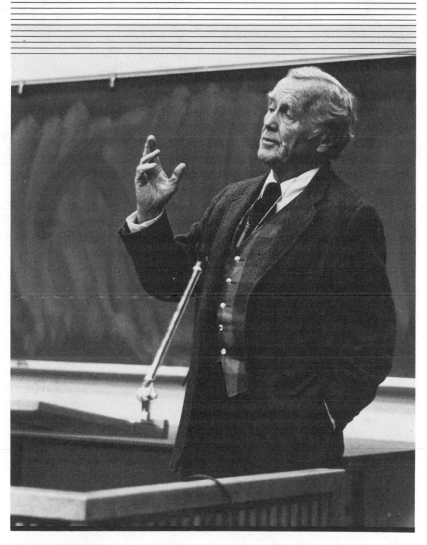

DELIVERY
CHAPTER 15

We have now gone through the process of finding a suitable topic, analyzing the topic and the audience, adapting the topic to the audience by constructing a suitable organization, and supporting the ideas. The final step comes when you face the audience and, using suitable verbal and nonverbal communication, present the speech. We discussed the basic principles of language usage in Chapter 3, and here we will only note some of the ways in which the delivery of the speech translates words into an oral message composed of both verbal and nonverbal elements.

Delivery is the presentation of the speech and consists of the paralinguistic, kinesic, and proxemic factors that the speaker employs to communicate with the audience. It includes the way the speaker uses voice elements such as pitch, rate, loudness, articulation, and pronunciation; delivery also includes body movement such as posture, gesture, eye contact, and facial expression.

APPROACHES TO DELIVERY

Over the years scholars who study public speaking have argued about which of the two general approaches to delivery is better. One approach stresses thinking the thought as you speak it and feeling the emotion as you express it. The idea is that you should work from the inside out, because the best way to decide how to express disgust, for instance, is to feel disgusted, and then you will naturally find the vocal intonations and gestures to communicate that emotion. You have heard of "method" acting; this is much the same approach. The second approach is one where you study, plan, and rehearse the nonverbal communication carefully. In this approach, you work more from the outside in, on the assumption that most speakers are somewhat clumsy and inept and that for them to trust to feeling alone will only result in mumbling monotony and awkward gestures. In the second approach it is often helpful to have the advice of someone trained to tell you how effectively you are speaking.

Much of the controversy comes down to the question of how much and in what manner you should rehearse your speech. The advantage of concentrating on your meaning, as in the first approach, is that when you do it well, you appear natural and direct, unstudied; you project a lively sense of here-and-now communicativeness. The disadvantage is that if you have not worked on the basic skills of voice, articulation, and gesture, you may not have the techniques to enjoy the advantages of the approach. Few of us are natural actors or speakers. You do not want to appear inarticulate, inept, and unprepared.

The advantages of rehearsing key lines and gestures carefully are that when you do it well, you *appear* spontaneous, expressive, and confident. You project grace and an attractive vocal presence. The disadvantages are that, poorly done, you may come across as a kind of wooden-gestured, singsong-voiced, mechanical person, almost devoid of personality and vitality.

Both approaches can work, if done well; both have problems to keep in mind as you experiment to see which appears to work better for you. Obviously, we feel that someone trained to help people become effective speakers can help you get better faster as you experiment. Many really effective speakers we know use elements of both approaches. Either approach should include practice in basic skills in delivery and careful rehearsal before you deliver your speech.

In Chapter 2 we described a speaker's main rehearsal options. Speakers may write out their manuscripts and read them; they may prepare the speech and memorize it, word for word; or, they may prepare an outline and speak extemporaneously. If you read from manuscript or deliver the speech from memory, it is essential that you rehearse the speech a number of times. As you rehearse, watch your language for difficult phrases. You should practice different ways of saying the lines in order to make the key ideas stand out. Make sure your posture, gestures, and facial expressions support your meaning. Strive for naturalness. The best art conceals itself. If the audience gets nonverbal clues that you have labored long and hard over your delivery, you will have failed to some extent. Try to convey the illusion that the lines and gestures that you have rehearsed a dozen times are spontaneous, spur-of-the-moment reactions to the situation.

Rehearsal is also important in extemporaneous speaking. Here you do not have to overcome the barrier of the written manuscript or the memorized speech, but your delivery may be rough as you fumble for a word, repeat yourself, look away awkwardly, or start a gesture and stop it in a jerky way. Rehearsal can make the words flow more easily, even though you have not memorized them and can smooth out and polish your delivery.

When you write or memorize a speech, you can go over the language very carefully to make sure that you are taking the connotative and denotative aspects into account and to define, name, and describe things in a way designed to achieve your objectives. You must be careful, however, not to produce a written essay rather than a speech. A paragraph that reads well may not sound good when spoken to an audience. Sometimes a speech that works for an audience seems unduly redundant when read silently. Written and oral language usage differ; your ear cannot reread a confusing sentence.

We strongly urge that you get into the practice of recording speeches and listening to them to see for yourself how well your ideas come through. Better yet, ask someone who has not seen your manuscript to listen to the tape and then tell you what he or she got out of it. Even when you expect to speak extemporaneously, you will have some time for rehearsal; give some thought to specific word choice and sentence structure as well as the nonverbal elements of your speech. If a particularly effective phrase occurs to you, add it to your outline in the margin; you may want to use it when the time comes.

PRINCIPLES OF EFFECTIVE DELIVERY

The first principle of effective delivery is to avoid distractions. One important goal in delivering your speech should be to communicate as effectively as possible with the audience. A basic principle of delivery is that any feature of your nonverbal communication that serves to distract the audience from the message is undesirable. You should work to rid yourself of all such distractions. Those of us who lecture to college classes have learned again and again how tempting it is for audience members to be distracted by nonverbal tics and random movements. We have run across the student who carefully notes down every "uh" and "err" and reports to his friends after class that the "speech" instructor used 52 "uhs" during the course of the hour. We know of students who discuss the speaker's tendency to pace back and forth in random fashion, to lean on the podium, to look at the floor or out the window, to purse her lips or look at her notes, fool with her pencil.

Among the more distracting features of a speaker's delivery are regular vocal tricks, facial tics, or physical movements, such as swaying from foot to foot, which have no relation to what the speaker is saying. The technical term for "uhs" and "errs" is *vocalized pauses*. Vocalized pauses are among the most disturbing features of delivery and can be remedied with some attention and practice. Many times speakers use words much as they might use vocalized pauses. Some years ago students experienced a "you know" epidemic of large proportions. We heard some speeches in which *every* idea was cluttered with "you knows." Other terms go in and out of style. "Man" is another term that often serves only as a distraction when used as a verbal crutch. Overused, *any* word or phrase can become a distraction.

Many times we are unaware of the aimless patterns of voice and gesture that distract our audience. If you have an opportunity to see yourself giving a speech on videotape, it is often a revelation.

The second principle of effective delivery is to speak in a manner that is appropriate to the topic, the audience, and the occasion. If you are speaking to a small audience of 25 in a classroom, your manner should be different from what it would be if you were speaking to 2500 people in an auditorium or to 25,000 people at an open-air rally. Public-address systems enable us to speak in more conversational tones to the largest of audiences, but the larger audience requires a broader and more impressive manner. The broad gesture, which seems appropriate before the large rally audience, would seem overwhelming in the small classroom. Likewise, the manner of delivery appropriate to a highly emotional occasion would be inappropriate to a calm or solemn occasion. There are cultural expectations for every speech occasion, and the rule is to use an appropriate manner of delivery, one that fits the audience and the occasion. There will be more regarding this in the concluding chapter.

The third principle of effective delivery is to use nonverbal elements to reinforce the meanings in your message. The way you orchestrate the vocal melody and the accompanying body movements in relation to your words can strengthen or weaken your communicativeness. A good delivery will make it easier for the audience members to listen to and decode your message.

The fourth principle is that your manner should increase your credibility as a person. Much of your credibility, or believability, as a source of ideas and advice depends upon the kind of person you seem to be. Members of your audience who are unacquainted with you or who only know you by reputation will often decide whether you are likable, trustworthy, active, and knowledgeable on the basis of your nonverbal communication.

Speakers can use nonverbal suggestion to make themselves more influential with their listeners, more persuasive. You should work hard to appear to be in charge of the situation and your material, though in a relaxed and friendly way, not in a dictatorial or wise-guy manner. Remember that we are more likely to be persuaded by someone we accept as a person—a person we feel we could like. If the speaker's manner conveys the impression that he is calm, confident, sincere, and honest, we are more likely to trust and believe him. In a question-and-answer period after a formal speech, or in any face-to-face communication event, if the speaker's manner of fielding questions, dealing with disagreements, and handling challenges is confident, her credibility with the listeners is increased. If, under such stress, she loses her temper, her credibility often correspondingly plunges. If, further, the speaker can communicate to the listener that she genuinely appreciates questions and respects the questioner, and if she responds fairly and candidly to the best of her ability, admitting honestly when she is stumped, she tends to build good will. If the speaker's manner suggests that she has something to hide, or if she hedges in such a way that she appears insecure and afraid of making a mistake, then her ethos is damaged. All these instances refer mostly to the manner in which the speaker conducts herself, to her nonverbal signals.

If a person communicates verbally and nonverbally that he is trying to control us, that he is trying to outwit us and make us do something he wants but that we do not know about, that he is not really interested in us but in what he can get out of us, that he thinks he is a lot better and smarter than we are, or that he is so set in his ways he will not be changed, no matter how wrong others may feel him to be, then we are likely to reject him as a person and to reject his message as well. He will not persuade us, because we do not think much of him or his ideas.

On the other hand, if the speaker communicates verbally and nonverbally that he is absolutely fair, candid, and honest; that he is not defensive about his status or his expertness; that he is deeply involved with and dedicated to our common objectives; that he is willing to make personal sacrifices for our common good; that he is competent; that his advice is good and is given in our best interest; then his ethos is likely to be persuasive for us. He just may persuade us as he speaks, because he inspires confidence that he knows what he is talking about and wants to share his knowhow with us for our own good.

IMPROVING VOICE AND ARTICULATION

We happen to teach in an urban area where the general American dialect is spoken. We find that most of our students taking a first course in speech communication have never listened critically to their own voices; furthermore, they are rarely enthusiastic about the idea of recording their voices and having their classmates and instructor respond to what they hear. On the other hand, once the exercise has been done, they are as enthusiastic as they had been apathetic, and they say, "Everybody ought to do that." Few of these students are aware of the almost universal monotony with which they habitually speak. Comparing the energy level they use in making vocal sounds with the levels produced by trained radio actors, for example, our students find themselves always "in the valley," rarely on the peaks. They find they punctuate their thoughts less effectively than they had thought; they hear sloppy articulation, and they do not like hearing it. When they realize that their voices are not projecting the vocal image they had thought they were, they usually want to work on them to try to make their results more in line with their intentions.

Voice and articulation problems can generally be divided into two categories: those that are the result of some illness or of malformation of the parts of the body that produce speech; and those, far more numerous, that are the result of habits of speaking which do not utilize the vocal mechanism as well as possible. A tone-deaf person will probably never be a fine singer, but even a person endowed with a fine musical ear needs training to reach maximum potential. If you have a severe articulation problem you should consult a trained speech clinician or correctionist. The advice we give here is directed at the vast majority of students who have perfectly normal voices but wish to retrain faulty speech habits to make their voices more expressive and to increase their effectiveness at nonverbal communication.

The procedure for improving speech

The same general procedure can be used to retrain most bad speech habits, whether they are associated with poor use of pitch, time, or loudness, with poor articulation or poor voice quality. The first step in any program of improvement is to train the ear to hear the errors. Most of us are so used to speaking that we ignore the way we sound. Few students are aware of the common voice problems. Because speaking is, by nature, imitative, we speak as our friends speak and copy one another's bad habits of articulation and lack of variety.

An excellent way to hear yourself is to record your voice and play the tape back while you listen critically. You ought to take advantage of every opportunity to tape relatively long passages and listen to them. Eventually, however, you must come to the point where you can monitor your own speech—*while* you are speaking. The feedback principle discussed in Chapter 1 is relevant here. You must become the actor in a feedback loop with the objective of improving your own voice. Your ear becomes the perceptor, and the sounds you utter are continually monitored to allow you to bring your practice on target.

The steps in the process go something like this:

1 Train your ear to hear the problem.
2 Gain control of the problem by learning to produce a sample of poor speech whenever you want to.
3 Learn to produce the better sound.
4 Practice the good sound and the poor sound, thus increasing the power of your ear to discriminate, and at the same time teaching your vocal mechanisms how it feels to produce better speech.
5 Once you can control your vocalization so that you can produce poor speech and good speech whenever you wish, begin to introduce the new speech habits into conversation with others—during lunch, for example.
6 Gradually you will find the new speech more comfortable, and as it becomes more habitual you can introduce it more often into your daily routine.

Eventually, you will use your new speaking voice without having to think about it consciously, and you can concentrate on the ideas you are framing in your message, assured now that you are using the best vocal technique you can to communicate your ideas and feelings nonverbally.

This general pattern can be used to correct slovenly articulation of certain sounds, particularly the tendency to substitute easy sounds for more difficult ones, such as /i/ for /e/ and /d/ for /t/. The general pattern can be used to correct monotony of pitch, time, and loudness. It also works with voice quality problems, as well as with difficulties of rate, which are the easiest to remedy.

If a person speaks too rapidly, for example, careful attention to speaking more slowly, drawing out the vowel sounds in a smooth way during drill sessions, will soon enable him to train his ear. One can speak more rapidly or more slowly without difficulty. A good feedback loop can bring the rate on target quickly. Often a person who speaks rapidly also speaks in a jerky, staccato fashion, so that the articulatory mechanism—the tongue, teeth, and lips, in particular—are asked to form the consonants so rapidly that they are poorly articulated. Slowing the rate and forming the consonants more carefully many times solves an articulation problem as well as a rate problem. Generally, a good rate for reading to audiences is between 140 and 185 words per minute. Daily speaking should not exceed this maximum, and speaking slower than 140 words per minute should be restricted to occasions when one is addressing a large crowd and must overcome problems of general noise, echo, and the like.

A good drill for breaking the monotony of time, pitch, and loudness is to read a passage first in a monotone and then with great expressiveness, much as a Shakespearean actor might read an emotional speech from a play. Overdoing the flexibility of your voice in drill sessions does two good things for your nonverbal communication: (1) It forces your vocal equipment to stretch its range, just as daily exercise stretches muscles and makes them more flexible; and (2) it teaches your ear to discriminate changes in emphasis at the same time it teaches your vocal equipment how these new sounds feel.

IMPROVING GESTURES AND MOVEMENT

Posture

The way a speaker stands and holds his shoulders and his head as he speaks communicates a good deal nonverbally to the audience. If the speaker is delivering a speech in a relatively formal setting, the audience expects him to stand erect, with his weight evenly balanced on both feet. The feet should be relatively close together, with one foot slightly in front of the other.

The speaker should not lean on the speaker's stand, slouch first on one foot and then the other, rock back and forth or from side to side, or stand with feet widespread.

If the speaker is in a relatively informal setting, and if he wishes to communicate nonverbally that he does not want to give a carefully prepared speech, but plans to ramble on a bit and throw out a few ideas and then ask for questions and comments, he may sit on the edge of a table, sit in a chair, lean on the speaker's stand, take off his coat, and so on.

Facial expression

One of the most important tools any speaker has for nonverbal communication with an audience is his range of facial expressions. Smiles, grins, smirks, frowns, grimaces, and raised eyebrows can all add emphasis or, conversely, suggest that the descriptive words in the message are to be discounted. Unfortunately, one of the beginner's most common reactions to nervousness is failure to use facial expressions. As a result, the anxious speaker often talks in a monotone, sighs a great deal, and has a blank expression on his face.

The person who is vivacious in conversation, whose face is alive every second in animated talk with one or two others, often tones down his facial expressions when giving a public speech. He should do just the opposite. A slight smile or grin is often lost on an audience 12 feet or more away. Thus, you ought to overdo the smile, the grin, the frown when you are giving a public speech in a good-sized room or auditorium. You have to overdo your platform personality to achieve the effect you ordinarily produce in the more informal and intimate situations.

Eye contact

One of the most expressive regions of the face is the area around the eyes. Again and again the eyewitnesses who reported their impressions of such great American speakers as Daniel Webster, Henry Clay, Stephen Douglas, and William Jennings Bryan noted the arresting and powerful effect of the speakers' eyes.

Generally the speaker ought to give the illusion that he is looking directly at the members of the audience. To be sure, direct eye contact may be a culturebound nonverbal convention, and you may wish to modify the advice for special situations. However, you are well advised to look a middle-class white North American audience in the eye.

In almost all situations, random eye movements are distracting. Looking over the listeners' heads for no clear purpose, looking out the window, looking at the corner of the room, looking at the floor, or looking always at your speech notes can prove distracting. When the speaker looks away from the audience for the greater part of his speech, he has no way of judging its response, of utilizing the feedback from nonverbal cues.

Gesture

The beginning speaker often makes an unsettling discovery when he gets in front of an audience. He finds that attached to his shoulders are two arms to which he normally pays little attention, but which now suddenly cannot be ignored. At the ends of his arms are two conspicuous hands. His first thought is to hide his hands, so he puts them both behind his back. When he does this, he feels tied up, and every move he makes with his shoulders seems awkward. He then tries to hide his hands in his pockets, but he still feels restricted, and his hands seem as obvious and as useless as ever. He may fold his arms over his chest or try to hold them rigidly by his sides, in the hope that nobody will notice them, but there is no hiding either the arms or the hands. The only solution is for the speaker to learn to use his arms and hands to make gestures in support of the material in his speech.

Once the beginner realizes he must move his hands and arms, he may make a second mistake by keeping his elbows close to his sides, using the forearms for short, jerky gestures. His nonverbal communication at this point is that he wants to use some gestures but feels inhibited in front of his listeners.

You can get the feel of good ways to gesture by practicing at home in front of a mirror. When you practice gestures suitable for a speech, you should make them broader than you first feel necessary. Experiment with gesturing with both arms. Remember to use the space above your shoulders, particularly if you are speaking from a stage and are some distance from your audience. Move your hands to express ideas. Make sure the movement flows through the entire arm to the tips of your fingers. Do not let your hands and fingers flop about loosely; do not use gestures that distract from, rather than add to, the meaning of what you are saying.

The entire body can gesture to suggest nonverbal meanings. The speaker may hunch his shoulders and crouch to suggest a certain mood or feeling. He may step toward the audience, pull back, turn to one side or another, or stand on tiptoe. A good speaker may use the techniques of pantomime, the art of getting across emotions, actions, and feelings by mute gestures. He may turn slightly, crouch, and make an imaginary pistol out of his extended index finger to suggest to the audience the character of a holdup man in a story. He might next turn, stand rigidly erect, and hold both hands high, this time suggesting his own response to the feeling of having the gun in his back.

THE USE OF NOTES

The question of whether to have notes for a public speech may seem a minor matter. Yet in the hands of a speaker who does not know how best to use them, notes can inhibit eye contact, facial expression, posture, and gesturing, and thereby affect the speaker's total skill at nonverbal communication. Many speech instructors prefer that students not use notes in class, simply because notes hinder development of good habits of nonverbal communication through body language. Some instructors also feel that beginning speakers should learn to keep the outline of their ideas in mind, without notes, as they speak. We do not use notes in most informal communication situations. We may use notes for formal speaking situations, however, and the Teleprompter and other devices provide ready notes, even whole speeches, for television performers. It seems to us that the situations calling for speeches without any notes are rare. However, listeners are impressed when a speaker uses no notes, and you should keep this in mind for your most polished and important speeches. If you can develop a way to prepare speeches that allows you to keep the main points of your outline in mind, you can usually easily remember the examples and other supporting material that fit under the main point. If you can speak extemporaneously without notes, you can keep your eyes on the audience and gesture more freely.

Many students find it difficult to speak without notes, and plan to use notes in the speaking they will do after they finish the class, so they prefer learning to speak well using them. The most important point about using notes in a speech is not to pretend that you have no notes. Few things a speaker can do distract an audience as much as the pretense that she has no notes. Sometimes a speaker writes her notes on small cards and stacks them on the speaker's stand or holds them hidden in the palm of her hand. She cannot fool anyone. The first time she sneaks a look at her notes the audience picks up the cue and watches for her to steal another look; she may create more suspense with this nonverbal behavior than with what she is trying to say! So if you need notes, bring them out into the open, then use them naturally, trying not to cut down on eye contact and facial expressiveness any more than necessary. Perhaps in the instance of quoting a statistic or a special sentence from some authority, the speaker can even hold up the notes and point to the place where she has her information; this communicates nonverbally that what she is saying is absolutely correct and she has it written down to make sure she says it correctly.

Avoid the common pitfalls of using notes. Do not look at them whenever you feel embarrassed; look at the audience, keep your poise, and pause to collect yourself. To the audience, your poised look at them as you pause communicates that you are about to say something important and are thinking about exactly the right way to say it best. Do not play with your notes; a nervous speaker with something in his hand is often tempted to fold it, roll it, tap it, or bend it. The audience may, again, become more interested in what you may do next with your note cards than in what you are saying.

Do not clutch your notes tightly in front of you with both hands; you cannot gesture with your hands if they are in this rigid position. Hold the notes in one hand and use the other arm and hand for gesturing, although you may certainly gesture with both arms if it seems appropriate—the notes, held up in one hand, will not distract from the gesture; if anything, a vigorous arm gesture that includes the display of notes may communicate that you are prepared, you have in your hand what you are going to say, and you are very much in charge of the situation.

The more imagination you can develop to enable you to see yourself as the audience does, the better your nonverbal communication will become.

Nonverbal communication is sometimes called the silent language. We are all vaguely aware of the implications of gesture, facial expression, and body attitudes when we talk with people from day to day. When we are involved in public communication events, we need to become more sophisticated about the implications of nonverbal body-motion codes so that if we are speaking, we know what to do to make our nonverbal communication support our intention. If we are viewing and hearing someone else speak, we need to be aware of the many signals given by the speaker's body, eyes, and vocal intonations. All these are elements of nonverbal communication, and they are important components of messages; there is much truth in the saying, "What you *do* speaks so loud, I can't hear what you *say*."

KEY IDEAS CHAPTER 15

• Delivery includes the way the speaker uses voice elements (such as pitch, rate, loudness, articulation, and pronunciation) and body movements (such as posture, gesture, eye contact, and facial expression).

• One approach to delivering a speech is to think the thought and feel the emotion at the time of presentation.

• Another approach is to study, plan, and rehearse the delivery carefully.

• Either basic approach or some combination of the two can work for a speaker if he or she learns to use it well.

• No matter what form of preparation a speaker uses—manuscript, memorization, or outline—rehearsal is essential.

• The goal of rehearsal of the speech should be a delivery that appears to be natural and spontaneous.

• Any feature of your nonverbal communication that distracts your audience from the message is undesirable.

• Your delivery should be adjusted so it is appropriate to the topic, audience, and occasion.

• Your delivery should reinforce the meanings in your message.

• Your delivery should increase your credibility as a message source.

• The same general procedure can be used to retrain most bad speech habits.

• The key to improving voice and articulation is to train the ear to hear the problem.

• One of the most important tools any speaker has for communicating with the audience is the skillful use of facial expressions.

• Generally the speaker ought to give the illusion that he or she is looking directly at the members of the audience.

• You can get the feel of good ways to gesture by practicing at home in front of a mirror.

• The most important point about using notes in a speech is not to pretend that you have no notes.

• The more imagination you can develop to enable you to see yourself as the audience does, the better your delivery will become.

SUGGESTED PROJECTS

1 • Select an emotional passage from a human interest story, novel, or short story and prepare a three-minute (450 or so words) oral reading. Rehearse carefully and experiment with various approaches to communicating ideas and feelings. Read your selection to the class, striving for an illusion of naturalness and spontaneity.

2 • Select some person that you admire very much and write a three-minute speech about him or her. Commit your speech to memory and polish the delivery in rehearsal. Deliver your speech to the class, striving to communicate directly with your audience.

3 • Pick a dramatic personal experience that touched you emotionally. With or without notes prepare to tell the class about your experience in extemporaneous fashion. The experience can be as violent as an automobile accident or as tranquil as the sunset on a wilderness area lake. Try to make the audience experience your feelings at the time.

SUGGESTED READINGS

Eisonson, Jon. *Voice and Diction: A Program for Improvement.* 4th ed. New York: Macmillan, 1979.

Fairbanks, Grant. *Voice and Articulation Drillbook.* 2d ed. New York: Harper & Row, 1960.

Jeffrey, Robert C., and Owen Peterson. *Speech: A Text with Adapted Readings.* 3d Ed. New York: Harper & Row, 1980.

PERSUASION
CHAPTER 16

No aspect of communication is more important to our daily lives than persuasion. We are urged to vote for political candidates, to support reforms, to buy products, and to establish relationships with other people. The message with persuasive intent comes at us in two-person conversations and interviews; in face-to-face small-group conferences; in public speeches and business presentations; in newspapers, magazines, letters; in films, radio shows, and television programs. Billboards proclaim suggestions about how we should act or believe; neon signs entice us to drink, eat, or buy. The lyrics of popular songs sell a point of view or a lifestyle. We go to a job interview and try to persuade the interviewer to hire us. We take a job as a salesman and try to get a customer to make a purchase. We see an attractive person and try to persuade her or him to go to a movie with us.

PERSUASION DEFINED

Persuasion is sometimes called changing behavior. It can also be defined as changing attitudes or belief, as winning friends, influencing people, gaining cooperation, or selling a product or an idea. When we talk somebody into doing something, we have persuaded him. When we suggest ideas or beliefs or argue for a position with evidence and logic in such a way that the listeners change their behavior, attitudes, or beliefs, we have persuaded them.

We will define *persuasion* as communication to influence choice. When we speak to inform (make a point clear), we often provide the listener with information that opens up new horizons and increases choices, but when we speak to persuade we try to influence the listener's choices and narrow them to the one we prefer.

Notice that persuasion is communication intended to get a response from the receiver, to change the listener's attitude or beliefs. The source of the message, the person giving a persuasive comment or making a persuasive speech, has a specific purpose in mind and drafts the persuasive message to achieve that goal.

Persuasion is not the same as force. We can control human beings to some extent with the use of force or the threat of force. If you are forced to do something, your options are closed. Coercion eliminates choice, while persuasion influences it. Coercion does not require artistry. "Do this or I will bash in your head" may get results but requires little skill—only the brute strength and the desire to deliver the blow. A good salesperson, on the other hand, is skillful and has developed the art of persuasion to a high level. If selling were as easy as bashing in heads, more people would be making $50,000 a year in commissions.

Persuasion is not the same as inducing somebody to do something by offering a powerful reward. A father might get his son to cut his hair by promising him a new car. Offering a large reward is similar to offering a threat of force. The boss who says, "Come to work on Saturday or I will fire you," is operating on the same level as the one who says, "Come to work on Saturday and I will give you a bonus." Neither offering a large reward nor threatening punishment involves much communication skill or selling ability.

THE PERSUASIVE POWER OF PERSONALITY

Persuasion and personal relationships

One of the most important factors for persuasion in a communication situation is the quality of the personal relationships that are established. If the people who are discussing a topic like and trust one another, attempts of either one to influence the other are more likely to succeed.

Persuasion often consists of advice. When we receive advice, we usually face some risky choices. Many of the big decisions in life pose some risks. Should I enlist in the army? Should I take a job with Pulver Motors? Should I get married? Should I go to college? Should I take a shot of heroin? When the choices are risky and I need advice, I turn to someone I trust. Trust assumes that the other person will give me advice that seems to her best for me. When I trust a person, I can count on her strength, integrity, sincerity, and expertness, and on her concern for me.

Persuasion and likability

Often liking and trusting go together, but they are not necessarily always connected. We might find some people likable but not trustworthy in important matters because we know they are forgetful, unreliable, or easily swayed by emotions. On the other hand, some people whose advice we take and whom we trust are not likable. We might trust a certain medical doctor because we know she is well trained, sober, and a talented physician, even though we do not like her much as a person.

Nonetheless, if we like a person, we are tempted to believe and accept her ideas and advice. We often *feel* better about taking the advice of someone we like than about accepting the recommendation of someone we dislike. An important part of the study of persuasion, therefore, concerns how people who talk with one another come to *like* one another.

Physical beauty is a factor in being likable. Peoples' ideas about what is beautiful are as individual as people. Just the same, Americans spend billions of dollars each year in the search for beauty because, for many, physical attractiveness is the key to popularity and friendship. Physical beauty is not enough by itself to assure likability, but other things being equal, the beautiful people have an advantage. Slogans such as "slim is beautiful" and "black is beautiful" clearly tie physical beauty to persuasive messages. Advertisers often use the persuasive power of handsome men and beautiful women shown using the product or simply being present in the same picture with an advertising slogan. The persuasive message is clear enough: "Beautiful people use this product; buy this product and you too will be beautiful."

Speaking ability is a factor in being likable. A pleasant, flexible, resonant voice quality communicates a dynamic personality, an alive and vibrant person. The person who can find the right word at the right time and who can express an idea clearly and with interesting examples or analogies draws attention and interest. The person with a lively and vivid imagination, who can make small talk, spin out dreams or fantasies, dramatize characters, tell interesting stories, and ask unusual questions, is interesting and can be likable.

Listening ability is a factor in being likable. Listening is a real talent and is often underestimated. The person who is willing to listen to others and find out who they are, what they are interested in, and what they are worried about is often liked. Genuinely good listeners are always welcome.

The importance of our attitude toward others

All the basic personality characteristics mentioned above, such as physical appearance and speaking and listening ability, enter into our significant communications, but equally important is the attitude people bring to their interpersonal communications. The salesman who seems interested in us only as long as he thinks we will buy something so he can make a commission irritates us. People who use the others in a working group for their own ends or who treat others like things rather than like authentic persons seldom create trust and liking.

An attitude of willingness and ability to help creates a feeling of trust and liking in others. A genuine offer of help is a powerful force of persuasion. A good salesman often has a sincere and dedicated desire to help the customer. Well-managed stores instruct the salespeople to ask, "May I help you?" The may-I-help attitude in reverse works to build trust also. "I *need* your help" is another persuasive message. A person who asks for help, accepts it without bitterness, and then thanks us makes us feel good. When people have helped one another, they feel freer to ask for help when they need it. When we create a climate of trust, we often accept the people we are talking with for themselves *as they are*. Acceptance does not mean approval of everything said or done by the participants in a communication; it means that the worth and importance of each person are unquestioned.

People who wish to persuade others in order to exploit them often try to cover up their real intentions. In face-to-face situations like the interview or small-group meeting such persuasive tricks usually fail. No matter how hard the manipulator tries to make the others believe he is sincere, unselfish, and dedicated to the welfare of all, his facial expression, vocal intonations, and bodily posture and gestures give him away. Others come to think of the manipulator as slick, oily, phony, insincere. If a person is only pretending to be interested in another, the nonverbal messages often communicate his real feelings. A common example of pretended interest is the child who courts another child only to ride his new bicycle. The result is that the receiver dislikes the person more than if the speaker had been honest in the first place.

Sometimes, a speaker's nonverbal cues create a wrong impression so that she fails to establish friendship and trust without knowing why. Often if several people are having trouble talking with one another because of unintended nonverbal mannerisms, they can discuss the things that bother them and come to an understanding.

PERSUASION AND SOURCE COMPETENCE

In addition to being likable and working to engender trust, the speaker should suggest competence, expertness, and credibility if his or her advice is to be persuasive. We expect a competent person's talk to contain a wealth of good and relevant information about the topic under discussion. The speaker who is clear, whose comments are easy to follow because they are well organized, whose language is precise, and who has a fluent and expressive way of speaking further suggests to us that he is competent. This is as true of the person talking to us face to face as of the person giving a public speech.

PERSUASION AND SOURCE CONVICTION

Finally, a powerful force for persuasion is the speaker's deep personal conviction that he is right. The first person a good sales representative persuades is herself. The father who discusses the dangers of the use of tobacco and advises his son not to start smoking as he himself drags on a cigarette is not persuasive. The persuasive power of dedicated reformers is in large part a result of their willingness to make great personal sacrifices for the cause. William Lloyd Garrison, a leading figure in the fight to free the slaves in the nineteenth century, once wrote of his own part in the battle to abolish slavery:

> It is my shame that I have done so little for the people of color; yea, before God, I feel humbled that my feelings are so cold, and my language so weak. A

few white victims must be sacrificed to open the eyes of this nation, and to show the tyranny of our laws. I expect and am willing to be persecuted, imprisoned, and bound for advocating African rights; and I should deserve to be a slave myself if I shrunk from that duty or danger.

Since Garrison was writing from a jail cell in Baltimore, his sincerity was obvious and his credibility was increased. One of Martin Luther King, Jr.,'s most persuasive messages was his "Letter from Birmingham City Jail."

PERSUASION AND THE SPEAKER'S REPUTATION

Two factors influence the public speaker's ability to persuade his listeners: his reputation and the particular speech he is making. When we study the persuasiveness of well-known public figures, therefore, we must examine both the effect of the speaker's reputation and the impact of the message itself. If we hear from others of a basketball player's skill and high scoring ability, his reputation affects the way we watch the start of the game, but our final opinion is also influenced by how well he lives up to his reputation in the game we are watching. The reputation of a speaker influences our acceptance of his ideas, but our final decision usually depends upon what he says to us.

Scholars have used a number of different terms to stand for the concept of the source's reputation. A popular term is *image*. Most politicians have professional help in building an image (reputation) that will gain votes. Business firms, motion-picture stars, rock musicians, government agencies, and other institutions often try to create a favorable image of themselves.

Another term for the speaker's reputation often used in communication research is *source credibility*. A large number of studies have examined the influence of a source's reputation on audience attitudes. The researchers first gave the experimental subjects a test to find out their attitude on a topic. Next the investigators told different groups of subjects that different people (sources) had produced the message they were about to hear. (The message was tape-recorded, so it was the same for each group.) They then played the message to the subjects and tested them again to determine whether listening to the recording had changed the listeners' attitudes. Since the content of the message was the same (controlled), the investigators argued that measurable changes in the attitudes from group to group resulted from the fact that each group believed a different person had been speaking.

Advertisers talk of image, communication researchers refer to source credibility, while students of rhetoric use the term *ethos* for much the same concept. Because the Greeks studied the arts of rhetoric thoroughly, we often still use their terms: *ethos*, according to Aristotle, refers to a person's *character*—his disposition to act in certain ways.

A communicator's ethos or image is not static. Rather, when people talk with one another, they develop images related to that talk. For example, in a two-person conversation between John and Mary, their images of each other grow out of what they say to each other and how they say it. The images involved in conversations are thus more like motion pictures than like still snapshots in which a given message source has one image now and forever and in which that image has a certain persuasive impact regardless of the receiver of the messages.

The personality of the listener influences the effect of a persuasive message, as well. Research reveals that listener scores on dogmatism tests (which show how bullheaded or inflexible a person is) or personality inventories correlate with how much listeners change their attitudes after hearing a message.

A listener's prior opinion of a speaker comes from many sources: previous in-person communications between them, what others have said to the listener about the speaker, what the listener has read about the speaker, and biographic information the listener may know about the speaker. Sources of information need not be individuals, of course. We receive communication from organizations, as well, and they too have prior reputations. The CIA has a reputation that affects all messages sent out by that particular unit of government, just as the John Birch Society, the Ku Klux Klan, Exxon Oil, the Communist Party, the Republican Party, and the American Nazi Party have images or reputations that affect the persuasive impact of messages they send.

Consider the images of two mythical candidates as they have been created on television and in the national publications. One is a senatorial candidate named Wayland, who is said to be young, slim, attractive, educated at Radcliffe College, dynamic, polished, a woman who inherited wealth but who has been giving her life to public service. Photographs of Wayland and her husband attending cultural and social events often appear in the slick magazines. They have several attractive young children. Wayland has appeared more and more frequently in recent months on television news shows in brief scenes that show her stepping off airplanes, talking informally to reporters at airports, or speaking before audiences. Her voice is pleasant, her manner serious but with some lightness and humor. She has a good smile and looks like someone you would enjoy knowing. Wayland's enemies say she is a lightweight and has gotten as far as she has largely through the power of her inherited wealth and social connections. There are ugly rumors about an impending divorce and about her extramarital sex life. Wayland is a liberal and strongly committed to international arms limitation.

Wayland's opponent, also mythical, is the incumbent Senator Homer

Beardsley. Beardsley is approaching 60 but is said by his friends to be amazingly vigorous and young at heart. He is frequently shown jogging, playing tennis, and chopping wood for the fireplace of his cabin in the western mountains. Beardsley is a self-made man, the son of a poor tenant farmer; he worked his way through college and law school, won a scholarship, and went abroad to study. Beardsley is said to be a brilliant man, but he has some difficulty expressing himself in speeches. He is a man of few words, and he has something of a poker face. He is by no means a charmer. He has the reputation of being a powerful member of senate committees, although he does not get many headlines. Mrs. Beardsley is a plain but pleasant woman who likes to recall her farm background. They both enjoy country music and camping trips in wilderness areas. Their children are grown; they have grandchildren. Beardsley has been a strong defender of what he calls "preparedness" and is suspicious of all plans to disarm the country.

Some students in a speech class (with our myth in mind) are presenting a debate on arms limitation, and the student speaking *for* limitations quotes candidate Wayland. The student speaking *against* limitations quotes Senator Beardsley. The reputation of each authority influences your, the listener's, response to the statements. However, should Wayland appear on campus to give a speech, her reputation would be a factor as you *begin* to listen to her, but her platform personality and her demonstration of the personality traits others have attributed to her would be important factors in your final image of the speaker.

THE BUILDING OF IMAGES

Building a good image of candidates and institutions is the object of much organized persuasive campaigning. As an individual, you are projecting a public image every day. You can learn much about how your own image appears to others and how you can improve your projection of it by studying the professional imagemakers' techniques. What are they primarily interested in doing? Professional persuaders often go to great lengths to discover attractive images for clients. Obviously, you are also trying to project your own image in the most favorable way.

Interestingly enough, images for persuasive impact vary from audience to audience and from culture to culture. You will certainly try to project your most responsible image to your father when you ask for the family car for the evening, but 10 minutes later, on the telephone, you may try to project your most exciting, devil-may-care image to the date you expect to pick up in an hour. Consider our mythical political candidates once more. Did you find Wayland's image more attractive than Beardsley's? If so, you might well be from the suburbs of a metropolitan area. If you found Beardsley more attractive, you are probably from a small town, rural, or midwestern area. Psychologists tell us that we identify with people with whom we feel we have much in common. In this instance, the word *identification* refers to the feeling that you and another person could walk a while in each other's shoes. Consider a candidate who is black, was raised in an urban ghetto, went to college on a basketball scholarship, became a star in the National Basketball Association, and subsequently worked with ghetto youths and became a militant advocate of minority rights. Would you find his image attractive? Anyone wise in the arts of persuasion takes a close look at the image he or she wishes to project and then works hard to find out what images will be attractive to the audience he or she hopes to persuade.

From all this, however, you must not conclude that imagemakers are creating false impressions of candidates or institutions. Persuasion must work within the limits of possibility. The basic personality of the candidate, or the nature of the institution being "sold," forms a framework within which the persuaders must operate. The best public-relations firm in the world cannot make Homer Beardsley appear to be a member of the jet set or socialite Wayland appear as a blue-collar worker. If a public realizes it has been fooled, the reaction is always swift and disastrous for the unwise candidate. All the persuaders can do—but this is of considerable value to candidates and to you as an individual—is to learn what is attractive in a personality being "sold" and to help a person stress the attractive portions of his or her image and minimize the less attractive elements.

Our society has been undergoing a refreshing scourging of phonies. If you consider it hypocritical to sell yourself when you wish to persuade, you should remember that there are times when people believe in a cause strongly and find that their personalities are alienating people; they will then work hard to change their images in order to build more favorable response for the cause they are promoting. Accenting the positive is no sin; accenting what does not exist, on the other hand, is unethical. If a potential candidate sells himself to the voters as a churchgoing, sober man, when in fact he never goes to church and drinks heavily in secret, he will be found out and his ethos will be damaged.

What happens when we know little or nothing about the source of the communication? We often decide how much to accept from such a source on the basis of the stereotypes we have all built in our minds since childhood.

We accept or reject messages because they come from people whose roles in society we accept or reject. We know that many professional people have spent years acquiring the knowledge needed to label themselves landscape architects, medical doctors, lawyers, certified public accountants, or college instructors, and when they speak to us as professionals we tend to accept what they say as being useful (truthful or persuasive) whether or not we find them personally attractive. We are accepting the image of the expert rather than the image as a personality, and we accept messages from such experts more readily when they are speaking about their particular area of competence. When a professor of economics argues that the Federal Reserve Board is following the wrong policy to get the country out of a recession, we listen to her and tend to think she knows what she is talking about. We expect her judgment to be professional and based on careful research. When this same professor argues that the salaries of economics professors ought to be increased, we may not accept her message as being as persuasive, since in this second instance, she is speaking as a person with vested self-interest and not as a scholar making an objective study of a subject. The authors watched with interest one evening as a well-known surgeon nearly tore up his hat in anger and frustration after the elementary school building committee wisely declined his carefully worked out plans for the new school. Used to having his judgments accepted immediately in his day-to-day hospital world, his expertise dropped dramatically when he spoke as another parent in the school meeting. The parents preferred the opinions of the teachers, administrators, architects, and city planners present, and wisely so. Experts, to be persuasive, have to stay within their area of competence.

DIRECT KNOWLEDGE OF THE SOURCE

In the final analysis, of course, a great deal of any speaker's ethos is generated by how he talks and what he says. Any speaker can do much to make his image more attractive right at the moment he is communicating.

What the speaker says, her verbal message, certainly has a considerable effect on whether we like and trust her, whether we accept what she is saying and are persuaded by her. If the speaker is to be trusted, she must say things that reveal her to be unselfish, interested in us, guided by a suitable code of ethics. (A suitable code of ethics would vary somewhat from situation to situation, depending on the speaker and the audience.)

The speaker may well create an advantage by reminding the audience of factors in her background, experience, and training that make her particularly competent to discuss the topic. This should not be done in a boastful way, of course. Often the speaker's expertise is known beforehand, either from advance publicity or from an introduction before she speaks.

The speaker may also imply her status. For example, she can add as she talks about what kind of tires we should use on our cars, "I've been racing stock cars for some years, and I've found that. . . ." A speaker can dramatize his or her expertise as in the following example. A woman, a special counselor in the welfare department, was being introduced as a speaker to a group of young mothers, all newly receiving benefits in the form of aid to dependent children. These mothers were more than a little wary of listening to another expert tell them how to manage their lives, particularly their finances, now that they were on welfare. The program chairperson introduced the speaker as a woman who had earned a degree in social work from the university and whose experience in the field was extensive. The listeners were only mildly impressed. The speaker won their attention and hearts at once when she began. "Fifteen years ago I was sitting in your seat. I'll tell you how I got up here, and I'll tell you how you can get yourself back on your own two feet, and I know that's where you want to be. I *know* each of you wants to do the absolute best you can for your children, and for yourself, and that's why you are here." Wiping away the feelings of guilt that had washed over the young mothers as they had filled out the myriad papers necessary to obtain public assistance, the speaker had immediately told them: "You are great women with problems; I had the same problem a while back, and I learned a lot of answers, which I am going to pass on to you."

If speakers can rise above the self-absorption that comes when they are the focus of attention and can work to raise the status of their listeners with genuine compliments about the organization the audience represents, warm comments about individuals in the audience, or requests for help and advice (giving every indication that they plan to take such suggestions seriously), then they will certainly build good will.

One final element always useful in constructing the persuasive ethos of a speaker comes from the fact that we all like to laugh. If a speaker can amuse us, if she can share her sense of humor with us, we are going to find her more likable. If she can communicate to us that she takes the subject, but not herself, seriously, we will be drawn toward her. If her humor is gentle rather than cutting or sarcastic, if she turns her humor back on herself rather than using it against others, we will trust her more. A person who can amuse her audience seems secure and in command of the situation. You must be careful not to overdo the use of humor, of course, particularly if you have a serious point to make. People love comics and clowns and try to place in that role any person who has some talent for comedy. The rewards for amusing speakers are great—laughter, congeniality, and the knowledge that they are well liked. But just as experts must stay in their area of expertness, so comics are expected to stay comics. If clowns try to make a serious point, to give advice about important matters, we feel uncomfortable and tend to ignore their advice. Use humor in your persuasive speeches, then, but keep in mind your overall purpose. There is much persuasive power in the personality of the source of the message.

THE PERSUASIVE POWER OF SUGGESTION

Persuasion and aping behavior

People often do or believe something because other people around them are doing or believing it. Follow-the-leader behavior is so primitive, we will call it *aping* behavior because the stereotype of an ape is that it will mimic behavior. If a person walking down a street stops and peers up toward the sky, some people may walk on past the sky watcher, but several other people will stop to see what has caught his attention, and soon a knot of people will be standing, peering upward.

How often have you been a part of this next scene? A siren sounds in a quiet neighborhood. People go to their windows or doors or out on their porches to see what is happening. One person runs from a house and dashes up the street. Soon several more follow, and if enough of the watchers are pulled into the parade, the pressure for you to go along with them grows strong. You probably go, too.

When people communicate with one another in a small group for the first time, they develop ways of proceeding on the same follow-the-leader basis. Someone says, "Let's introduce ourselves." Someone else says, "Okay. You go first." The first person tells her name and then a good deal about her background and manages to convey to the others a good idea of the type of person she is: chatty, informal, and friendly. The group has a chance to laugh with her and relax a bit. Finally she says, "That's about it for me. How about you?" She looks with interest at the person next to her; she seems genuinely interested in what the others have to say. She has broken the ice. The next person then describes as interesting a version of "me" as he can, and as the introductions continue around the group, no one resents the time being taken because each feels his turn will come; everyone begins to feel comfortable about the group and each acquires a good notion of what the other members are like. But consider another group that does not get off to such a good start. One person says to another, "Why don't you tell us about yourself?" and the second person simply mumbles her name in an embarrassed way and seems to have nothing to add. She looks at the next person immediately, as though her name is all she need give, and so the next person gives his name, and so on, and the group members' first attempts to get acquainted are not notably successful. In both groups the results stem from aping behavior; what one person starts, the others follow.

Beliefs and ideas can develop in the same fashion. So can norms or ways of behaving. Laboratory studies have shown the extent to which the behavior of others persuades us to do things we otherwise would not do.

A candid film made in the 1960s included a scene in which, when actors planted in an employment office waiting room began taking off their clothes in a matter-of-fact way, as though this were the usual procedure in that situation, a number of unsuspecting clients, after initial reactions of surprise and bewilderment, also began to remove their clothes.

You are probably not enjoying this evidence of how often we simply ape others in how we behave, what we do, even what we think. But human beings *do* behave this way. Aping behavior is often harmless and normal. However, you should resist being manipulated by propaganda that is designed to induce you to ape behavior which, if you stopped to consider, you would *not* choose. You should particularly watch for the propagandist's use of the so-called "bandwagon" technique, which asserts that "everybody is doing it, so come on along."

Persuasion and following directions

Another common human behavior pattern is to do and believe as we are told. Again, this is an immediate and natural response. If one person gives another directions about what to do or what to believe, the second person tends to do or believe as directed. Directed behavior occurs without thinking. If the sign says "STOP," you stop. Often people are hardly aware of what has taken place when they unthinkingly accept directions. As parents, you will tell your children what to do. As children, you were told by your parents what to do. Much of our educational process is a matter of following directions. Carried to extreme lengths, controlling people by telling them what to do and think is like pushing buttons to direct the movements of a mechanical toy. Under deep hypnosis, people blindly follow the directions of the hypnotist, reacting much as a machine would to programmed instructions.

Even so-called "rational" human beings are surrounded by persuasive messages capitalizing upon this tendency to follow directions. Particularly on radio and television we are ordered to:

Buy Buick!
Buy bonds!
Elect John Doe!
Vote Republicrat!
Shop downtown!
Throw the rascals out!
Save today!

Persuasion and accepting suggestions

Directions, as shown above, are clear, blunt, and unequivocal. You are given no option. Directions are phrased and delivered as commands.

Suggestions, on the other hand, recommend a belief or an action, but are phrased in such a way that the receiver has an option, some choice about doing or not doing what is suggested. The direction "Quit your job!" becomes the suggestion "May I suggest that you consider resigning." Suggestion slips the idea into the mind more gently than the jarring direction, and although suggestions encourage the growth of the idea or action, they do so less directly.

Thinking up and developing good suggestion requires considerable artistry. Suggestion skillfully done is efficient. Suggestion puts positions or points into the mind so they are hard to attack logically. We have observed many student discussion groups trying to find a good topic to present as a group for a class discussion. One member suggests a topic, and immediately another makes a face, showing his disgust with the idea, and says, "Let's not do that. Let's do something new and interesting for a change." The first participant then has to present good reasons and make a big effort to overcome the effect of the second member's suggestion that the topic is trite and uninteresting.

The process of suggestion, however, like that of direction, involves getting the listener to accept without thinking an idea, belief, or action. Suggestion is one of the most commonly used persuasive techniques in advertising and propaganda. See if you can think up a strong suggestion in behalf of some service or product in 25 words or less. Can you better these paraphrases of Madison Avenue masterpieces? "Glamour toilet tissue is like facial tissue. It doesn't *feel* like toilet paper." "If she kisses you once, will she kiss you twice?" "Clean odor, the Cologne of Mouthwashes." One we have always liked is the brief persuasive spiel of the hawker selling cheap inflatable pillows to people attending the big show in the state fair ground grandstand. "Four hours on a board," he drones. "Four hours on a board. May we suggest a pillow?"

Many of the people who bought pillows after hearing about the four hours on a board probably never consciously reasoned through their decision. This board-and-pillow example is of further interest because the hawker's spiel contains the two major kinds of suggestion used in persuasion, direct and indirect. The sentence, "May we suggest a pillow?" is *direct suggestion,* telling the potential customers what the seller wants them to do. The phrase, "Four hours on a board" is *indirect suggestion* that the potential customers will be uncomfortable shortly if they do not buy the pillow and, moreover, will be quite comfortable throughout the show if they do.

Directions and suggestions may be positive or negative. Positive persuasion results when a belief or a course of action is urged. "Save today at the Daisy sale!" Negative direction and suggestion urges the listener not to believe, or not to do something, such as in the slogan, "If you smoke, stop! If you don't smoke, don't start!" Positive suggestion and strong direct urgings have persuasive impact. Negative suggestions or directions are often less effective than positive ones. Negative urgings call attention to the belief or action you do *not* want to encourage and, in so doing, may arouse a curiosity about the subject that had not been in the listener's mind before. There is a line from a Carl Sandburg poem we often quoted to one another when our children were toddlers. The line well describes the unwanted effects of negative suggestion. Paraphrased a little, it reads, "Why does the child put molasses on the cat when the one thing I told the child *not* to do was put molasses on the cat?" The sign "Do Not Open This Door" often prompts more than one person to open the door simply out of curiosity. You would be wise to consider *all* possible results when you use negative suggestions in persuasive communication.

When speakers hint at a point without actually saying it, the suggestion they are using is indirect. The listener is led to discover the point rather than told directly about it. If a propaganda campaign maintains a steady barrage of indirect suggestion over a long time, the listeners may gradually come to believe something or begin to form a new attitude, almost without knowing what has been happening to them. When television was still advertising cigarettes, one brand was sold for some time as the cigarette for sophisticates. Its advertisements showed a woman dressed in the current high fashion, surrounded by luxurious furnishings, holding this particular brand in a long cigarette holder. Then, the company decided to change the cigarette's image, and a whole new advertising campaign was launched. Sophistication was out, and the ads now showed virile he-men working in oil fields, punching cattle, fighting forest fires, logging, or building huge bridges in high mountains. Gradually many viewers came to associate this brand of cigarettes with strong young outdoorsmen. Little was said in either campaign about the cigarette's flavor or its nicotine content. Both advertising pitches were expensive campaigns of indirect suggestion designed to persuade people to smoke the brand if they, too, wanted to be, at first, sophisticated, and later, ruggedly masculine.

Indirect suggestion and dramatizing

In Chapter 12 we discussed the importance of discovering the rhetorical visions of the members of your audience as you analyze their values and motives. Here we turn to the ways speakers use narratives and dramatizations to adapt to the rhetorical visions of the audience members and convey a position by indirect suggestion.

One powerful means of persuasion is the dramatization of interpretative scripts that hook into the audience's dreams (rhetorical visions). Often the speaker will portray his or her position in a persuasive speech in terms of real people acting in such a way that their behavior explains what happened. Once you have discovered the interpretative scripts of the listeners, you can search for ways to dramatize your subject that fit into their rhetorical visions.

Successful persuasion not only relies on real-life people but also uses fictitious characters who serve as hypothetical examples and who have admirable or hateful characteristics. Superman brings certain qualities to mind. So does Caspar Milquetoast. Finally, a persuasive speaker may use the figure of speech called *personification* to create emotional responses to abstract propositions. When a speaker uses personification, he endows an abstract idea, institution, or government with human characteristics so it begins to act like a person in a drama. Mark Twain once suggested that a lie could travel around the world while the truth was still pulling on its boots. Suggesting that truth can pull on its boots gives truth the attributes of a person. In nineteenth-century oratory, the personification of such abstract notions as *truth, virtue, beauty,* and *eloquence* was common.

Persuasive messages may contain personifications of abstractions such as the United States of America in the form of Liberty or Uncle Sam or of Great Britain in the person of John Bull. Political cartoonists, who often work with suggestion to achieve their persuasive impact, frequently personify John Q. Public or give the atomic bomb the characteristics of a human being.

In addition to characters, a propaganda or persuasive campaign must provide a setting for the drama. Watch several television commercials or clip several advertisements from a magazine. Notice the scene or location of the action. Although only a small number of people still work as cowhands in our country, a high percentage of characters in advertising campaigns ride horses, wear large western hats, and herd and brand cattle. Many commercial advertisements are set in "pluperfect" homes— gorgeous, lovely, and in perfect order. Much political persuasion derives its impact from the particular setting in which the drama takes place. The John F. Kennedy drama of Camelot was played out at Hyannisport, Palm Springs, and the White House. Jesse Jackson's Operation Breadbasket was set in the black ghettos of Chicago. Skillful propagandists planning a dramatic action for symbolic effect take pains to select the proper scene for their drama. Do you demonstrate in front of the federal building, or at the site of a large nuclear energy plant? Do you go to Washington, D.C., and march on the Pentagon, or do you go to the state capital? In the 1950s, foes of school integration in the South bombed black churches rather than schools. Friends of integration encouraged black students to enroll at the University of Alabama. In the 1960s foes of capitalism bombed Bank of America branch offices. In the 1970s farmers seeking better conditions drove their tractors to Washington, D.C.

Finally, the characters placed in a scene and situation must participate in a dramatic action that arouses our emotions and causes us to become involved imaginatively in what is happening. Persuaders often can take actual events and with a bit of imagination remake them into dramatic actions to fit their purposes. Persuaders and propagandists are in an important sense dream merchants, and to the extent they can catch their audiences up into a dream, they can often persuade them to act and believe in certain ways. One legend has it that in the early days of the automobile, the tendency was to advertise cars in terms of engineering details and facts about their performance. Then an advertising genius developed an ad consisting of a photograph of a handsome young man in his driving togs and goggles, his scarf flying in the wind, a beautiful girl at his side, driving an open car on a road that led across a green valley to the mountains beyond. When asked what in the world he was trying to sell with such a layout, he is alleged to have replied, "A dream"; and modern advertising was on its way.

The heroes of our public dreams are likable and believable and tend to have a good ethos for us. The villains of our dramatization of events can seldom persuade us. Thus the dramatic interpretation of events provides the audience with emotional involvement as well as with credible sources. The positive and negative suggestions inherent in an attractive drama presented as part of a persuasive or propaganda campaign are among the most powerful forces for changing attitudes and behavior.

As consumers of persuasion, and as persuaders ourselves, we should be much aware of the importance of public dreams in relation to positive and negative suggestion. We should learn to look for the rhetorical visions that seem to be operating currently in our culture, for the interpretative scripts change as events around us reshape our priorities. Much of advertising and of the selling of political candidates is shaped by what the dream merchants think the public is buying this year.

We should be alert consumers of persuasion and constantly evaluate messages according to the guidelines presented in Chapter 6. As we develop our own persuasive efforts, we should be aware that even the most skillful dream merchants cannot always predict the public's response to their campaign. Nor is what we see and hear in the mass media necessarily the most persuasive communication we receive.

Sometimes we have a too-simple view of how persuasion and propaganda work in the mass media. Early scholars of radio and television thought mass persuasion flowed directly from the radio or TV receiver to the listener. When, for example, the president went on television and talked directly to the American public, scholars assumed this had a direct and persuasive impact on the viewer-listener. Subsequent research found that the one-step view of mass persuasion was too simple; it revealed that the persuasive impact of television occurs in at least two steps: the persuasion first affects opinion leaders and then is processed in small-group conversations. Thus most people feel the influence of television at second hand, as the ideas and dreams suggested by the tube are talked about in conversations with family and friends.

The small group is important not only because it is a consumer of persuasion but also because the dramatic themes that become public are often first created within a small group. Gradually these successful group fantasies are worked into the mass media, are broadcast, and are again processed and vitalized in other groups.

Much of our motivation to be and to do is contained within the dreams that become real and exciting to us. Our rhetorical vision is often shaped by the positive and negative suggestion inherent in the messages of the mass media; many of our personal fantasies are these messages after they have been discussed, recreated, reshaped in our talk with other people we like and enjoy; some of our dreams are the product of shared group fantasies.

We are not necessarily persuaded by reason. We are often persuaded by suggestion that ties in with or creates our rhetorical visions. To limit communication to factual information is to deny the powerful influence we all feel when those things we hold most dear, our innermost hopes and dreams, are involved.

KEY IDEAS CHAPTER 16

• **Persuasion is communication designed to influence choice. Coercion, like persuasion, restricts choice but, unlike persuasion, requires little artistry.**

• **Little persuasive skill is involved in offering a reward or threatening punishment.**

• **Much persuasion is dependent on the quality of the personal relationships established among the people involved in a communication.**

• **When the choices are risky and people need advice, they turn to someone they can trust.**

• **A genuine offer to help is a powerful force for persuasion.**

• **We tend to believe people who we think are competent, expert, and interested in our welfare.**

• **A powerful force for persuasion is a person's deep personal conviction that he is right: Sincerity is persuasive.**

• **The image of a public figure is closely related to his or her credibility as a source of messages.**

• **Organizations and business corporations also have images that affect their believability when they issue corporate messages.**

• The persuasive impact of a public figure's image varies from audience to audience.

• If a public realizes it has been fooled by misleading image building, the reaction is usually swift and disastrous for those involved.

• We accept persuasive messages from some sources because they have professional credentials that we respect.

• Much of people's ethos is created by how they talk and act in our presence.

• A message source creates a credible image to a large extent by nonverbal communication suggesting that he or she is interested in the listener, expert in the subject, and admirable as a person.

• Funny people are not listened to on serious matters, but a judicious use of humor in a speech increases a speaker's crediblity as a human being.

• The principle of aping behavior is simple: What one person starts, others tend to follow.

• People tend to do and believe as they are told.

• Suggestion plants positions or points in the mind so they are hard to attack logically.

• Whereas direct suggestion tells listeners clearly what they may do or believe, indirect suggestion only hints at it.

• Negative forms of persuasion sometimes backfire, because listeners may be tempted to do what they are told not to do.

• Real people often make the best characters in fantasy themes for propaganda and persuasion.

• When speakers use the figure of speech called personification, they endow an abstract idea or institution with human characteristics.

• Fantasy themes often gain part of their suggestive force from the location or setting of the drama.

• Persuaders often use actual events as the basis for fantasy themes intended to change attitudes and behavior.

• Persuaders are in an important sense dream merchants, in that they can propagate a certain dream and can sell products and ideas that promise to fulfill the dream.

• Mass-media persuasion has its first impact on opinion leaders and, through them, influences the general public, by means of small-group conversations.

• The small group is not only a consumer of public dreams but also a generator of small-group fantasies, which later become public dreams.

SUGGESTED PROJECTS

1 • Select some important personal decision, such as which college to attend, whether to get married, whether to buy a car, or which career to pursue. Think of the one person whose advice you would be most likely to accept in regard to the decision. Make a list of reasons why this person is a credible authority for you in regard to this particular decision.

2 • Write a short paper in which you describe and discuss six techniques of indirect suggestion that you have noticed in current television ads or in magazines and newspapers.

3 • Select a hypothetical target audience for a persuasive campaign. Analyze the main rhetorical visions that the majority of the audience will have for the topic of your effort. For example, take a campus issue such as grading practices or tuition costs. What are the present rhetorical visions in the student body relating to grading? Develop several interpretative scripts that you could use in your campaign to provide positive persuasive suggestion in support of your topic.

SUGGESTED READINGS

Bales, Robert F. *Personality and Interpersonal Behavior.* New York: Holt, Rinehart and Winston, 1970.

Brembeck, Winston, and William S. Howell. *Persuasion: A Means of Social Influence.* 2d ed. Englewood Cliffs, N.J.: Prentice-Hall, 1976.

Cronkhite, Gary. *Persuasion: Speech and Behavioral Change.* Indianapolis: Bobbs-Merrill, 1966.

Larson, Charles U. *Persuasion: Reception and Responsibility.* Belmont, Calif.: Wadsworth, 1973.

PUBLIC-SPEAKING TYPES AND OCCASIONS
CHAPTER 17

Throughout Part Three of this book we have stressed that in our culture the public speech is an established communicative occasion with a long tradition going back to our earliest history. Indeed, if we could take a time machine back to a meetinghouse in New England in the seventeenth century and listen to what was going on, we would soon be able to tell that a Protestant minister was delivering a sermon. There is much similarity in the main features of public-speaking occasions and in the nature of the speaking itself down through the years. The similarities carry over into different geographical regions as well. You could attend a college lecture in California, in Florida, in New Mexico, or in New York and soon be able to tell that they were all of a type and that they were all given for a similar occasion.

Just as we learn the general grammatical usage and dialect features of how to use a language, so we learn the general usages of people in public speaking occasions and can communicate more easily because we do know what to expect.

Although there are some common general features to all public-speaking occasions, there are more specific requirements for special types and occasions. If we learn the details that have to do with the persuasive speech, the informative speech, the organizational presentation, and the more specialized types of speaking, we can do an even better job of listening to and giving such speeches. In this chapter we describe the major speaking types and occasions.

THE PERSUASIVE SPEECH

The participants in one common public-speaking situation come with the general expectation that the speaker will deliver a persuasive message. The audience expects a persuasive message when a speaker known to take a definite stand is scheduled to talk on a controversial subject. Our discussion of the persuasive speech will concentrate on the stylistic features of the message.

The persuasive speech tends to influence the listener's choices and to narrow audience response to the one the speaker prefers. Notice that the speaker designs the persuasive speech to arouse a specific response or change of attitude from the listener.

Persuasion and motivation

The concept of motive, properly defined, can be used not only as a tool to criticize persuasive speaking but also to help the person preparing a speech. Our concern here is with motive as what, in fact, drives members of the audience to act the way they do. Many people talk of motivating other people. When a salesperson says she must motivate the customer to buy the product and a teacher says he must motivate the student to study for a test, they seem to be saying that they can install within the customer or the student a motor that will impel the customer to buy and the student to study. We must realize that whatever basic motives the listeners possess are in them already, and as persuasive speakers, we have to adapt to the motives present in the audience. We cannot install motives in people, because motives develop in a complex way, usually over a period of time. People's motives are influenced by their heredity, their upbringing, and the people after whom they have decided to model themselves.

People may develop further wants, motives, and goals while sharing a fantasy in a meeting or in a series of deep conversations with other people, but when they go to hear a persuasive speech, their motive structure is largely formed. The speaker has little hope of changing that structure. When we manage to persuade a member of an audience, we do so largely by attaching our suggestions to the motives already present. Only by hooking into previously held motives can we make individuals in an audience want to do or believe what we are trying to persuade them to do or believe.

People tend to do what they want, even though, upon careful study of the facts, what they want at the moment may not always be the best thing in the long run. A good automobile salesperson tries to make the customer *want* his car first; then he suggests logical reasons why the person should buy it. The salesperson often suggests, "Why don't you get in and drive it around awhile?" He hopes that when the customer gets behind the wheel and drives the car, he will come to want to have the car for his own. Persuasive speakers should carefully evaluate the wants of their audience and then present their ideas in such a way that they make the audience *want* to do what they suggest.

Dealing with audience habits

We all perform much of our daily routine out of habit, those learned behavior patterns that are repeated so often they become almost involuntary. When you first started senior high school, or later, college, your old habits and patterns were torn up; you had to develop new ones. Usually such periods of our lives are troublesome for us. We do not know where to go next, what to do. We often feel homesick for the good old days, or really for the good old ways. When you analyze the audience for your persuasive speech, remember that if you can show that by following your advice the members of the audience can continue in the same comfortable ways, they will often choose your suggestion. On the other hand, if you want to change things, you will have to shake up your listeners and make them believe that their present habits cause serious trouble and that they must change their ways. If a person is in the habit of smoking cigarettes, then before you can persuade him to change his habit, you have to prove to him that he may be in for serious trouble if he does not stop smoking. You must remember that your persuasive message may "cost" the listener a comfortable habit; you have to be ready to meet the challenge of his resistance to change.

The two types of persuasive speech

Persuasive speeches arise in two main situations. First, a number of people have grown increasingly restless with the way something is being done. They are unsatisfied with some basic part of their lives. These people begin to think up new and, to them, better ways to do something about it. They are now ready to attempt to persuade other people to support their drive for a change. Once a substantial number of people begin to argue and persuade the community to change things, the second situation arises: Another group becomes disturbed because it feels the present situation is satisfactory, and fears the proponents of change will succeed. This group begins to take steps to persuade the community to reject the proposals for new programs. Persuasive speeches are given either (1) to get the audience to work for, vote for, or in some way help adopt a new law, program, or way of doing things, or (2) to get the audience to work against, vote against, or in some way prevent the adoption of a new law, program, or way of doing things.

The speech for change. If you are disturbed or upset by the way things are going and wish to advocate change, you should develop a speech outline that has three main parts. The first point in a persuasive speech for change is "Things are a mess." Take the topic of the rate of inflation. Someone who wishes to change it should begin with the point, "The present rate of inflation is a mess," and then use the basic building blocks of communication (a point to be proved and the evidence, examples, statistics, and testimony of experts that support the point) to build his case against current economic conditions. The second point in a persuasive speech for change is "Here is my program to solve the problem." In developing this point, the speaker for change explains his recommendations. He describes his recommended changes and urges the audience to take some positive action to help get the changes made. He may say, "My program for solving this mess is to lower interest rates and balance the federal budget. You can help in this regard by signing the petition I have here in my hand." The third point in a persuasive speech for change is "If you do as I say, here is what is in it for you." The speaker then describes in graphic detail the benefits that will accrue if the listeners follow his advice and support his proposal.

Persuasive Speech to Change Things

I. Things are a mess.
   A. Point to be proved (statistics, testimony, examples)
   B. Point to be proved (statistics, testimony, examples)
II. Here is my program to solve the problem.
   A. Point to be made clear (examples, analogies, narrations)
   B. Point to be made clear (examples, analogies, narrations)
III. Here is what is in it *for you* if you adopt my program.

Notice that this basic framework can easily be expanded to use the actuating pattern explained in Chapter 13.

Of course, you will not find many occasions when the exact phrases "Things are a mess" and "Here is my program to solve the problem" can be used in your speech. You will need to phrase the points differently for each specific occasion.

The proof of the case tends to come in the first point, where the speaker describes the present conditions and explains the nature of the problem. The persuasive impact tends to come in the third point, where the speaker describes how the wants of the audience will be satisfied by the new program. Here, in shorthand form, is a quick, persuasive speech:

Your present car is a mess. The paint is scratched, the tires are shot, the motor needs overhauling. The repairs will soon cost more than new-car payments, and in the meantime you can't count on your transportation. Here's my program for you. Let me put you into this neat little Rattlesnake four-cylinder convertible. You not only get dependable transportation, but you get a whole new outlook on life. The women who won't date you now will begin to flock around you. You'll get a new sense of zest for life as you tool down the freeway in this sweet little sports car.

The speech against change. The speaker who wishes to persuade an audience *not* to adopt a new proposal has several different options in planning her speech. Essentially, the basic outline consists of three points that take issue with the three main points of the speech advocating the change. Thus the first point is "Things are going along just fine"; the second point is "The proposal would not work"; and the third point is "The proposal would make things a lot rougher on you." The speaker need not use all three points, however. For some arguments, she may select only one and argue simply that things are just fine and submit two or three major reasons for believing change is unnecessary. She may pick several points and argue, for example, that there is no need for a proposal as drastic as the one under consideration, and even if there were a need, this plan would not help matters any.

Let us see how the entire outline works:

Persuasive Speech Against Changing Things

I. Things are going along just fine.
   A. Point to be proved (evidence)
   B. Point to be proved (evidence)

II. The proposal would not work.
   A. Point to be proved (evidence)
   B. Point to be proved (evidence)
III. The proposal would make things a lot rougher on you.
   A. Point to be proved (evidence)
   B. Point to be proved (evidence)

The persuasive part of the speech against a proposal can come in the first point, if the speaker describes the desirable aspects of the way things are and makes the audience appreciate and want to keep the good things they have. Of course, the speaker can also be persuasive in the third point, by presenting the dangers in vivid and graphic terms, so that the audience is repelled by the results of the new plan as the opponent presents them.

THE INFORMATIVE SPEECH

Another common public-speaking situation is one in which a speaker has important information or knowhow to give to an audience. The audience comes to learn from the expert. The speech form expected under the above circumstances is the *speech to inform.*

In our culture, we expect a lecture to be an objective and many-sided view of the material. The lecturer does not intend to narrow the choices of the listener but rather aims to open up new horizons and give the listeners new perspectives for viewing the topic. Of course, few of the real-life speeches we attend are just what we expect them to be. Every speaker has some biases, and often is not as objective as the model suggests. Still, though we tolerate some departure from the ideal cultural norm, if a speaker advertised as a lecturer gives, instead, a powerful persuasive pitch for a pet project, we are disturbed by this violation of a cultural norm.

The informative speaker is supposed to encourage feedback and strive to achieve understanding by answering questions in a complete and open way. We expect the speaker's language to be a clear and careful reporting of denotative meanings and descriptions of factual information. While we anticipate that the persuasive speaker will select language to slant the speech in favor of his bias, we expect the informative speaker to use language in a way that represents various positions and arguments fairly; his tone is "These are the facts, and these are the various ways people look at the subject, and you can draw your own conclusions after I have given you all the information."

THE PRESENTATION

The presentation is a speech form that has emerged within the last few decades to meet the needs of our highly developed urban culture. Most of us now work in organizations, institutions, or corporations. Representatives from various groups within the company, the church, the governmental agency, or the school need to give and get information in formal communication settings officially approved by the organization involved. Because these official speeches are so important, the people preparing them have called upon the latest communication technology to aid in their preparation. Recent developments in film, audiotape recording, television or videotape, photography, and graphic arts, stimulated by the use of commercial advertising on television, are used in preparing a presentation. Music and sound effects may be employed. The result is that the presentation is essentially a multimedia communication. The speaker uses every trick in the book and even tries to invent new gimmicks to make his or her message effective and persuasive.

Supervisors or employers with the power to do so usually authorize a given presentation, assign the people to work on it, and decide who will actually give it. The person who gives the presentation is often not a professional speaker, because the organizational position and status of the message source are important parts of the presentation. Thus, even though the vice-president in charge of personnel is not a particularly able speaker, she may have to give a presentation because the content of the message is such that someone in a position of authority in personnel has to deliver the speech. All of us who come to work in business and industry, in governmental, educational, or religious institutions, may well expect to deliver presentations at certain key times in our careers.

How you give a presentation on the job can be crucial; when you present yourself and your ideas about your particular specialty to your peers and your superiors, they will make judgments about your skill, understanding, and competence on the job. Also, many of the highest-level decisions are influenced by presentations. Lower-management people often work up proposals and make a presentation of their recommendations to the higher-level people within the organization, who make a final decision.

Sometimes presentations are given repeatedly, especially for purposes of public relations. A company representative might give a presentation to visitors touring a plant. Another representative might go out to groups and schools in the community and give a presentation about the organization. The most common situation, however, and the more critical or important occasion, is the instance in which a presentation is prepared with a definite persuasive purpose, with a specific audience in mind. The audience for a presentation may be one or two people only, as is the case when a salesperson for combination doors and windows gives an elaborate presentation in a customer's living room, complete with models of various windows, a series of brochures, slides of installations, and a demonstration of the way the various models of the windows work. More usually, of course, presentations are given to groups of people ranging in size from five to twenty, or even, occasionally, hundreds.

Presentations are the most carefully prepared, rehearsed, and tested messages given by members of organizations. Quite often, the organization's top management and best specialists review a presentation before it is given. The dry-run rehearsal is the rule rather than the exception in presentational speaking.

Aids in making presentations

One effective way to make a presentation is to have the audience directly experience the material in the message. In order to do this, the speaker could take the audience on a field trip, or he or she could bring an illustrative event to the audience. Suppose a person is making a presentation about the teaching of reading to children in an inner-city school. He might take the audience to the school and have them observe the teaching as it is going on. He could, on the other hand, have a teacher and some pupils from the school come before the audience to demonstrate the teaching there.

Another way to allow the audience to participate in the presentation is to have it take part in a simulation or model of a process being discussed. For example, members of the audience might go to a planetarium and see, projected overhead, a simulation of the heavens, or they might operate an automobile simulator while the speaker adds verbal information about highway safety.

A number of multimedia aids are useful even though they do not furnish the audience with the active participation that often yields the highest interest and understanding; there is the *demonstration*, which allows the audience to be present while the speaker participates, as when a speaker mixes and bakes a cake while talking about the merits of a new cake mix and rapid-baking oven.

Exhibits are displays that resemble a demonstration without as much direct intervention from the speaker. The presentation associated with an exhibit usually involves the speaker's taking the audience on a guided tour of the exhibit. The speaker may pause at certain stations along the tour and demonstrate a process, for example, or recreate a historical event. Exhibits may consist of an unlimited variety of materials, including posters, models, mockups, objects, chalkboards, recorded sounds, videotape playbacks, and still or motion pictures.

Closed-circuit television and audiotape-recording equipment are extremely useful aids to the presentation. The speaker can produce one reel of videotape, for instance, which has on it photographs, diagrams, graphs, charts, filmstrips, slides, clips from motion pictures, models, mockups, scenes recorded on location, posters, cartoons, interviews, excerpts from speeches, and her own narration or comments. The speaker may also give her presentation and incorporate segments of videotape as she proceeds. A speaker may use audiotape in much the same way, to supplement a demonstration or exhibit or to illustrate a point in a presentation.

Motion pictures provide excellent aids for a presentational speaker, but at a considerably greater expense than videotape. A person making a presentation may be able to find segments of commercially prepared film that are suitable for incorporation in his speech. The expense of shooting and editing film for a given presentation is so high that only extremely important presentations use specially prepared film segments.

Still pictures, graphs, charts, line drawings, and cartoons are dependable and useful techniques for communicating messages. Carefully developed and integrated into a well-prepared presentation, these aids are often used in our modern organizations.

Speakers continue to use the old reliable aids to presentation, such as the chalkboard (blackboard), which anyone studying presentational speaking should learn to use well. Large cards with information on them can be placed on an easel beside a speaker so that all members of the audience can read whatever diagrams, charts, illustrations, or photographs the speaker wishes to use. A flip chart is a good aid in giving presentations; this consists of a pad of newsprint-sized paper, mounted on an easel and designed to be flipped back and forth to show various charts or diagrams as needed. The speaker can also have blank flip cards, on which he writes visual aids with a heavy marking pen as he gives his verbal message.

The flannel board is a large board covered with fabric; the speaker can prepare display items backed with the same material so they will stick to the cloth on the board. The speaker can place illustrations, figures, and so forth, on the board as he speaks.

Speakers often supplement their presentations by using slides or filmstrips projected on a screen. Still pictures may show people, events, fossils, geologic features of the earth—whatever would be useful. Graphs, charts, diagrams, maps, and other graphics are easy to see when projected on a screen with a slide projector, and slides are easy to store and carry. One of the most useful devices is the overhead projector, which throws an image of whatever is drawn on a transparent surface upon a screen in front of the audience. The speaker can prepare drawings and diagrams on the transparencies in advance, or she can write on a transparent sheet while she speaks, much as she would use a pad of paper, and the writing will be projected onto a screen in front of the audience.

The presentation in the future

More and more evidence is accumulating that the presentation is the public speech of the future in our culture. The brief persuasive commercial messages on television have become a popular art form and the style-setting edge of communication in our society. Children who start watching television at an early age are often so intrigued by the commercials that some of their first words and songs are those they learn from television advertising. As a spinoff from the large investment of money and talent in television commercials, we now have a well-developed multimedia technology of persuasive and effective communication. More and more organizations are drawing on the multimedia knowledge for aid in the development of important presentations. The presentational techniques developed in business have enormous implications for the whole field of education. The truly gifted lecturer is probably as rare and difficult to find as a gifted golfer or chef, but with the wealth of presentational aids available, many more people can give highly effective messages that will both instruct and impress listeners.

SPEECHES ABOUT PEOPLE

Persuasion is often concerned with the human personality. People are interested in personalities. We come under the spell of striking and dramatic people, and we grow to love or hate individuals until they dominate our thoughts and dreams. Chapter 16, on persuasion, gave detailed descriptions of the techniques of suggestion speakers can use to project an image of a person to an audience. On some occasions in our culture the audience expects that almost the entire speech will be devoted to biographic information, praising or blaming that individual's life and character.

The eulogy

The technical name for a speech devoted entirely to praise of a person is a *eulogy*. When someone dies, often a speaker gives a funeral eulogy describing the deceased's life and interpreting its meaning in a favorable way. Usually speeches about people present them in a favorable light. Sometimes, however, a speaker devotes an entire speech to damning a person, and the name for a speech that cuts down a person in this manner is a *dyslogy*. Few dyslogies are given in the United States, although in many political campaigns there is a large element of personal attack against the opposition by the partisans.

On some occasions people gather to hear a speech celebrating their history, heritage, culture, or community. Often the speech to build group cohesion consists largely of praising heroes and attacking villains. Certain key people, such as the founders of an organization, club, fraternity, company, state, or nation, become the focus of attention, and the speaker praises these people for values the community wishes to celebrate and recall. The typical nineteenth-century Fourth of July address in the United States was such a speech form. The speaker would praise the "Founders of the Constitution" and the "Signers of the Declaration of Independence." Many Fourth of July orations included eulogies of George Washington.

Although relatively few people find themselves called on to give eulogies, many of us are called on to give short speeches in praise of a person; we refer to the duty that often falls to an officer of a club or organization, the job of introducing a featured speaker at a meeting. The speech of introduction is another culturally developed message form.

The speech of introduction

The audience expects a *speech of introduction* to be brief, but it also expects certain things to be taken care of in this speech. The listeners expect the introduction to tell them enough about the main speaker to enable them to evaluate his or her expertness and to make them more eager to hear the speech. Usually the audience expects the person giving the introductory remarks to say only favorable or complimentary things about the speaker. A good speech of introduction, however, should be more than a simple listing of accomplishments ("He has written fourteen articles and three books, holds eight degrees, and has won twelve honors and seven national awards"); it should recognize the uniqueness of the audience and occasion and reveal some part of the speaker's personality that warms the audience to the individual.

The good speech of introduction, in our culture, avoids too much praise of the speaker. Most audiences tend to become embarrassed when one person overdoes the praise of another person who is also on the speaker's platform. (The exception to this cultural norm is the political convention or rally. We expect and tolerate outrageous flattery in partisan political meetings. There are also ethnic groups in our culture that practice more public personal praise. In considering this matter if you are to make an introduction, you must rely on an analysis of your particular audience.) Experienced speakers live in fear of the inexperienced person who gives them a glowing introduction no one could live up to! More than one speaker has had to use some stock retort to acknowledge an overblown introduction without publicly embarrassing the person who gave it. One such retort we heard was, "Thank you for that great introduction. I was wondering where you heard all those things, and then I remembered my mother knew I was speaking here tonight."

If possible, the best procedure if you are making an introduction is to check with the speaker ahead of time to find out what material the speaker would particularly like to have included in the introduction. In this way the introduction can tie in with what the speaker plans to say and help set the tone the speaker plans to use. Moreover, once you meet the speaker, even briefly, you have a better idea of what remarks she will prefer and what remarks she might find embarrassing. If you have an introduction written out in advance, she can check it out for herself.

The speech of welcome

At times in our culture a meeting or a conference has an opening session that features a speech of welcome to all the delegates. A *speech of welcome* is expected to deal with the person or organization sponsoring the meeting and giving the welcome (for example, "On behalf of the college . . ."), with the people receiving the welcome ("I am particularly pleased to talk with students dedicated to ending pollution"); or with the occasion ("We are most pleased to be the site for this vitally important workshop in changing attitudes toward the human environment"). Generally we expect the speech of welcome to praise the hosts, guests, and occasion. The speaker aims to make the guests feel that they are important and the event is significant. Like a speech of introduction, the welcoming speech should be brief.

Both the introduction and the welcoming speech serve a primarily ritualistic function. A ritual is a set way of doing something that has long been the habit of a group, an organization, or a culture. Both speaker and audience will be satisfied with a brief, routine comment. All of us, however, appreciate a touch of originality and artistry in our ritual speeches, and we appreciate a speech of welcome that both fulfills the needs of the occasion and goes on to do more. An assistant to the mayor of New Orleans managed this some years ago when he gave a welcoming speech on behalf of the city to the members of the national Speech Communication Association convention. The speaker was a black man who began in the expected way by praising New Orleans much in the style of a tourist advertisement. He praised the tourist attractions, the charm and history of the city. Then, with a quick transition, he caught the audience by surprise and began describing the seamy side of New Orleans. He talked about the poverty, racial injustice, and crime. Many audience members found themselves sitting forward in their chairs at this unexpected turn in his remarks. The speaker then concluded with an optimistic note that the citizens of New Orleans were working on all these problems, and that a new day would dawn. His skillful blend of the expected plus the unexpected aroused the admiration of the teachers of public speaking who heard him; he had definitely made a routine speech of welcome into a much more memorable, though brief, message.

The speech in honor of achievement

The final sort of speech about people that we will discuss is the speech of praise which is given when an individual wins an award or is honored for past achievements. Again, the speaker making the award or noting the occasion is primarily praising good motives, honorable actions, good character, and effective work.

KEY IDEAS CHAPTER 17

• Every culture needs to have the right spokesperson say some formal words at important periods in the life of the family, institution, community, or nation.

• In the United States all forms of public speaking are prized, cultivated, and practiced.

• The public speech is a cultural event with clearly understood rules and customs in most societies.

• Although there are some general features common to all public-speaking occasions in our culture, there are more specific requirements for special types and occasions.

• The participants in one common public-speaking situation come with the expectation that the speaker will deliver a persuasive message.

• The persuasive speech aims to influence the listeners' choices and to narrow audience responses to the one the speaker recommends.

• The speaker should remember that people tend to do what they want at a given moment, even if the evidence indicates it will be bad for them in the long run.

• The speaker who wishes to change an audience's habitual routine has the burden of proving that change is necessary.

• Another common public-speaking situation is one in which a speaker has important information to give to the audience.

• The audience attending a speech to inform comes to learn from the expert.

• In our culture, we expect a lecture to be an objective and many-sided view of the material.

• A new speech form has emerged in the last few decades to meet the needs of an urban corporate culture—the multimedia presentation.

• Presentations are the most carefully prepared, rehearsed, and tested messages given by members of organizations.

• On some occasions in our culture the audience expects that the entire speech will be devoted to discussing, praising, or blaming a person's life and character.

• The eulogy is a speech devoted to praising a person.

• The speech of introduction is a special speech form in our culture.

• Many speeches in praise of individuals serve a primarily ritualistic function.

SUGGESTED PROJECTS

1 • This is to be your most thoroughly prepared, carefully written, and well-rehearsed speech—the equivalent of an oral term paper. Select a topic that you feel strongly about and prepare a five- to eight-minute persuasive speech for delivery in class.

2 • Select a topic area in which you have special knowledge which your classmates are unlikely to share. Do not pick something like the proper way to serve in tennis. If you know how computers are used to project voting outcomes during network coverage of elections or how the law of comparative cost advantages is supposed to work in economics, these would be good topics. Prepare a five- to eight-minute speech to inform for delivery to your class.

3 • Select a topic of some complexity that will require careful explanation for the audience to understand. Develop a multimedia presentation, using a range of visual and audio aids to help you clarify your ideas for your audiences.

4 • During one of the rounds of speeches or presentations suggested above, your instructor will assign you the task of giving a brief introduction to a classmate's speech.

5 • Select a person, living or dead, whom you admire or dislike and prepare a five-minute speech either praising or attacking that person.

SUGGESTED READINGS

Brembeck, Winston, and William S. Howell. *Persuasion: A Means of Social Influence.* 2d ed. Englewood Cliffs, N.J.: Prentice-Hall, 1976.

Howell, William S., and Ernest G. Bormann. *Presentational Speaking for Business and the Professions.* New York: Harper & Row, 1971.

Olbricht, Thomas. *Informative Speaking.* Glenview, Ill.: Scott Foresman, 1968.

INDEX

273

Ghostwriting, 81–82
Gibb, Jack, 72–73, 76
Grammar, 39, 41, 42
Great Britain, 253
Groups
  ad hoc, 145–146
  agenda in, 146, 147, 151
  attention span of, 150–151
  decision-making, 151–152
  roles in, 131–136
  structure in, 151–152
Group discussion, 143
Group size, 143

Habits, 260–261
Hamlet, 102
Hasty generalization, 209–210
Hawaii, 41
Hearsay evidence, 219
Hidden agenda, 114, 118
Howell, William S., 76, 203, 257, 271
Huff, Darrell, 223
Humor, 159, 248
Huseman, Richard C., 76
Hypothetical examples, 167–168,
  206–207, 211

Illumination in creativity, 164
Image, 243, 245–247
Impromptu speech, 196–197
Incubation in creativity, 164–166
Indirect suggestion, 251–255
Information, 34
Informative speech, 263
Intelligence quotient, 214–215
Interpersonal communication, listening and,
  67–74
Interpreting meaning. *See* Decode
Interviewing, 52, 112–116
Introduction, speech of, 268–269
Introduction for public speech, 193
Iran, 179–180
Irony, 50, 53, 54–55
Irwin, John V., 189

Jackson, Don D., 18
Jackson, Jesse, 253
Jackson, Mississippi, 216
Jeffrey, Robert C. 189, 203, 223, 237
Job interview, 113–116
John Birch Society, 244
Johnson, David W., 110
Johnson, Lyndon, 39
Jourard, Sidney M., 110

Kennedy, John F., 177, 253
Khomeini, Ayatollah Rhollah, 179, 180
Kidd, Virginia, 90
Kinesics, 46, 226, 232–234

King, Martin Luther, Jr., 243
Knapp, Mark L., 61, 123

Labov, William, 44
Larson, Charles U., 257
Leadership
  emergence of, 134–135
  formal, 137
  one-time meeting and, 144–148
Leathers, Dale, 61
Lewis, Thomas, 76
Listening
  active, 73–74
  creative, 70–71
  interpersonal communication and, 67–74
  likability and, 241
  public speaking and, 63–67
  supportive, 71–72
  therapeutic 71–72, 73–74
Logical analysis, 169–172
Logue, Cal M., 76
Long, Huey P., 81
Loudness, 16, 51

McCrosky, James C., 30
Manipulator, 135–136, 242
Manson, Charles, 209
Manuscript speaking, 25–26
Mass media, 80–81, 82, 84, 254–255
Mean, 218
Meaning, 105–106
Median, 218
Meetings
  briefing, 126
  consultative, 126
  decision-making, 126
  leading, 146–148
  participating in, 148–149
  planning, 145–146
  ritualistic, 125–126
Memorization of speeches, 227
Message, 5, 6, 7, 11, 13, 14
  double-edged, 54–55, 102
  public speaking, 160
  units of, 166–169
Middle East, 182
Mills, Glen E., 174
Minnesota, 159
Monotony, vocal, 230–232
Morse code, 14, 15
Mortensen, C. David, 18
Motive, 88, 259–260
Multimedia communication, 266–267
My Lai, 209

Name calling, 39
Naming, 37–38, 96
Narrative, 167–168, 212–213
New England, 182, 259

notes, use of, 234–236
outlining of, 200–202
posture, 232
proxemic factors in, 59
speaker-centered, 176
Puritans, 182

Questions, 70, 115

Radcliffe College, 244
Random sample, 216–217
Rate of speech, 16, 51–52
Real examples, 210–211, 212
Receiver of messages, 6, 7, 11, 14
interviews and, 115–116
listening and, 67–70
public speaking and, 160
two-person conversation and, 105
Reflective thinking, 197–198
Relationship communication, 116–122
Republican Party, 244
Residues, method of, 199
Revival speaking, 158–159
Rhetoric, 82
Rhetorical community, 85–87
Rhetorical criticism, 78, 82–89
Rhetorical vision, 85, 86, 87–89, 205,
179–184, 252–255
Ritualistic meetings, 125–126
Rogers, Carl R., 73–74, 100, 110
Roles in small groups
central persons, 135–136
changing membership and, 136
disagreer, 131
emergence of, 132–133
leadership, 134–135
stability of, 133–134
Roosevelt, Franklin D., 26
Rumor, 66–67, 104
Russia, 180–181, 182

Sandburg, Carl, 252
Sarcasm, 50–55
Schlafly, Phyllis, 183
Scott, Michael D., 30
Scott, Robert L., 91, 174, 224
Secondary tension, 130
Self-concept, 66
characterizing and, 96–97
identity crisis and, 97
interpersonal communication and, 97–98
interviews and, 110
naming and, 96
nature of, 96–97
perception and, 105
self-disclosure and, 99
Self-disclosure, 80, 99, 120–121
Self-image. See Self-concept
Shah of Iran, 179–180

Shakespeare, William, 102
Shapiro, George L., 76
Sheflen, Albert E., 61
Sheflen, Alice, 61
Shuy, Roger W., 44
Sign language, 15
Small-group communication, 57, 58, 71,
112, 149–152, 255
SMCR model of communication, 5–9,
67–70, 73, 160–161
Social climate, of groups, 129–131
Source of message, 5, 6, 7, 11, 14
competence and persuasion, 242–243
conviction and persuasion, 242–243
credibility and persuasion, 229–230,
243–245, 248
interviews and, 115–116
listening and, 67–70
public speaking and, 160
persuasion and, 242–248
in two-person conversations, 105
Source competence, 242–243
Source conviction, 242–243
Source credibility, 229–230, 243–245, 248
Speech Communication Association, 269
Sprague, Jan, 110
Stage fright. See Communication anxiety
State anxiety, 21–22
Statement-of-case pattern, 195–197
Statistics, 169, 213–217
Status, 59, 132–134
Steinem, Gloria, 183
Stevens, Leonard, 76
Stewart, Charles J., 123
Suggestion, 249–255
Supportive communication, 100–102, 115

Television, 178
Television commercials, 80–81
Territoriality, 57–58
Testimony, 169, 218–221
Topics
creative analysis of, 162–166
logical analysis of, 169–172
public speaking, 160
selection of, 161–162
Trait anxiety, 22–23
Transitions, 194
Trust, 71, 80, 100, 102, 120–121
Turner, Kathleen J., 91
Twain, Mark, 37

United States, 180, 182, 184, 219, 253
Unity in organization, 191
University of Alabama, 253

Verification in creativity, 164
Vietnam War, 98
Vocal characteristics, 48–51, 230–232

81 82 83 84 85 9 8 7 6 5 4 3 2 1